FOUR HUNDRED MILLION CUSTOMERS

The experiences—some happy, some
sad of an American in China, and
what they taught him.

By CARL CROW
Drawings by G. Sapojnikoff

To Helen

Table of Contents

Preface to the First Edition

With the vast number of books on China which have already been published and are being constantly produced, the advent of a new volume on this very interesting country places-the author on the defensive. The reading public is quite within its rights in asking him to explain why he thinks a new book necessary and why he has written it. With the shelves already crowded with books by writers on religion, by travellers, statesmen, humorists, philosophers, economists, and representatives of dozens of other branches of highly specialized knowledge, what hope have I, they may ask, to add anything to what has already been written and published, and why should I be audacious enough to attempt it?

My justification is found in my profession, which is that of an advertising and merchandising agent, and so represents a branch, if not of specialized knowledge, at least of specialized effort, which has not yet been represented by the many authors of books on China. Since the occupation is a comparatively new one, I perhaps should explain that we do not, as many laymen suppose, spend our time in selling advertising to anyone who can be induced to buy. Our entire efforts are devoted to helping our clients to sell their goods, paying particular attention to the part played by various forms of advertising. They pay us for this work and, since one of our vanities is to insist that we enjoy a professional standing, we use the term 'fees' in referring to our compensation. If we do our work efficiently, we should be able to give our clients expert advice on all manner of things, ranging from the color and wording of a label to the relative merits of the various newspapers published in any one of dozens of Chinese cities. We should be able to tell him whether or not there is any likelihood of his being-able to build up a profitable sale for his brand, and measure the strength and the weakness of the competition he has to face. We thrive or suffer adversity with the tips and clowns of our clients.

My work has naturally made my point of view that of one who looks on the Chinese as potential customers, to consider what articles they may purchase, how these articles should be packed and what advertising methods will be most effective in producing sales. My clients have sold everything from textile mills to perfumery. They have comprised many nationalities, English, American, German, French, Dutch, Belgian, Australian, Canadian, Japanese, Spanish, and one from the Duchy of Luxemburg. Each has had different problems to solve and different ideas as to how to solve them, but the main objective was always the same, to sell his goods to the Chinese. In order to do my work efficiently, I have had to study everything connected with China and to fit all kinds of knowledge into a merchandising pattern so as to make it useful to my clients. In this way, the studies of the advertising agent must range as wide as, though in a more humble field than, that of the anthropologist, for there is no information about the country and its people which may not at some time or other prove of value. It has been no hardship to me to study the Chinese, their character, history and institutions, for I am as keenly interested in them to-day as I was when I was thrilled by my first rickshaw ride, a quarter of a century ago. It is the sympathetic study of China that, to many foreigners who live here, accounts for the fascination of the country.

It is a country so vast and so complex that it can never become hackneyed – so little know that one may with encouraging frequency enjoy the thrill of the explorer by discovering some new fact which appears to have escaped the attention of thousands who have travelled the same road with less observant eyes.

This is my excuse and my justification. I hope the reader will find it acceptable and that this new point of view will give him a new understanding of the interesting, exasperating, puzzling, and, almost always, lovable Chinese people as I have know them.

Carl Crow.

No one liked the new cigarette

1. The Very Particular Customer

Although I had lived in China more than five years and had traveled about the country a great deal I really didn't begin to learn very much about the Chinese people until I established my advertising agency. The sole function of an advertising agent is to help a manufacturer sell his products. He must know what people want to buy, their buying habits, their preferences and prejudices. As soon as i began studying the problems of my first client the Chinese people began to project themselves on my mind in an entirely new way. They were no longer the members of a group of curious and friendly people in whom I had a detached and academic interest, but a nation of four hundred million potential customers with human needs and desires. It was my pleasant duty to learn what these needs and desires were—a fascinating study in which my interest never staled for each new problem solved brought others into focus. The seventeen problem solved brought others into focus.

The seventeen years I spent in the business were not long for with each year I came to know the Chinese people more intimately. My first experiences showed that I had really learned very little about the people and had accumulated a lot of completely fallacious ideas.

I had not been conducting my advertising agency many months before a visiting manufacturer who was looking for trade opportunities in China said to me: 'I suppose the Chinese will buy anything, provided the price is cheap enough.' That is an idea held by most people, even by some foreigners who live in China and should know better. Out of the depths of my ignorance i agreed with him. It is easy to see how one might come to that conclusion. No one gets more enjoyment out of a bargain than the Chinese, or will search further or haggle more ardently to get one, but, on the other hand, no one will more stubbornly and successfully resist attempts to sell him something he does not want, no matter what the price may be. Mere cheapness is not enough to make him change his tastes or forget his prejudices. That was the first lesson I learned in my study of the Chinese customer. The widely prevailing demand for a distinct type of cigarette affords a good example of this. Cigarettes have almost entirely replaced the old-fashioned water-pipe in China, and the annual sales run into the billions of units. Such American favorites as Camels, Lucky Strikes and Chesterfield- were all stocked in Shanghai, and sold for about two-thirds of the price charged for them at home, because the packets did not have to bear an internal revenue stamp and were free from other American taxes. These brands were sold, in fair to modest volume, to expatriate Americans, and to a few other foreigners, but not one packet out of a thousand was ever sold to a Chinese consumer. The price has nothing to do with this limited demand. Chinese prefer the flavor of the bright yellow 'Virginia' tobacco of which all popular British cigarettes are composed. All cigarettes made in China are of the British type. Chinese dislike the more aromatic blends of Virginia and Turkish or Virginia and Burley tobaccos which are used in the manufacture of all American cigarettes. Some experts in the tobacco business say that if a smoker ever changes from a straight Virginia to a blended cigarette he will never again become a straight Virginia smoker, that he will find them unsatisfactory after becoming accustomed to the more sophisticated blends. This must be true in America, where the blended cigarette and the theory both originated, for there the blended cigarettes have practically driven all others from the market.

One of our clients, the manufacturer of one of America's most famous brands, thought the same theory would work out in China, and we felt so sure he was right that we undertook his blended cigarette advertising with a good deal more than the usual enthusiasm inspired by a new and potentially large advertising account. Nothing was overlooked in launching the venture. Salesmen got the brand stocked everywhere, and it was advertised by every approved method we or the manufacturers could think of. They were so certain of success that they were willing to let next year's business pay for this year's advertising, and they were generous in their anticipation of what future profits would be. Thanks to the assistance given by their New York advertising agency, one of the best in America, the campaign we put on in China was far better than anything that had ever been seen there before. But, in spite of all that we could do, the cigarettes remained on the dealers' shelves. Maybe the hypothesis that anyone who changed to a blended cigarette would smoke that kind ever after really would prove correct in China, if given a fair trial. But we were never able to prove it. So far as we could discover, we never succeeded in getting a single Chinese to become a smoker of our brand of blended cigarettes, and so couldn't tell whether or not he would become a regular consumer once he got used to them. Any number tried to smoke them, but, after a few puffs, they found the taste both strange and odious and would not buy a second packet. The Chinese sales fell back to the zero point from which they had started, and the advertising campaign was dropped by common consent of everyone who had anything to do with it. The only satisfaction we got out of the experience was that everyone praised the advertising.

Not only do Chinese have very decided ideas as to what they like and dislike, but once they have become accustomed to a certain brand, no matter whether it be cigarettes, soap or tooth paste, they are the world's most loyal consumers, and will support a brand with a degree of unanimity and faithfulness which should bring tears of joy to the eyes of the manufacturer. There are, in every country, certain proprietary brands which are dominant in their field, but I doubt if any of them are so firmly entrenched as are some in China. In a very comprehensive market survey we found that a world famous British household soap enjoyed such popularity in parts of North China that nine out of ten shops which sold soap did not stock any other brand, though dozens of cheaper competing soaps were on sale in this territory and a few manufactured locally. Once in a while, when there had been a flood, or a drought, and the purchasing power of the local residents fell even lower than usual, he would buy a cheaper soap; but that was a temporary expedient, and with the return of a reasonable degree of prosperity he went back to his old favorite brand, which was also the favorite of his grandfather. A big and apparently impregnable market like this was just the sort of thing other manufacturers like to train their heavy batteries on, and many of them used up a lot of ammunition and made a lot of noise, but without results. No doubt many of them made a soap practically as good and offered it at a cheaper price, but not one of them ever built up a volume of sales big enough to let our clients know that there was any serious competition in the field. The consumer who occasionally tried the competing soap because of its cheaper price might fully appreciate its good qualities, but he was not sure the next cake would be so good. He had been fooled before by manufacturers who did not maintain the quality of their products, and was therefore suspicious. On the other

4

hand, he had full confidence in the old brand. He had used it for years, his father and his grandfather used it, and it had always been the same. The satisfactory domination of the North China market by this brand had a sound merchandising basis and was due to the high quality of the soap in a very difficult field. Most of the water in North China is extremely hard, and cheap soaps, which will produce a satisfactory lather in the soft rain-water of the Yangtsze Valley, curdle in this water, which comes from springs and wells and is full of alkali.

We once helped in an attempt to take some business away from a brand of cigarettes which, in another part of China, held about the same dominant position in the tobacco field that this brand enjoyed in the soap field. There is no secret about the blend of a cigarette which cannot be discovered by an expert, and our friends reproduced in their factory the blend of the popular brand with scientific exactness. In fact, to make doubly sure of success, they employed as their factory superintendent a man who had held a similar position in the competitor's company. Having perfected the blend, they improved the packet, making it, so far as cigarette packets go, a thing of beauty, with a gaudy landscape and with the red and gold lettering which the Chinese find so attractive. They packed the cigarettes in heavier tin foil and offered them at an appreciably lower price. A big advertising campaign was launched and crews of extra salesmen employed. A fair sale was built up. But we never succeeded, so far as we could learn, in getting a single consumer to change from the old brand to the new one. We knew that the two cigarettes tasted alike, because they were made in exactly the same way from identical proportions of the same grades and qualities of tobacco, and it was impossible for them to taste differently. But the consumer, taking a puff of one and then of the other, laughed at the idea that the taste was identical and kept on smoking the older and more expensive cigarette. Ours was only one of many attempts which were made by other manufacturers to take business away from this popular brand. In fact, when a new cigarette manufacturer entered the Chinese market that was usually the first thing he tried to do, but no one has ever been any more successful than we were.

It is because of the Chinese loyalty to a brand and their suspicion of any change that manufacturers are so reluctant to make any change in a packet, no matter how trivial. Though they put great faith in the integrity of a brand with which they are familiar, Chinese appear to be in constant fear that the manufacturer will take advantage of that faith and palm off inferior goods, or that someone will fool them with a closely imitated packet. The result is that the least change, even such an unimportant change as a street number, will arouse their suspicions and make them refuse to accept the goods. It is remarkable how quickly the Chinese will discover a small change in a packet or label, though it may be printed in a language they cannot read. One of the precautions they always take is to count the number of letters in a brand name to see if the total is correct. This test, however, is rather futile, for imitators know this and the number of letters in an imitation brand is always the same as the number in the genuine. In advertising, the picture of the packet must be an exact reproduction clown to the most minute detail. In the American advertising we placed in China we were very rarely able to use the pictures of packets sent to us by the manufacturer. They were quite suitable for advertising in other countries, but were either too sketchy or too inaccurate for China. In cigarette posters the packet was always shown opened so as to display the contents. This was done to show the bright yellow color of the tobacco and to offer visual evidence of the fact that the packet actually contained ten cigarettes. A Shanghai manufacturer once printed several hundred thousand posters before it was discovered that only nine cigarettes were shown protruding from the packet. That made the posters valueless for advertising and .they had to be destroyed.

It would be very felicitous to be able to give to advertising the credit for creating all or a major portion of the popular prejudices and preferences of the Chinese in favor of certain brands, but candor compels me to admit that most of the foreign brands which enjoyed a dominant position in China attained that position solely through reputable age; they were widely and profitably sold before there was any advertising in the country worthy of the name. That is true of the soap and cigarettes referred to above and of many other brands representing various lines of manufacture. Of course, the manufacturers of these pioneer products were fortunate enough to get their goods established and popularized before there was any competition, and they had a free field. When given an opportunity to buy their first cigarette and their first cake of soap the Chinese made their own investigations and came to their own conclusions without the aid of advertising and without any suggestions from the manufacturer. In fact, the reason for the popularity of some old brands remains something of a mystery to everyone who knows anything about merchandising in China. Take, for example, the brand of cigarettes which was so popular. If I had never heard of this cigarette, were shown a packet for the first time and asked my opinion as to the possibilities for its sale in China, I would have no hesitation in saying that the Chinese would never buy it. The same judgment would be passed on it, I believe, by almost everyone else who knows anything about the cigarette business. The quality of the cigarette was unquestioned, but nothing about the packet was right, according to present-day theories, and there were many things about it that were distinctly wrong. According to most merchandising experts, a cigarette which is poorly packed will never be widely sold, but in this instance the theory did not work. It was the biggest seller in China and in some places outsold all other brands by a proportion of three to one.

The made in Hamburg horse shoes offers a very interesting and illuminating example of the way the Chinese come to their own conclusions regarding the merits of a piece of merchandise and form an opinion from which it appears impossible to divorce them. At one time or another, almost every conceivable kind of merchandise has been shipped to China on the off chance that some use would be found for it and that a market would be built up. In the days when the sailing ships came out half empty and returned with their holds full of tea and other China produce, any cargo that would provide suitable ballast was welcome, and would be carried free or at very low freight rates. Among the strange items which came to China during this period was a shipment of old horse shoes from Hamburg—horse shoes which had been worn so thin that it was impossible to put new caulks on them. The consignee hoped they would find a sale, but he had very dubious ideas as to what they would be used for. All that he knew was that Chinese blacksmiths were always hammering useful objects out of all kinds of odds and ends of iron and steel, and he hoped they could make something saleable out of horse shoes.

Old horse shoes made good razor blades

This seemed quite a reasonable expectation, for the skill and inventiveness of the Chinese blacksmith is proverbial. The horse shoe dealer's hopes were soon justified, for the smiths discovered that the discarded shoes, when cut in two, provided ideal material for the manufacture of the Chinese razor, which is really nothing more than a glorified and very finely tempered knife with a blade that is thick and broad. There was a big and steady demand for these razors, and soon 'Hamburg horse shoes' became a staple article of commerce in the China trade.

Junk dealers in a great many other cities had old worn-out horse shoes they wanted to get rid of, and soon there were shipments to China from New York, Liverpool, Paris and many other places. But the Chinese blacksmiths were unanimous in refusing to purchase these substitutes'. They maintained that the great size and weight of the German draft horses, and the day by day hammering of the horse shoes on the cobbled streets of Hamburg, gave the old shoes a size and a temper which was just right for the manufacture of razors, and could not be duplicated in any other city. Hamburg became the old-horse-shoe center of the world and, unless the old shoes were shipped from there, they found no market. As a result, horse shoes from all quarters were assembled there for shipment and sale to China. The fact that horse shoes from Paris or New York which reached China in Hamburg bottoms were found to be entirely satisfactory proves, perhaps, that there was nothing in the original theory of the tempering effect of Hamburg's cobbles, but it was typical of the Chinese to discover, or to think that they had discovered, a definite superiority in the horse shoes from one particular city and then to slick to their convictions.

In the last few decades the China vogue in horse shoes has changed. Soon after the Republican Revolution caused the cutting of millions of Chinese queues, and made barbering a more serious business than it had ever been before, an enterprising Chinese who had lived in San Francisco established a pucka barber shop in Shanghai, with reclining chairs and a sign which looked like a giant stick of striped candy. Before this, barbers in China had carried their equipment about with them like scissors grinders. They would shave a wealthy customer in the privacy of his own court-yard, or set up a shop on the pavement to take care of the barbering needs of the more humble. The added expense of shop rental made it necessary for the modern barbers to charge higher prices, so, like good business men, they justified this in every way possible. They even washed the lather off the customer's face, instead of leaving him to do that for himself, as had been the good old custom. They also abandoned the use of the crude but efficient Chinese razor and bought Sheffield razors made in Japan. This gave the Chinese razor-makers a serious blow, so, with their razor business slumping, they began making knives and hatchets and cleavers out of the old horse shoes. The Hamburg product had been of just the right size for razors but was a little too small for these new uses. Then it was discovered that the draft horses of Liverpool, especially those which added grace and majesty to the brewery drays, provided much larger shoes, and Liverpool became the center of the world's old-horse-shoe trade. Hamburg shoes found no sale. Old metal dealers with stocks of Liverpool horse shoes on hand said that the streets of Hamburg were no longer cobbled and that therefore the horse shoes had lost the superior quality they formerly possessed.

Curiously enough, Hamburg became, and for a long time remained, the fortunate center for another peculiar Chinese preference. In certain parts of Belgium, there is a very white clay which is known by the trade name of lithopone. It is used all over the world as a basis for white paints and is sometimes used to adulterate white lead. Though the white clay comes from Belgium, it was introduced to China by German traders who bought the clay in Belgium, packed it in uniform wooden casks, and shipped it from Hamburg. By and by, the Belgians who had been selling the clay to the German merchants, learned that it was marketed in China and came to the conclusion that they might just as well make all the profits themselves instead of dividing them with the German go-betweens. Trouble started as soon as the first shipment arrived in Shanghai from Antwerp. The Chinese who had ordered the lithopone insisted that it was not according to specifications, the casks were of different design and did not bear the trade mark with which they were familiar, and, furthermore, it had not been shipped from Hamburg. It was obviously an imitation article with which the deceitful foreigner was trying to cheat them. They said they should have known that there was a trick of some sort when they were offered the cargo at a price lower than they had been paying. A chemical analysis made by the experts in the Chinese customs service showed the old and the new product to be identical, but that carried no weight with the Chinese paint manufacturers. They wanted Hamburg lithopone and would accept no substitutes. The Belgians finally had to close the transaction with what might be called 'a very handsome loss.' They never tried the experiment again. The Germans continued to buy from the Belgians, pack and ship from Hamburg. The Chinese purchasers had to pay extra shipping charges and a middleman's profit, but they were sure they were getting the genuine article; that is the way that business had always been done and they had no wish to change it.

Chinese are not the only people who deceive themselves with the idea that the point of shipment of cargo is identical with the point of origin and stick to absurd prejudices. Eggs are very cheap in China, compared to the price which prevails in most other countries, and in 1919 there was a roaring business in Chinese preserved and cold storage eggs which were exported to England and America. Although the volume of business done in each country was large, the consumption of eggs is of such tremendous proportions that the importation of a few million Chinese eggs did not affect the market to any appreciable degree. But for some reason there sprang up, in each country, a tremendous and bitter propaganda against Chinese eggs, which were alleged to harbor innumerable dangerous germs, to say nothing of other and more spectacular creatures. One farmer in England wrote a letter to his local paper, in which he said that when setting a hen, he had, out of curiosity, included a Chinese egg and that a snake had hatched. No one ever knew the kind of snake it was, because he had killed it at once. A great many English newspapers reprinted the story, and although dozens of scientists and practical chicken breeders wrote in to say that an egg which had been in cold storage couldn't even hatch a tadpole, the harm was done, and many English housewives would have nothing more to do with Chinese eggs, no matter how low the price. Bakeries, however, continued to buy them.

Propaganda in America against the Chinese egg did not go to the extreme of hatching out imaginary snakes but it was equally effective. The restrictions of pure food laws were invoked and, in a short time, the Chinese egg-business in each country was, though not exactly dead, sickly; it had ceased to be a major undertaking which would interest big business men. The Americans had been the first to go into the business, and they were the first to get out. Sadly they settled their hotel and club bills in Shanghai and went home. Some of them had to pay through the nose because of canceled contracts. The British egg dealers lived up to the good old British reputation for dogged persistence. They kept on shipping-eggs to England where there was, at most, a very limited market, and everyone who knew anything about the egg-business wondered why, in their stubborn and stupid playing of a losing game, they did not go broke. Finally the mystery was solved. The Chinese eggs were shipped to England, repacked and re-shipped to America, where they found ready acceptance as English eggs.

One would naturally assume that when it comes to such a common article of merchandise as a hand sewing needle, the selling methods, like the article itself, would be the same the world over, but things are different in China. If I had known this when my advertising agency was young, I could have saved one of my clients quite a lot of money instead of helping him to throw it away. This client was looking for a cheap premium article which he could give away to stimulate sales in a territory where competition was becoming troublesome. The premium, in order to be effective had to meet certain conditions. It had to be an article for which there was a universal demand, cheap in price, small and easily transportable, not perishable. I thought at the time that this would be a difficult, if not an impossible, order to fulfill, but we did our best, and I spent several hot afternoons poking about Chinese department stores looking for hints. I was about to give up when a cargo broker wandered into my office. He was a stupid fellow, otherwise he would have known that an advertising agency does not provide a logical market for odds and ends of cargo which some importer has been stuck with and wants to sell at a cheap price. He was apparently making an office to office canvass. That is what some stupid salesmen do and, as a result, turn up a lot of business which the smart salesmen don't get, because they are too smart to waste their time on what they know to be impossible prospects.

This proved to be a lucky day for the stupid salesman, for he was selling needles, a huge consignment of fine German needles which could be bought at bankrupt prices. I have forgotten what the reason was, and in any case, he didn't tell me the real one. But the price was convincing enough. I tried my best to maintain a discreet trading attitude while I got all the details and a few sample packets, and as soon as the broker was well out of sight, went to see my client. He agreed with me that the problem of a premium had been solved. The packet of twelve needles in assorted sizes met all the theoretical requirements. It was something that would be treasured by the poor, would be acceptable to the rich and be useful in every household. The first asking price was low enough and by the time my client's Scotch purchasing-agent got through with his negotiations the price was of course even lower. The cargo of needles changed ownership. If the salesman got anything like a decent commission, his living expenses were taken care of for some months to come.

As soon as the premiums were advertised and offered to the public, I began to learn something about the needle business. The only needles I had ever seen were, like these, put up in packets of twelve assorted sizes. My client, who was generous enough to share with me the responsibility for the stupid mistake I had dragged him into, had the same idea. As neither of us had ever seen or heard of anything but a packet of a dozen needles of assorted sizes we had both assumed that needles, like pups, are produced in litters. In most other countries, all other countries so far as I know, all needles are sold in that way, and a woman who was offered a packet as a premium for the purchase of a standard article at no increase in price would accept it without troubling to open the packet to see if all twelve needles were there. But not in China. There is an old adage about not looking a gift horse in the mouth, but no Chinese woman ever heard of it and, even if she had, she would forget about it when enjoying the fine frenzy of a shopping-expedition. She would not only look in his mouth and count his teeth but weigh and measure him and try to compute the value of his hide. The Chinese woman shopper takes no chances. If she is buying a piece of cloth she will not, like careless women in other countries, judge the quality by an examination of one end of the bolt. She measures out the length she wants and then goes over it inch by inch to see that the quality is uniform throughout.

That is what she did with our needles. First she opened up the packet to make sure that there were twelve needles. She found the count to be correct, but the twelve needles were all of different sizes, and she could use or wanted only one size. There was some trick in this, some devilish foreign attempt to palm off on her a dozen needles all but one of which were obviously too small or too large to be of any practical use. She appealed to the unfortunate salesman to show his honesty and fair dealing by exchanging the packet for twelve needles of the size she wanted. Of course he couldn't do that, so we lost a customer instead of gaining one. This was repeated every time the packet was offered, and finally the harassed salesmen got tired of the abuse and wouldn't bother with the premium any more. Needles soon became an unpopular subject of conversation between my client and myself. I never really inquired how they were finally disposed of, but I know we were all relieved when, we had heard the last of them.

There were approximately 2,000 million needles sold in China every year. As everyone, rich and poor, must use needles, and as no needles were manufactured in China, the annual sale provides some interesting statistical comparisons. If we assume that all women above the age of five or six spend a good part of their time in sewing, an assumption which I think is more accurate than most figures pertaining to China, then it will be seen, by a simple calculation, that the consumption of needles is approximately one per month per customer, which is just about right. A smaller number would not account for the millions of shirts, gowns and other garments, and a greater number would indicate a carelessness in use, or an extravagance in purchase, of which I am sure no Chinese woman would ever be guilty. These needles are not bought by the packet but by the piece, or, at most, three or four at a time. Each customer knows what size she wants and she is not interested in any other kind. Needles, mostly of Japanese and German manufacture, were not sold in packets of assorted sizes. Each packet was made up of one size. That was where our needle premium scheme went flat. To offer a Chinese woman a packet of twelve assorted sizes was like offering her a dozen pairs of shoes of assorted sizes. As only one pair would fit her she wouldn't be interested in the other eleven. That was the reason we had been able to buy the needles at such a bargain. A German manufacturer, who was attempting to break into the China market, had shipped them out in packets of assorted sizes and found them unmarketable

Chinese girls made their own decision about styles

2. Miss China Discovers Her Legs

My advertising agency in Shanghai placed the first lip-stick and vanishing cream advertising in Chinese papers a year or so after the end of the First World War and after that the promotion of the sale of cosmetics became an important part of our business. We placed the first big toilet soap campaign about the same time. I did not expect to find any romance in the advertising agency business, but we ran into it early and after that it became a part of our stock in trade. Thanks to our efforts and the liberal advertising appropriations of our clients, a good many Chinese girls were taught to put on vanishing cream as a base for powder and rouge and to use cold cream at night, rubbing it into the pores of the skin. We advised them that after a liberal use of soap the face should be washed with cold water. The only reason we did not tell them anything about 'cosmetic skin' was because it was impossible to translate that term into Chinese. We induced all the Chinese moving-picture stars to use the toilet soap we advertised and they wrote us discreet but convincing testimonials which formed the principal part of our advertising copy. It happened to be the same soap that was used by all the Hollywood stars, so, in our newspaper advertising, we pictured one Hollywood and one Chinese star together, but we devoted more space to the Chinese star. In our world, she was the more important,

17

though the Hollywood star earned more in a week than she did in a year. In our copy, we had to go rather cautiously on the subject, of unsightly pores, because the skin of Chinese women is of much finer texture than the skin of the foreign mem-sahibs and whatever pores she may have are no more unsightly than the pores in the skin of a baby. So we did not have to promise that the use of our cold cream and toilet soap will remove unsightly pores, but said that they would prevent them, which was a much safer proposition.

It must not be assumed that our first lip-stick and other cosmetic advertisements started Chinese girls on the cosmetic road to beauty. It would be very pleasant to harbor that thought but the facts do not justify it. Five thousand years ago, according to authentic Chinese history, Chinese girls were plucking useless hairs from their eyebrows, and putting rouge on their cheeks. It was probably an ancient custom even then. Old pictures show that, from century to century, there were changes in the style of applying rouge. Sometimes it was most prominent in the upper part of the cheek, at other times it was a vivid red circle marking the spot where the jaws were hinged. In some centuries it was used lavishly, sparingly in others, but it was always used. Dynasties have fallen and the country has been devastated by floods, famines and civil wars, but the cosmetic business has always flourished. When the savage hordes from the North overran China, as they did from time to time, the barbarian women at once copied the beauty methods of the Chinese, but in a coarse barbarian way. They covered their cheeks and sometimes their foreheads with the reddest rouge they could get. The surviving

Manchu women, representatives of the barbarians who invaded China in 1618, rouge their faces in a way that makes the Chinese woman shudder. Japanese women also learned their first beauty lessons from the Chinese and do not appear to have added any refinement of their own. They are more restrained than the Manchus in the use of rouge, but their prodigal application of rice powder often gives them the appearance of a cake that has been covered with icing.

Chinese women do not think much of them. They know that without the allurements of the *kimona, obi, tabi* and *geta* the sex-appeal of the Japanese woman would become a negligible quantity and that no Japanese woman would dare to wear the form-revealing Chinese gown.

The oldest retail shop I have ever been able to discover in China was an establishment in Hangchow, which was the Chinese equivalent of a beauty shop centuries ago, and, so far as I know, still does a thriving business in rouge, talcum and other aids to daintiness and beauty. A famous Hangchow poet, who, almost ten centuries ago, wrote sonnets in praise of the eyebrow pencil and the perfumed rouge of his lady, may have been referring to the wares of this identical shop. I once tried to get them to sell some rouge we were advertising, but, after trying out a few samples, they said they had come to the conclusion that we could offer nothing superior to the brands which were popular in Hangchow when Columbus found a continent blocking his way on his route to China. That, of course, was not the real reason, for you never get the real reason for anything in China except by earnest and expert research. They didn't want to stock our rouge because it was too expensive for middle-class customers. The high price of imported rouge did limit sales, but those who could afford to do so bought the brand we advertised, and the volume of business grew at a satisfactory rate.

The best Chinese customers for lip-sticks, rouge, or any other beauty aids are the married women and not the debutantes. Chinese wives discovered many centuries ago that, if they would make themselves attractive enough, their husbands would willingly employ servants to do the cooking and scrubbing. The result is that Chinese women are the most perfectly groomed in the world and, everything considered, enjoy the greatest measure of luxury. The wife of a clerk making the equivalent of $25 a month enjoys the convenience of a servant, usually a small slavey who will do the rough work for her. If the husband's income is larger, there are more servants. Many American women think they are fortunate if they can have a single servant to wash the dishes and help with the sweeping and dusting. Her Chinese sister, whose husband enjoys the same income, would never turn a hand at the housework and would have her own personal maid whose sole duty was to brush her hair, manicure her nails, and take care of her clothing.

Chinese wives have much more leisure

The Chinese women undoubtedly spend—and have spent for many centuries—a greater proportion of the family income on cosmetics than is spent by any other national group. The wealthy buy the most expensive of perfumes and cosmetics and in liberal quantities. Those who cannot afford these extravagances buy cheaper brands and in smaller quantities, but every woman, rich or poor, has a beauty kit. The middle-aged wife of a ricksha coolie always has among her possessions a bit of talcum powder and some rouge. She may use it only once or twice a year—at weddings and festivals—but she always has the comforting assurance that she can make herself beautiful any time she wants to take the trouble to do so. Only the aged widows deny themselves these vanities. The use of cosmetics might imply a desire to re-marry, which would be looked on as an indication of wantonness.

Before there had been any rouge or lip-stick advertising in China, Shanghai girls discovered an aid to beauty which their sisters in other countries had all overlooked. An importer of rubber goods noticed that there was a surprisingly large sale for the small hot water bags which were used to relieve the pains of toothache or neuralgia. As fast as he brought in a new shipment, all were sold out, and it seemed to him that a good part of Shanghai was suffering from toothache, until he found that Chinese girls were using them to make their cheeks rosy. Bags filled with hot water were concealed in their muffs and, by applying heat to the cheek, a natural rosy glow was produced which was all the more captivating because it had not been there a few moments before. It was the nearest approach to an artificial maidenly blush that one could imagine. Of course, this beauty aid was not entirely satisfactory, because it could only be used in cold weather. The next season muffs went out of style and so did the miniature hot water bags. This had, for us, the satisfactory result of increasing the sales of compacts and rouge.

Our clients got only a small part of the increased cosmetic business which eventually resulted from our advertising. When we started to exploit a new product in China, we could never be certain about the sales, but we could always be certain of one thing, and that was that if it was possible to do so some Chinese or Japanese manufacturer would start making a similar article and selling it at a cheaper price. This is what happened as soon as we began to advertise vanishing cream, rouge and lipsticks. Most of the small cosmetic manufacturers rode along in the tail wind of our advertising, but a fair proportion of the others did some advertising of their own. One Chinese manufacturer was so encouraged by his early sales that he plunged on a whirlwind campaign which, to the surprise of everyone, proved successful, and he built up a big and prosperous business. In the meantime our toilet soap advertising was appearing in big spaces in all the leading newspapers and magazines. The net result of all this publicity on the subject of beauty was to change the attitude and, to a certain extent the psychology, of the Chinese women. Before this all beauty aids had been a feminine mystery, like midwifery, but as soon as they were given publicity they became genteel and respectable Chinese girls, for the first time, began to powder their noses in public with no sense of shame, and their horizons immediately broadened. They had been kept in seclusion for several thousand years, but as. soon as they discovered that they could make up their faces in the presence of men and that the men, thought it a graceful and intriguing gesture there was no holding them back. The Chinese woman had broken out of the inner courtyards of the Chinese home and nothing will ever put her back again.

The great revolution in woman's dress followed as a logical and inevitable sequence. When I first came to China almost all the women wore trousers. They were not the baggy or scanty two-legged affairs which foreign ladies wore on the beach with an eye to their sex appeal, but trousers as decorous as any pair that a cabinet member ever thrust his legs into. The most perfect picture of feminine respectability I have ever seen was provided by a trousered Chinese Sunday School teacher explaining Bible texts to her trousered girl pupils. I hadn't seen my old Sunday School teacher for a matter of fifteen years or more, and my recollection of her was rather hazy, but she had always been my ideal of respectability.

I couldn't help comparing the two, and I am sorry I had to do it, for my dearly beloved and highly respectable old spinster with her billowy skirts, has, ever since then, presented a new picture to my mind. She is no longer the most respectable looking woman I ever knew, for the trousered Chinese lady has replaced her on my little private pedestal.

Some time after the end of the First World War, the women in America and England began wearing short skirts; in a very short time the ladies' tailors in Shanghai were using only two-thirds of the material they had formerly used and were charging the same prices. We weren't very happy over the new style, because one of our oldest and favorite accounts was a Manchester firm, which we could truthfully advertise as making the finest and most beautiful calico in the world. It was obvious that short skirts meant a reduced consumption of calico, therefore less sales, therefore less advertising. But when most of the foreign women living in Shanghai blossomed out in knee-length skirts, I felt a little more hopeful about the calico business. As the ladies with ugly legs outnumbered those with pretty legs by more than ten to one, it seemed logical to assume that, in the end, the style preferences of the owner of ugly legs would prevail and force their more fortunate sisters back into long-skirts.

There was one season when our hopes were encouraged by the fact that skirts were lengthened a little but by the time the next season rolled around it was obvious that the will of the ladies with pretty legs had prevailed.

However, the calico consumption of foreign women in China did not amount to very much. The important question, so far as we were concerned, was what the Chinese girls were going to do about these new styles. Most of the fashionable ones had already begun to wear skirts, that being one of the manifestations of modernity which followed the overthrow of the Manchus; but the more old-fashioned ones were still wearing trousers. We didn't have to wait very long for their decision after they had had a chance to see what other women looked like from the knees downward. They observed the passable legs of the French women, the generally unattractive legs of the British and American, the fat legs of the German and Scandinavian, the atrociously ugly legs of the Japanese, and came to a sudden though centuries belated realization of the fact that here was an asset which had been overlooked. The naturally small feet and the beautiful hands of Chinese women have driven lovers to poetry and suicide. Lips, hair, eyes and teeth had been fittingly celebrated in the literature of forty centuries but legs had never been mentioned. The girls decided that legs had been neglected entirely too long and that they would put them into circulation without any further delay.

The logical thing for those who were wearing trousers to have done would have been to put themselves into short pants. A few tried it, but these looked excessively masculine and immodest. As the result of paternal governmental regulations, growing Middle School girls were already wearing knee-high skirts, which were constantly climbing up their thighs, so that style was out of the question. Then they hit on a very happy solution, a long skirt with the left side slit to a point above the knee so that every alternate step revealed the contours of a beautiful leg. Old-fashioned fathers and a few jealous husbands raised the very devil about this scandalous style, but the girls liked it so well that the next season they slit both sides of the skirt and, with minor alterations, that remained the style. Some add a touch reminiscent of the old trousered days by. wearing, underneath the skirt, wide trousers of brocaded silk, but most of them just wear high-heeled shoes and silk stockings. A few of the foreign ladies of Shanghai copied the Chinese style, but the result was not entirely successful.

For several years we had been discussing with our Manchester friends the idea of getting out a style book for Chinese women. This had been suggested to us by the fact that some of the small up-country papers sometimes borrowed the blocks and published our vanishing-cream advertising free, because we always saw to it that that the girls in the illustrations were dressed in the latest Shanghai styles, and smart up-country ladies gave these pictures to their tailors to copy. However, we weren't quite sure we could compile a complete style book and our clients were a little dubious about the whole project, so the matter was discussed from time to time and nothing done. Then, quite unexpectedly, we received instructions to go ahead with the style book, and were worrying about- what Ave were going to put into it, when we got advance information about the slit skirts. We had to work fast, but before the spring demand for calico arrived we had published the first fashion book China had ever seen, in which we showed how attractively the new style skirts would look when made up with our client's calico. Because of its lucky timeliness the book was a great success. Some copies found their way to Java and Siam and there was such a demand for them in the large colonies of Chinese expatriates that we printed up extra editions for each of these places. For several years after that we published annual fashion books, and we always featured the slit skirt, sometimes introducing, on our own initiative, some novelty such as having the slit on one side a little higher than on the other. It was always great fun to check up and see how far our ideas were carried out. We were never entirely successful in getting our suggestions adopted, but, on the other hand, they were never entirely ignored. Chinese publishers saw that there was money to be made in fashion books and soon there were a number of them on the market and we went out of the fashion book business. But I am rather proud of the fact that we brought out the first one and that we played our small part in revealing- the most beautiful leg the world has ever seen. About the time that Miss China discovered her legs, she also discovered that there was no reason why she should lace her slender body so tightly as to produce a flat-chested effect which was as unnatural in a way as the bound feet of past generations. For once science and fashion agreed, for Chinese doctors said that the women would be healthier if they allowed a natural bust development; so curves and legs enjoyed a simultaneous vogue which, it appears, will be permanent. The Chinese women like it, and the men are quite willing to let them have their own way. While the Chinese girl finds her new curves quite satisfactory she knows that anything can be carried to an extreme, and. the result is that among the many beauties of China, there is no one who remotely resembles Mae West. They couldn't look like her, even with a blond wig. Every time there was a Mae West show in Shanghai, the Chinese girls flocked to it, but they attended to marvel rather than to admire, and left the performance with the comforting satisfaction that they were not as other women. They know that if there were any old maids in China they would be plump and generously curved.

I once received a letter from one of our associates in Australia, outlining the possibilities of a new advertising-account we might get. It was a preparation which would make fat women thin. Enclosed were some cuttings of advertisements showing the copy which had made a financial success of this remedy in Australia and New Zealand. One of the pieces of copy which intrigued me very much included the picture and testimonial of a beautiful blonde lady voluptuously stream-lined, who, according to the testimonial, had lost the love of her husband and the admiration of her friends, had, in fact, become a virtual outcast in society because she had carelessly allowed herself to put on twenty pounds in weight. Then she took a course of this marvellous medicine, lost not only the wicked twenty pounds, but a few additional pounds and was again a slim blonde beauty, adored by her husband, the envy of her friends, and invited everywhere in Sydney.

Here was a remedy on which anyone in China could make a fortune except for the fact that there are no customers, because there are no fat women. There used to be a popular song to the effect that nobody loved a fat man. What the wag had in his mind, but did not dare say in those squeamish pre-War days, was that no one loves a fat woman, except the man who married one when she was slim and so cannot change his affection without some difficult emotional and sentimental adjustments. The Chinese husband is never faced by a problem of that sort, because his wife never allows herself to get fat. They never go on a diet or take reducing exercises to restore their girlish figures, because they never lose them. The mother of five or six husky children will usually be as slim as a schoolgirl.

With all of these changes in styles there is one fundamental attitude of the Chinese woman on the subject of clothes which has remained unchanged from the time of Cleopatra. She dresses to attract the admiration of men, and especially to hold the admiration of her husband. The foreign woman dresses for the benefit of her sisters, hoping that her new ensemble will be admired by her friends and acquaintances, nor would it be a matter of great regret on her part, if some should be made miserable through the extremity of their jealousy and envy. Whether or not her husband is pleased is a matter of relatively small importance. He has to pay for the gown anyway. The point of view of the Chinese woman is just the reverse. She dresses with the idea of pleasing her husband. Her prettiest dresses are worn in her own home. If she is admired by other women, she accepts the compliment with all the greater pleasure because she has not striven for it. I suppose the foreign woman has a lot more fun and excitement in her endeavors to outdress and outbeautify her sisters, but I am sure the Chinese wife has a much easier time of it when it comes to the problem of getting her dress allowance increased.

These changing styles had repercussions in the business world of China which no one could have foreseen at the time. The silk weavers were the first to be hit. They had a more or less standardized product, and although one of them might produce a new pattern at uncertain intervals, when the fancy struck him, their shelves were pretty well filled with good old standard stuff which the Chinese woman bought year after year without any idea of demanding something new until the old gown wore out. They would never have thought of a gown going out of style.

Now the Chinese women demanded something new and began to find the old stock passe. The beautiful new patterns our Manchester friends offered each year added to, if they did not create, this feminine unrest. The silk weavers and dealers soon found that if they wanted to keep their business they would have to get out some new designs every season or stir up their dye pots so as to produce new colors on old patterns. In the meantime some of their old steady sellers began to move slowly and then came to a dead stop. Some pieces had to be shipped to remote parts of the country to find buyers among women who were still staidly old fashioned.

The pawnbrokers also got a jolt. Pawnbroking is an old and highly respectable business in China, and usually a very prosperous one. While in other countries a visit to a pawnbroker is supposed to imply a rather desperate needs for funds, that is not the case in China. Chinese can see no reason why they should bother to store their winter clothing during the summer months when the pawnshop proprietor will not only do this for them, but will lend them a small sum for the privilege. The result is that at each change of season, the pawnshops do a big business lending money on clothing and redeeming old garments. To the pawnbrokers a silk gown had always been a silk gown whose re-sale value could be accurately appraised. Then the changes in style began to come in, and he was confronted with the unprecedented situation that a gown of known value last spring was a totally unsaleable object this autumn. Much against his will, the pawnbroker now has to study ladies' styles and become a fashion expert. I wonder what he would think if he knew that he had been brought to this sorry state through the sale in China of New York lip-sticks and Manchester calico!

Once in a long time he may actually make a sale

3. Fortunes Through Profitless Sales

In every town, and in almost every part of every town in China, one would find in operation, on any sunny day, the smallest and most modest retail establishments on earth. The stock was sometimes displayed on a makeshift trestle board counter, but as frequently it would be found on a square of bamboo matting spread on the ground. Rarely did either the trestle board counter or she matting cover more than a single square yard. The pitiful stock invariably consisted of what appeared to be the most useless collection of articles it is possible to imagine — crooked nails, rusty screws, defective buttons, broken door knobs, cracked saucers, a couple of empty cigarette tins. It was just the sort of a nondescript collection of rubbish that a child might collect in an attempt to 'play shop' on an ambitious scale and that is really all that it was — a playtime store —- but the players were old men instead of children. Every fine morning I could see these ancient playboy merchants trudging to their favorite corners carrying their precious cargo with them. There they assembled their stock, carefully separating rusty screws from crooked nails, and there they sat all day in the sun. If it was a rainy day the shops did not open. Theirs was a pleasant life. They saw the moving

29

picture of the crowds on the street, passed the time of day with an acquaintance, chatted with competing merchants, and once in a long time they actually made a sale. Someone might find himself in need of just the piece of rubbish he saw displayed and bought it for a few coppers. But these old merchants did not have to worry about their customers or make any reports on sales volume. A son or grandson provided them with bed and board and they kept shop for the fun of the thing, just as old gentlemen in other parts of the world play golf or pitch horse shoes or go to offices where they are no longer needed. Perhaps some of them had wanted all their lives to be shopkeepers and were able to gratify their ambition only when in their dotage. If that is the way they wanted to spend their time, their children saw that they were allowed to do so, for in China the whims of old men are gratified just as the whims of babies are.

To a great many foreign manufacturers the activities of the regular shopkeepers appear just about as futile and whimsical as this — so far as profits to the shopkeeper are concerned. Whenever any proprietary article became popular in China, either because of its merits or because of advertising, though usually because of both, we could be sure that it would only be a question of a few weeks until it would be selling in many retail shops at a price not only below the advertised price, but frequently below the wholesale or replacement cost. These price reductions developed and spread rapidly. There was no secrecy or privacy about the small retail shop in China; the fronts of most of them were open to the street so that a merchant, without leaving his own counter, not only saw all that was going on in his competitor's shop across the way, but could observe almost every individual transaction. If he noticed that a standard brand of toilet soap was selling very rapidly, he lost no time about moving his stock of that brand up to the front counter and hanging out a sign offering it at a cent or two below the normal price or the price offered by his competitor. The competing merchant usually countered with a further price reduction, and so the competition would go on until they reached a profit-sacrificing price below which they dared not venture. News of these price reductions spread up and down the streets and into other streets, and soon the whole town would be selling the soap below cost.

One would think that this price-slashing would create more sales of soap and therefore be good for the soap business. This was true in so far as it created a greater aggregate sale, of soap, but it did not do the price-slashed brand any good. The merchant made no profit on it, therefore was not interested in selling it. He displayed the soap, hung out signs telling of the cheap price, but when a customer came into the shop he tried to sell him every other brand rather than the one which he appeared to be pushing. He might even go so far as to say that this brand was not so good as it used to be, that he could no longer recommend it, and that that was the reason for the cut price. If the price cutting-kept up, the brand finally acquired a bad name as being one on which no profit could be made. The dealers would stock it, if there was an insistent demand tor it, but they did so resentfully and under compulsion and made no attempt to sell it. Advertising had to carry the double burden of creating a demand for the product which was strong enough to counteract the antagonism of the dealer. Merchandising became a vicious circle. The more popular a brand became the more the price was cut, the more unprofitable it became to the dealer and the harder he would attempt to sell other brands.

It may sound very absurd, but it is no exaggeration to say that one of the problems faced by every manufacturer of a popular and widely advertised proprietary article in China was to compel the dealer to sell it at a profit to himself, and no one has ever been able to do this with complete success. The big cigarette companies went farther than anyone towards solving this problem; they had an elaborate system of deferred discounts, secret rebates, and free goods deals. These rebates, discounts or free goods deals were genuinely secret in that the beneficiary did not know what they were until the time came to collect them. The goods were sold to the dealer at a fixed price per case, but with the understanding that at a time when, presumably, the dealer has sold out his entire stock to consumers, he would be given a premium consisting of a cash rebate on his purchases or some free goods. Some manufacturers made the scheme very complicated, and more enticing, by means of monthly allowances of this kind followed by one grand final rebate just before Chinese New Year, when everyone was supposed to liquidate all his obligations and when cash was urgently needed by almost all, and was especially useful to merchants. No matter how keen the competition might be, the dealers who had bought and paid for goods on these bizarre terms did not dare to go very far in their price cutting, for if they did, they might end up with a loss. This sales policy required a lot of combined juggling and tight-rope walking on the part of the manufacturer, and a single misstep might mean a disastrous spill. The most skillful performer was the one who could make the original sales price high enough to enable him to give the dealers a surprisingly liberal allowance and still leave a satisfactory margin of profit for himself. And, of course that might lead to trouble, for the dealer who got an unexpectedly big rebate this season would expect a similar pleasant surprise next season and there would be heart burnings and resentment if he were disappointed.

The cutting of prices to below the wholesale or replacement cost affected only a comparatively few brands in retail shops, but there were a great many wholesale dealers in a number of lines who, as a matter of ordinary business practice, sold goods at exactly the same price they paid for them and, what is more, they prospered and amassed fortunes by this fantastic comic opera policy.

Incredible as it may sound, this method of growing wealthy was really very simple and very easily explained. The wholesale cigarette dealer, for example, was given credit for ninety days by the manufacturer and, if he was a big and important dealer, the manufacturer would not be too harsh and unbending with him about payment on the due date. The days of grace which are customarily allowed to creditors all over the world were more flexible in China and often turned out to be weeks or months. The wholesaler extended credit of one month to the more reliable retail dealers, but not more than one month, while he sold for cash to the small dealers and hawkers. It doesn't take very much of a mathematician to see that if he took three months' credit for himself, gave not more than one month's credit to other's, and had a monthly turnover of $5,000, he would at all times be cash in hand to the amount of two months' business, or $10,000.

All Chinese believe that anyone who has $10,000 at his command must be either a fool or very unlucky if he does not make a fortune. There were any number of legitimate enterprises he could go into which would enable him to make his capital earn money with a rapidity that was unknown in countries where more capital is available and interest rates lower. If he was conservative, he would become a banker and lend small sums at high rates of interest. Just how high these rates might be is indicated by a lawsuit in Shanghai in which the plaintiff claimed the return of his principal, plus compound interest at 10% a month, which he said he could easily have made. The judge considered this claim to be extravagant and did not allow it, but if the creditor had claimed, let us say, 2% a month, compounded monthly, there is little doubt but that the decision would have been in his favor. It was possible to get even higher interest rates on small short term loans at New Year, and the wholesaler could, without taking any dangerous risks, double his money in a few years. If he wanted to go into a more venturesome line of business, but one promising more liberal returns, he might finance a chain or retail shops or one or more wholesale establishments in different lines, thus doubling, trebling and 'quadrupling his working capital. By purchasing land and erecting small shops, he could secure profitable rentals, possession of the land gave him more credit which enabled him to purchase more land and build more shops, and so on ad infinitum.

The cigarette business was only one of many which enabled fortunes to be made through profitless sales. China imported quite a large quantity of fresh fruits from America, principally oranges. An old custom had been established of selling this fruit to local dealers on thirty days' credit which, in practice, meant the importer hoped to be paid for it in thirty days, but usually had to wait very much longer. As soon as the retailer received a shipment of oranges he sold them out as rapidly as possible, offering them, in his shop, at a price which was a little below cost and often sending hawkers to make office to office calls. As his sales were all for cash, he soon accumulated funds which he would not have to repay until some uncertain time in the future. With this he bought for cash fresh fruit from Northern China, which constituted the bulk of his business, and if he was lucky and the season and the market were favorable, he might be able to turn the stock over several times and take two or three profits before it was necessary to pay for the original stock of oranges. In the meantime the American fruit dealers had been financing all the fruit business of Shanghai and unwittingly aiding the sale of all competing fruits.

With, their smaller turnover and more restricted line of credit, the small retail merchant did not enjoy these golden opportunities to make profits out of the use of someone else's cash, but did business and often thrived on a margin of profit which would be the despair of merchants in any other country. He was able to do this because his fixed expenses were very low. Needing some space to store advertising material, and to house some workmen, we once rented a shop in Ningpo; the monthly rental was six Chinese dollars, which was about two dollars in U.S. currency at that time. According to standards in other countries, it was not a very pretentious establishment, but it was typical of the shops in which nine-tenths of the wares of China were sold. The main room was 12 feet wide and about 18 feet deep, windowless and doorless so that the whole front was open for the display of goods in the day time and closed by shutters at night. In the back was a small stone-paved court-yard separating the shop from the kitchen, and above were several sleeping-rooms.

With a shop like this, where the taxes were infinitesimal, the shopkeeper had not only adequate business quarters, but a shelter for his family, who invariably lived on the premises, and all he had to worry about was to make enough profits to provide food and clothing and meet the rent. The question of capital was usually very easily solved, for he could get some goods on consignment; even if he had to put up cash, the entire outlay would not be more than a few hundred Chinese dollars. It was remarkable what a brave showing could be made on the shelves for a very small investment through the judicious display of empty cartons. One never saw a shop which did not present the appearance of being crammed with saleable merchandise from floor to ceiling, but if the shelves were inspected it would, in many cases, be found that most of the cartons were empty.

No matter how small his establishment, the shopkeeper would have at least one assistant. In small shops in other countries the proprietor would depend on his wife for help, but the Chinese wife, except of the very lowest class, has seldom allowed economic pressure to interfere with what she considers to be her most important business, and that is the business of being a wife. She is not, like her Japanese sister, a worker by day and a woman by night, or will she tamely submit to the ill-treatment which is often the lot of the Japanese wife. She will care for her husband devotedly, bear him innumerable children without complaining, trim his toenails and wash his shirt, but she will not, unless it is absolutely necessary, help him to make a living. The Chinese husband accepts this dogma with equanimity, if not with outright approval. He never makes any attempt to shirk or divide his responsibility as a bread-winner and is what is known in homely phrase as a 'good provider.' That is the reason that among the women of Siam, Burma, Malaya, and various other places in the Far East, Chinese are in great demand as husbands and so arc able to marry the prettiest girls.

The employment of an assistant did not mean the beginning of an expensive pay roll, because the assistant drew no wages. If there was a vacant room in the house he was allowed to sleep in it. If not, he slept on the floor of the shop. He shared the family meals, but with a certain discretion and restraint, especially when there were bits of expensive food such as pork or chicken in the communal bowl. He would be provided with the necessary clothing and, if business prospers, he may get an extra cotton gown at Chinese New Year and perhaps a little cash. There was, on either side, no thought of injustice in this arrangement. The boy was not-only being given food and shelter, thereby relieving- his parents of this burden, but also an opportunity to learn a business. By and by he might become a shopkeeper himself and thus achieve the ambition which appears to dominate half the Chinese race.

As the business grew and the shop was enlarged, new assistants would be engaged, and there were always more of them than were ever kept busy or could conceivably be needed. It was a very rare occurrence to walk into any retail shop where there are not twice as many clerks as customers. When he added to his staff, the shopkeeper did not select his assistants by any such haphazard method of picking out boys because of his estimate of their intelligence, industry and honesty. No matter how carefully one might investigate the matter, one could never be sure that the new employee would have any or all of these characteristics or would use them to the advantage of his employer if he had. The Chinese shopkeeper had a system of choosing employees which was much more efficient. Looking about the neighborhood from which his customers were drawn, he noted that the Wong family was large and prosperous and that he was not getting any of their business. As soon as matters could be arranged, a young and humble member of the Wong family was introduced into the shop on the presumption, which usually proved to be correct, that a fair share of the Wong family business would follow. In like manner a Chow, a Ling and a Chang would be added to the staff, the only limit being the number of families in the neighborhood whose trade might be large enough to be profitable. When not busy, which was most of the time, these lads might be seen keeping an observant eye on the street to see whether or not any of their relatives strayed into a competing shop, and when they did, the matter became a problem for family adjustment.

Eventually, after some years of service, and the control of a profitable volume of family trade, the assistant might be given a small wage, and at a still more remote time eventually might be taken into partnership. Whatever the wage, it would barely cover actual living expenses, but if the year had been a profitable one, the bonus at New Year was often very liberal. If the Wong-family prospered and their trade was big enough, the probabilities were that instead of working up to partnership with his old employer Wong, financed by his family, would start a shop of his own, in which case the Wong family business moved over in mass to the new shop. That, as a matter of fact, was the logical and usual development and accounts for the fact that though there were many shops in China, there were very few large ones. In most cases, the few large shops in existence were made possible only by the fact that the family was so large and prosperous that little if any outside help needed to be employed.

While the Chinese merchant offers visual evidence of his prosperity by leaving cargo about where it can be easily seen, he seldom invests any money in new show cases, plate glass windows, or similar vanities which bring joy to the heart of the American retailer. There are two reasons for this, which are just about as different as two reasons can be. If he has prospered he does not want to disturb the lucky influences which surround him by any changes in the shop or office. The other reason is more practical. Merchandise is something that can be sold, presumably at a profit, but in any case is marketable. Equipment, such as show cases and desks, form a permanent investment and as such are likely to give a bad impression among the customers of the shop. Obviously the man who has spent a few thousand dollars on things of this sort must get his money back one way or another and eventually the customer must pay the bill. It stands to reason that the man with expensive tastes of this kind is going to be more avaricious for profits than the one who is content with a shabby shop, and the buyer had better beware of him.

A great many tourists who came to Shanghai made it a point to visit a silk shop which was world famous for its products. And justly famous, for no other roof in the world covered such a wealth of beautiful fabrics. Beside them the treasures of many Fifth Avenue establishments were cheap and tawdry.

Heavily armed guards indicate his wealth

But the exterior of the shop gave no hint of wealth. It was located in an obscure street, there were no plate glass windows and the paint was so old that it might originally have been one of several different colors. Inside the shop the floors were of cheap wood, very much worn and somewhat splintered. It would be difficult to find anywhere in the United States such cheap construction, and few American office boys are required to sit .at a desk so shabby as that occupied by the manager. At an auction sale the entire stock of furniture and fixtures would probably have brought less than a fairly good secondhand motor-car sold in the same way. But what a wealth of silk was piled on the cheap pine counters! And what a big and prosperous business they did. Even on a dull day, the proceeds would much more than cover the cost of all the shop furniture and fixtures.

A few blocks farther up the same street was the office of one of the biggest tobacco concerns in the country, one of the most prosperous to be found anywhere. The entrance was cluttered with packing boxes which the visitor had to step around. The stairs to the offices above were narrow, steep and dark. Offices were small and crowded and the whole place resembled nothing so much as a carelessly designed rabbit warren which has been built large enough to allow human beings to move about in it. The only evidence of wealth and prosperity about the whole place was the presence of several heavily armed Russian guards who were there to protect the very wealthy proprietor from kidnappers. These gentry knew that he could easily pay a ransom of a million. It was in these quarters that this tobacco millionaire made his humble start, it was here that he grew wealthy and nothing could induce him to change. He would not even allow a window in his private office to be enlarged so as to provide more light and air.

It was a privilege to be able to visit the great advertising agencies in New York. Here business was housed with all the art and skill of the architect and the interior decorator. In London, Paris and Berlin, the offices of some of the big agencies were so striking that one who has once visited them would always remember them. But I can't imagine any Chinese advertiser ever placing his account with one of these gloriously housed agencies. The moment he stepped across the threshold he would instinctively compute the price of the rugs, the cost of the modernistic furniture, the salary of the charming girl at the reception desk. He could come to but one conclusion. 'Too much overhead expenses! Too much window dressing! These things cost money and someone must pay for them. It will not be me. I will take my account to some concern where they will sell me advertising instead of interior decorations.'

Fashions and ideas change in China just as in other parts of the world. And so fashions in the matter of offices changed while I was living there. Chinese who were educated abroad had something to do with it, the real estate boom in Shanghai probably had more. The students who were educated in America came back, with the plate glass and steel furniture complex and the idea that China's progress depended on the adoption of these window dressing methods. A few of them convinced their fathers, but most of them failed.

The fact that Shanghai was ripe for a big real estate development occurred to some financiers, dingy old buildings were pulled down and newer, finer and more expensive ones put up for which we had to pay a higher rent. With elevators instead of stairs, plate glass windows and all the other appurtenances of modern office housing, it was only natural that there should be a change in the furniture style of the city and some became quite modern in every respect. But with a few exceptions these very handsome offices, and the superior furniture with which they were equipped, were occupied by foreigners. As the construction of the new buildings made parts of the old buildings tenantless the Chinese moved into them at even cheaper rents than the premises had formerly brought. The Chinese occupation of modern offices with good furniture awaited the problematical time when Shanghai would be so thoroughly rebuilt that there were no more shabby buildings available and all the secondhand furniture shops would have gone out of business.

Although the lads who worked in the retail shops seldom received any fixed wages, that does not mean that the)' had no spending money. This, in some shops, might be quite liberal. By very old and inalienable custom, everything which came into a shop except the stock itself constituted salvage belonging to the assistants. This included all cases, barrels, crates, and other packing material, samples of merchandise and all advertising matter. Packing cases provided the richest prizes. The nails were carefully removed, the lumber sorted out and sold. It brought a good price. With unimportant exceptions, all lumber in China was imported and, when shipped to interior parts, where there was no local supply, the high freight charges made lumber excessively dear. The individual boards in a packing case might be worth in some parts of China four or five times the value of the lumber when it came from the overseas mill. For a Chinese living in the interior to chop up a packing case for kindling would be as absurd as for people living in countries where wood is more plentiful to chop up pieces of furniture for the same purpose.

A good many manufacturers who tried to economize in the cost of packing cases in China found the experiment an expensive one. If a shop stocked two competing brands of sardines, let us say, one packed in a case with a re-sale value of 30 cents and the other in a case with a re-sale value of half that amount, there was no question about which brand would receive the concerted selling-efforts of the shop staff. The brand with the 15 cent case would be shoved into an out-of-the-way corner and the other would be thrust on the attention of the customer. There were few fiber board boxes in use in China. They were manufactured there and were widely used for export packing, but few manufacturers dared to use them in shipping goods to interior points in China. They had no re-sale value and any goods packed in them would meet the determined opposition of the men who actually sold the goods. On the other hand, some manufacturers deliberately used heavier and more expensive cases than necessary in order to provide a higher re-sale value. The additional cost was added to the wholesale price, passed on to the customers, the assistants got the benefit and everyone was con ten led. The man who tried to establish a sale for his products in China and was not thoroughly familiar with the re-sale value of his packing cases and other containers had not learned one of the kindergarten lessons in Chinese merchandising. On the other hand, the manufacturer who could devise a practical packing case or other container with a low production cost and a high re-sale value was well on the road to success and might even build up a very large and profitable business without the aid of an advertising agent.

Free samples which were given to the retailer for distribution to his customers fell into the same category with packing material and, if the quantity was liberal enough, were of even greater value, not as a means of promoting sales but as a means of filling the pockets of the salesmen. With their hard common sense, born of the necessity of salvaging every stray copper diat appears to be homeless, Chinese cannot understand why anything should be given away and, if an article, even a sample which was supposed to be free, had any value, they were perfectly walling to pay for it. The result was that when some hopeful manufacturer sent samples to a retailer, the assistants sold them, and the proceeds purchased many cigarettes. As the most logical customers were people who were already using this brand of tooth paste, let us say, the samples were usually sold to them at a very low price, so that all the manufacturer accomplished was to kill the sale of some of his regular size packages and turn a profit into a loss. Also he had established a very bad precedent, because once the assistants found out that a manufacturer was foolish enough to give away good saleable merchandise they never gave up exerting pressure on him for more and more samples.

When I was in business in Shanghai I often read in the American advertising journals of a successful sampling scheme by which the manufacturer of some new product had made his brand well known almost overnight through a princely distribution of full-size packages as samples. In all cases the scheme was fundamentally the same. A coupon was to be clipped from the paper and presented at certain designated places, in exchange for a package of the article advertised. Sometimes the reader was told to present the coupon to any dealer who, by arrangement with the manufacturer, gave the sample packages out of stock and the manufacturer later reimbursed the dealer by paying for the coupons at the full retail price of the goods given away.

It must be a good plan or so many manufacturers wouldn't use it. I But I shudder to think what would have happened if we had tried anything like that in China.

We had two experiences, with modifications, of this wholesale free sampling and both were sad. In the first one, which happened just after the First World War, an old and highly respectable and very conservative British firm had taken over the .agency for a New York house which manufactured talcum powder, cheap perfumery and other such knick-knacks. The New York manufacturers, full of the self-confidence and exuberance of post War prosperity, sent to Shanghai thousands of samples and full details of the method they had used to popularize their product in city after city in America. It was nothing more nor less than an invitation to all readers to come in with a coupon and get a sample consisting of miniatures of talcum powder, scent, soap and toothpaste.

The assets taken over with the perfumery agency by this British firm included our services as advertising agents, and we were called in to put the scheme into execution. We argued against the free offer and suggested that a small charge of ten cents be made for the samples. The manager of this rather aristocratic old firm had always before dealt in big and important articles such as cotton goods, machinery and dye stuffs and had been a little chagrined when his London directors had compelled him to take on this cosmetic line. Our suggestion that he charge for the samples threw him into a very natural rage. Did we think, he demanded, that he was running a retail shop? Did we think that, because they had taken on this line of muck they were reduced to the necessity of cadging postage stamps and asking-coolies for coppers? In the end, the free offer was advertised, but we purposely advertised it in only one of the local papers, the one which had the smallest circulation and which we assumed would bring the poorest results.

Before the agent's office opened on the morning following the appearance of the advertisement a good-sized crowd had assembled; an hour later the street was blocked. They couldn't give out the samples fast enough and the crowd grew unruly. Someone threw a brick through a plate glass window. The police were called out to clear the street so that traffic could get through. In the end, the manager was hauled before the police court on a charge of obstructing traffic and fined £5.

We took part in a similar scheme several years later and thought we would work out a system which would, at least, obviate the necessity of an appearance in a police court. The idea was to give ever) one a full-sized cake of a new brand of toilet soap in exchange for a coupon clipped from a newspaper. Arrangements were made for distribution of the samples at forty different points so that, no matter how great the demand, it would be scattered over a wide area and cause no serious trouble. In order to avoid counterfeiting of the coupons, and other nefarious plots, the scheme was kept a complete secret to all but a few executives. The first copy sent to the papers contained no hint of a free scheme, but at the last moment we substituted a new block and went to bed feeling that we had been rather clever.

The next day we found out that we had not been quite clever enough. While, the papers were being printed someone discovered the free offer and soon every newsboy in Shanghai knew of it. They promptly increased their orders for papers so that some 10,000 extra copies were printed. Then the boys clipped the coupons from all the papers, delivered or sold the mutilated papers and were all ready for us when the coupon redemption was to begin at 8 o'clock.

Of course, we had specified that only one sample would be given to any one person, which was a very fine theory but nothing more than a foolish gesture in actual practice. When we tried to enforce it the newsboys, with pockets full of coupons, merely employed gangs of small boys and paid them a copper for each coupon they redeemed. In fact this suited the racketeers very well, for they sat in a near-by tea house which provided a convenient place for the assembly of the tablets of soap which were costing them practically nothing. Before the day was over, we had given away several thousand dollars' worth of valuable samples and so far as we could judge, more than nine tenths of them went to the newsboys. They sold the samples to dealers who offered them to the public at a very cheap price; the new brand was completely and thoroughly dead in less than six months from the date of its birth.

When we shipped advertising matter to any point in China, we always tried to avoid assessment of duty by-declaring it to the customs as being of 'no commercial value.' That phrase, which is a common one in shipping-documents covering advertising material, was entirely false so far as China was concerned. It is impossible for me to conceive of anything which has no commercial value. The lowliest circular or handbill could be put to some useful purposes for which it was never intended. Its most common use would be for wrapping paper, or, pasted together" with others of its fellows, it would make good inner soles for shoes. There is an old story to the effect that that was how the tracts of religious societies found such a wide circulation. If printed on one side only, the circular served as writing paper or made a very satisfactory envelope. Colored hangers found a fairly good sale and sometimes at really remarkable prices. We once produced a large lithographed hanger for an American cigarette company which sold readily at 25 cents, actually a few cents more than the cost of production. Chinese bought these hangers as works of art and used them to decorate their homes, and saw nothing especially objectionable in the fact that they might advertise a cigarette or a brand of cod liver oil. In Shanghai, and every other large city, there were dealers whose sole stock consisted of these advertising calendars and hangers. Metal signs were valuable, especially those of heavy enamel which British advertisers used on the London buses and therefore assumed to be suitable for use in any other part of the world. These made really good small stoves. One shop in Soochow for years sold stoves of this kind, made from Scotch whisky signs. The proprietor of the shop appeared to have an inexhaustible supply of raw material, probably he had a nephew who worked for some Englishman with a whisky agency.

Very few of these shop assistants would be able to pass a test for efficiency which would enable them to qualify for work in a smart New York store, but they all, apparently by instinct, did one thing that would bring joy to the heart of any retail merchant in other countries. When you handed one of them a note or a coin he immediately confirmed its denomination. He would hold it in front of you and say: 'five dollars' or 'ten dollars' as the case may be. There were never any arguments or misunderstandings in China from customers who insisted that they should have change for a ten dollar bill instead of a five. The manager of a Milwaukee department store who was visiting Shanghai told me he had spent thousands of dollars trying to teach his sales girls to do this but had never succeeded. He visited a lot of the retail shops of Shanghai and I think he made many small purchases just for the joy of having the assistants verify the denomination of the note he had given them. When he finally left China to return to America, he told me that he had not been able to find a single sales-man who had failed.

Street sweeping coolies tidied up the Shanghai War

4. Starvation for the Sea-Gulls

A Chinese friend who spent a good deal of time in my office made a trip to Dairen and returned to Shanghai very much impressed by the evident prosperity of that paradise of the Japanese smuggler. The very modern wharves and docks did not impress him as they would a foreign visitor with a keen eye to such things, for his point of view was human rather than mechanical. He discoursed at length about the warm garments in which everyone appeared to be clothed, and the heaped bowls of food which seemed to be the portion of every laborer in this modern and prosperous smugglers' cove. He was so enthusiastic about it that for days he talked of nothing else. When someone in the office expressed the opinion that he had overdrawn the picture a bit, he adduced one final and convincing bit of evidence. The people of Dairen, he said, were so prosperous that the streets of the city were littered with cigarette butts and no one bothered to pick them up.

There were no cigarette butts littering the pavements of the purely Chinese sections of Shanghai. By the time a smoker got through with his cigarette there, as in other parts of China, there was so little of it left that if he took another puff he would burn his lips. What was left could only be called a butt because of the etymological difficulty of finding another appropriate name for it. Foreign smokers were more wasteful. Most of them tossed a cigarette away when there was a good half inch left, and others were even more extravagant. But there was no waste. This flotsam of the pavement was observed by keen-eyed old men who, with a prong on the end of a stick, picked up the commercially valuable butts and deposited them in a can. On rainy days, when the salvage end of his business was a total loss, he removed the charred ends, shredded the tobacco from the papers, and with this material rolled by hand a lot of readily marketable cigarettes. In the matter of net income, it was the most profitable cigarette business in the world. There was no expense either for materials or advertising and every cent the manufacturer took in was just so much clear gain.

During the Japanese war on Shanghai in 1933, there was a tremendous expenditure of ammunition of all kinds, ranging from heavy shells to machine gun bullets. In fact, some of the Shanghai foreigners developed the theory that the Japanese had a lot of old ammunition on hand and had decided to use it up on the live targets provided by Chinese and so gain some useful military experience. In the fighting which took place in the Hongkew section of the International Settlement of Shanghai, there was a lavish and apparently useless expenditure of ammunition. There were no Chinese soldiers in Hongkew, and never had been any, but the Japanese riflemen and machine gunners took shots at every moving object, and the artillerymen showed considerable skill in putting shells through some Chinese houses and leaving uninjured adjacent structures in which Japanese money was invested. A great many inoffensive Chinese civilians were killed.

While the Japanese were enjoying this bloody military holiday, everyone moved out of this area, even the police stations were closed, and the streets were deserted except for the presence of Japanese troops. The one branch of municipal service which was at all times in the greatest danger, but which continued to operate during the entire war, was the street cleaning department. The coolies who swept the streets of Hongkew were ordered to come in for duty in a safer part of the settlement, but they ignored the order, or pretended they had never received it, and stuck to their old post. A good part of the time they remained hidden in comparatively safe places, but when there was a lull in the Japanese target practice, and it appeared to be safe to do so, they swarmed out with their brooms and baskets to salvage the rich harvest of empty brass shells and other abandoned articles of warfare. This was probably the only opportunity they had ever had to sweep off the streets anything of the least possible value. Ordinarily early risers gave the streets a pretty thorough going over and picked up the more important scraps of paper before the street cleaners started to work. Here they had a rich field with no competition and they made the most of it. When, a few hours after the fighting was definitely over, an army of Shanghai souvenir hunters swarmed into the war zone, they didn't find even so much as an empty machine gun clip. The 'Shanghai war' was, in this respect, probably the most tidy war that was ever fought, because every morning the bullets were not whistling about them, the street cleaning coolies were on the job and left the battle area as clean as a freshly swept kitchen floor.

The harbor of Shanghai was not only one of the most important and busiest but one of the cleanest in the world. The water was not the brilliant blue to be found in other more favored places, it was a murky yellow.

However, on the surface of the water would be found none of the flotsam and jetsam of other harbors, no broken fruit crates, half-submerged gunny sacks, decayed oranges, and odds and ends of lumber floating about. All these things were valuable and they were rescued from the harbor by the salvage boats which plied about. Most tourists, in their ignorance, referred to these respectable craft as 'beggar boats' or 'scavenger boats.' These derogatory terms were both inaccurate and unjust. In their limited way, the work done by these Shanghai salvagers was just as reputable as that done by bigger concerns with steam tugs, stockholders and boards of directors. The difference was only one of size and the importance of the undertakings. They were modest, both in equipment and personnel. The boat was flat-bottomed and small enough to be navigated by a single pair of oars. The crew invariably consisted of the skipper, who was also the owner, his wife and such children as were too young to be usefully employed ashore. The energies of the entire family were devoted to the rescue of wrecks from the sea.

Shanghai salvage boats are always ready

It was because they did their work so thoroughly that there were no sea-gulls in Shanghai. These useful scavengers thrive on the thrifty coasts of Scotland, but they would starve to death on the Whangpoo river. There is a fanciful story to the effect that migrating gulls occasionally called at Shanghai but always hurried away to warn the confraternity that no matter how short the rations may be, the members had better stay where they were, for here there were no rations at all.

As soon as a big merchantman or gunboat dropped anchor in Shanghai, one or more of the little salvage boats always anchored in a strategic position to catch everything that came from the garbage chute. It was customary in the British and American navies to delay clearing the galleys for a day or so before arriving in Shanghai. This allowed for the accumulation of an amazing amount of empty bottles and cans and sometimes food which has been condemned by the navy doctors. Members of the crew saved up their old clothing to add to the largesse and so provide riches for the human gulls of Shanghai. When one of these richly laden gunboats steamed into port, the salvage boats came swarming about just as the Arab pirates of the Barbary Coast came around the clipper ships a century ago. Each skipper did his best to get there first; there was foul and abusive language, and a lot of unfair and reckless seamanship.

The crews of the British and American gunboats watched these races with keen interest and rewarded the winner with the richest prizes by giving him the best garbage the galley afforded. But he was not allowed to take everything. After the garbage chute had disgorged what appeared to be a just and appropriate amount of salvage, he was ordered away so as to give somebody else a chance. From the time the gunboat arrived in Shanghai until it left, it was always surrounded by these small salvage boats. Nothing escaped them. The bottles and cans were readily marketable and the food would fatten pigs and chickens. Everything in China has some intrinsic value and can be turned into cash.

Every foreign household provided a rich supply of salvage which was the perquisite of the house coolie. In fact, the zeal and avidity with which house coolies collected every discarded object around the house often appeared to indicate that the principal function of the household was to keep him supplied with saleable empty bottles, cans, old newspapers and discarded garments. Clothing was seldom too old to find a ready sale, but if it was, the garment was reduced to its component parts. The cloth could then be patched together and reconstructed to form almost anything from a shirt to an overcoat. A few of the buttons might be chipped or cracked, and while these defects would lessen the market value they did not destroy it. If there were any dress-making activities going on around the house every scrap of cloth was saved. If the cloth could not be used in any other way several layers of scraps were pasted together and made very serviceable shoe soles. The sails of a great many Yangstze River junks were composed of old flour sacks. Some cans were valuable just as they were. The solder was melted from others, producing from each a rectangular piece of serviceable tin, which could be put to any number of uses. If you got enough of them you could put a tin roof on your house, lapping the individual pieces like shingles. Even bits of broken window panes had a value, as carpenters used broken glass to finish woodwork. Our house coolie searched the waste basket every day for old manuscript pages I had thrown away. He had no foolish idea that pages bearing my handwriting would ever have any historical value or become collectors' items, but he knew that as only one side of the paper had been written on, only half of the usefulness of the writing paper had been destroyed and that what was left found a ready sale to students. Stubby ends of lead pencils probably reached the same market. He even saved old film negatives, though I can't imagine what use was ever found for them unless for kindling fires.

Hundreds of garbage coolies pushed their carts around Shanghai and collected the refuse from the households of three million people. Theirs was a melancholy occupation, not because of its humbleness, but because of its humdrum lack of opportunity. They knew that never, by any chance, would there be an empty beer bottle, an old pair of shoes or a broken-down chair in their carts. They knew that even if an old newspaper was found there, it would be so torn or crumpled as to have lost its re-sale value. The servants of the household always saw to it that nothing that was by any possibility useful or saleable ever escaped them.

Since the Chinese boys and cooks were as a rule far better housewives than any of the foreign ladies of Shanghai, the latter gracefully surrendered the management of the household to the servants and thus had plenty of time to play bridge. Life for them was one perpetual series of week-ends, which started on Thursday morning and ended on Wednesday night. Shanghai was probably the only place in the world where bridge games started at 9 o'clock in the morning, the wife going to her bridge game at the same time as her husband I went to his office. The quantity of slightly soiled playing cards produced in Shanghai was prodigious and provided the wherewithal to purchase many an extra piece of pork for the enjoyment of the thrifty house coolies. They also provided the ricksha coolies with unbelievably cheap cards, for each card was cut in two pieces thereby making two packs out of one and providing a pack which fitted into the small pockets of a Chinese jacket. If you examine a pack of cards closely, you will note that each card can be cut in half without in any way destroying its utility.

One of the most interesting streets in Shanghai was Peking Road, famous for its second-hand shops. Some of the more aristocratic establishments dealt only in second-hand furniture; if one was lucky and a careful purchaser, fine antiques at very reasonable prices might at times be picked up. In the less pretentious places would be found some of the salvage from the foreign households. Here one might also purchase antique silk hats, riding boots, saddles, golf balls, and slightly worn collars. Some of the shops specialized in odds and ends of motor-cars, radiators, engines, steering wheels, and old tires. In other shops there were stray parts collected from launches: marine engines, binnacle lights, bells, lanterns and life preservers. One would think that only by an almost miraculous coincidence could anyone find in this assortment of highly specialized rubbish anything that would be needed, but I passed these shops several times a day on my way to and from the office, and I saw that sales were constantly being made. I once bought a second-hand bear trap there, not because I had any need for it, but because I was so surprised to find one on sale. Very probably anyone with patience enough to hunt for the parts and skill enough to assemble them could have built himself a complete motorcar out of the materials to be found on Peking Road.

When I say that everything in China has some value, that statement is a little more comprehensive than one might think, for it includes counterfeit coins. Before 1933, when the coinage of silver dollars became uniform through the operation of a central mint, there were quite a number of provincial mints operating and, in addition to the coins they produced, a great many Mexican and a few old Spanish dollars were in circulation. As directors of the various provincial mints had different ideas as to what should constitute the proper weight and fineness of a dollar, and also changed their minds from time to time, we had dollars of many different values. In any transaction involving the payment or the collection of a quantity of dollars, it was necessary to specify which dollars were to be used, or to come to an agreement as to the relative value of the different kinds of coins. As travelers usually carried a confusing assortment of dollars around with them, the Chinese Government Railway had posted in most of its principal stations an official list setting forth the discount at which various provincial dollars would be accepted. At the bottom of the list there was a line reading:

'Counterfeit coins accepted at market rate.'

When the Chinese government began issuing paper currency which was backed by a sound specie reserve we were relieved of the necessity of carrying around several pounds of silver dollars for spending money. Before that time it was not at all unusual to locate, among the mementos of last night's visit to a cabaret or night club, one or two dollars of doubtful parentage whose silver tinkle was somewhat dulled. But the fact that they were not of pure silver, or contained no silver at all, did not by any means destroy their value. It wasn't necessary to slyly pass them off on someone else. We merely took them to an exchange shop where the experts would determine their value very carefully and give a fair price for them. The exchange shops, when they had accumulated a quantity of these coins, would sell them to the Chinese mint, receiving the market price for the silver content.

Of course, the reason for this lenient attitude on the subject of counterfeit coinage was found in the fact that Chinese coins were never worth any more than the value of the metal they contained. A lump of silver weighing five pounds was worth approximately the same as five pounds of silver dollars, provided the fineness of the silver was the same. The older silver dollars had stamped on them the exact weight of the piece so that there could be no misunderstanding as to what it was worth.

A number of years ago two wealthy brothers, whose Bagdad ancestors had made several fortunes out of the opium business, fell heir to one of the numerous foreign language newspapers of Shanghai. They didn't know anything about the publishing business, but, fortunately for them and for all concerned, they had plenty of money, so they could afford the luxury of playing at running a newspaper. They stuck with it for several years and never lost their amateur standing as publishers. One of their favorite stunts was to get out special editions, and some of them were very successful. A few of the advertisers in Shanghai, including almost all our clients, had learned that about the only thing extraordinary about a special issue was the extra revenue it brought to the publisher, but there were enough dupes to give Shanghai the world's record, month by month and year by year, for special editions. Daily papers were published in six different languages and each has different pretexts for special editions. The numerous weeklies also had a special issue on the slightest provocation. The only people who did not get them out were the publishers of annual directories.

Encouraged by their success in smaller enterprises, these inexperienced publishers decided to get out a special issue which would make all previous attempts, either by themselves or others, trivial and insignificant, and to set a record which would be very difficult to beat. They employed extra advertising and circulation canvassers, made discreet cuts in rates to stingy advertisers and, in the end, produced one Sunday morning the biggest daily newspaper I have ever seen. Being an old fogey about such matters, I never placed any business in these special editions unless compelled to do so by my clients, and this Gargantuan edition had appeared without any help from us. The advertising manager was so proud of his success that he couldn't resist the temptation to do a little gloating, so he came around a few days later to tell me what a wonderful opportunity I had missed because the sale of this Sunday paper had been twice that of the ordinary issues and very much greater than that of any other foreign language newspaper that had ever been published in China.

He had fairly convincing proofs of his claim about the circulation of the paper, but they were entirely unnecessary so far as I was concerned, because I already had a guilty knowledge of the sales of their paper which was embarrassing to me. When I got to the office on the Monday morning, after the big edition came out, I found the place full of copies of the giant newspaper. It didn't take very long to find out what had happened, though I never would have known that anything had happened if I had arrived in the office half an hour later for, by that time, all the Sunday papers would have been delivered to the old paper dealer who had contracted to buy them. What had happened was this. A couple of coolies in my office, who through selling office waste paper had an expert knowledge of the market value of old newspaper, had learned of the amazing number of pages this issue was to obtain, had computed the weight and made the profitable discovery that they could buy copies of this paper at the regular newsstand at street sale prices and re-sell them to the old-paper dealers at a profit of about $25 for each thousand copies. They formed a syndicate to finance the enterprise, got some friends to help them in their operations, and as fast as the papers came off the press they bought them. They did the job so thoroughly that although deliveries were made to the regular subscribers, it is doubtful if a single copy got into the hands of any other bona fide readers. I heard rumors around the office that the coolies made about $300 on the deal.

The Yin and the Yang form a perfect whole

5. Sales Without Salesmen

When a new field marshal of industry arrived in Shanghai to storm the citadels of Chinese trade, one of the first things he usually thought of doing was to organize some shock troops of Chinese salesmen and put things over in a big way with no loss of time. That was usually what he had done at home with great success and he did not see why the same program could not be carried out in China. If he had picked up any acquaintances on the boat who told him anything about the way business was conducted in Shanghai, he would have learned that competing firms had not gone very far in the employment of this obvious aid to sales, and it appeared that the door of opportunity was wide open to anyone who knew how to organize and train a sales force. A great many came to us with the request to help them to get things started by recommending one or more good salesmen to form the nucleus of their organization. When confronted by a request of this sort, I always had to make the same reply, which was perfectly truthful, though often unconvincing to men who thought in terms of salesmanship:

'I am sorry I can't help you, for if I knew where I I could find a good Chinese salesman, I would employ I him myself.'

The fact that there are no Chinese salesmen requires some detailed explanation. A great deal of Chinese philosophy is based on the idea of the dual principle in nature, which they know as the yin and the yang. There is male and female, sun and moon, heat and cold and so on through innumerable combinations of complementary forces, which, in combination, form the perfect whole. The yin and the yang principle, which is as old as China itself, operates in many countries where it was never heard of and applies to situations which were undreamed of by the old Chinese philosophers. The philosophical principle is so complete and perfect and all embracing that it includes the relationship between the crust and fruit of a pie, the butter and bread of a sandwich, the whisky and soda of a drink. These commonplace comparisons have nothing to do with the philosophy and are mentioned only for the purpose of showing the universal application. For example, it is obvious that good orators could not develop without good listeners. The quality of oratory all over the world started to decline when people began to read newspapers instead of going to political meetings. This is an example of the application of the positive yang principle of oratory and the negative yin principle of auditors, the two in combination forming a perfect whole. Anthropologists might elaborate this ancient philosophical principle until one could find in it a complete explanation of the influence of environment.

America has produced the greatest race of salesmen the world has ever known because American psychology, for reasons I do not understand and will not attempt to explain, has made this development possible. Perhaps the decline in audiences at political meetings turned to the more restricted field of salesmanship those whose temperaments demanded an opportunity for vocal self expression. At any rate, selling and being sold to is a great American vocation. Just as my fellow countrymen enjoy the ministrations of a barber and a bootblack, they revel in the visits of salesmen. It appears to me that a great many American businessmen enjoy getting settled into a comfortable chair and letting a good salesman turn himself loose on them. They appraise his technique with the eye. and the ear of a connoisseur, enjoy a good performance and are irritated by a poor one. If this is not true, then why does such a tremendous proportion of the population find profitable employment talking people into buying something that they should know, without aid from anyone, whether or not they need or want it? It has all the appearance of being a contest in which both get the keenest enjoyment. The buyer says, in effect:

'I have a whale of a lot of sales resistance this morning. Jump in and see what you can do about it.'

Then if the salesman is good enough he wins, the fountain pen is brought out and another signature goes on the dotted line. In listening to stories or sales which have been made, often told by the man who did the buying, one cannot escape the conviction that in most cases it was the technique of the salesman rather than the price or quality of the goods that was- the deciding factor.

On one of my visits to America after an uninterrupted residence of more than ten years in China, I had a deuce of a time buying a hat and some neckties of which I was very much in need because, it appeared to me, no one would let me buy anything; they insisted on selling things to me. I had been out of America so long that I had but a hazy memory of some of our most treasured institutions. I remember the hat episode very well. I went, into a shop in Herald Square and, in order to make my position perfectly clear in the matter, announced that I proposed to buy a hat. I did not explain that I had a rather definite idea of what I wanted in the way of head gear, for I presumed that would be taken for granted, and that, in any event, I would be consulted in the matter and my ideas given some consideration. But apparently that was not the procedure demanded by efficient business methods. The smart young man gave me a most appraising glance and, seizing a hat from the shelf, began presenting more selling points than I thought a single hat could possibly possess.

Having been away from my native land for a long time and accustomed to the complaisant and non-resistant attitude of the Chinese, these aggressive tactics were new and rather disconcerting to me; but I was determined to buy a hat instead of having one sold to me, so I said to the salesman:

'I came in here to buy a hat and fully intend to do so. If you will quit trying to sell me the one you prefer and allow me to look around, I will undoubtedly find one which suits me and will buy it.'

Some look on the salesman's face must have telegraphed a signal of distress to the floor manager, for he came rushing over to inquire if he could do anything for me. I started to repeat what I had told the salesman but got no farther than:

'I came in here to buy a hat—'

'Here is our very latest model—' said the floor manager.

'Never mind,' I said. 'I don't want a hat.'

Then my wife intervened, diplomatic relations were restored and I was sold a hat. I always disliked it and was glad when it got shabby enough to justify me in giving it to a ricksha coolie in Shanghai. The only way I was able to buy a tie with any degree of satisfaction to myself was to spot one in a shop window and rush in and buy it before the salesman had an opportunity to say anything.

I haven't told this story in order to prove that I am a crabbed old crank (which it probably does prove to most of my readers) but to indicate that Americans are, more than any other people, receptive to salesmanship, and so come back to an explanation of why there are few, if any, Chinese salesmen in China. The reason is that they haven't the proper mental material to work on and so are as helpless and useless as a carpenter without wood or a plumber without pipes. One of the joys of dinner at a good restaurant in most places in New York seems to be the ritual of allowing the head waiter to make up your mind what you want to eat, but I can't imagine any Chinese doing this. He knows just what he wants to eat and just what he wants to buy, or if he is dealing with something that is outside his range of experience, he will ask a friend who owns one. More than two thousand years ago, the great Chinese sage Confucius taught his fellow-countrymen to be suspicious of eloquence of any sort, which he branded as a subtle and deceptive form of insincerity, and they are especially suspicious of any form of eloquence that is designed to part them from their money. In fact, the Master held up for special condemnation the very type of person who would qualify today as an ideal salesman, that is a handsome, well-dressed man with a pleasing address. He warned his disciples to beware of people of this type because they were usually unprincipled and without conscience. Followers of the Master have amplified and confirmed this dictum and no one has ever said a word in defense of the salesman. The result is that the salesman follows a profession which is without honor in China. They make little distinction between the hawker and the salesman except to be more suspicious of the latter because he operates with more dangerous wiles and on a more expensive scale. It is impossible to conceive of a convention of Chinese salesmen, for everyone would be ashamed to attend it. Many Chinese employed by foreign firms would be proud of the title 'chief accountant,' 'assistant cashier,' or 'service manager,' and would prefer any of these to the title of 'sales manager.' There is, in fact, no such term as 'sales manager' in the Chinese language; when a translation is necessary the term 'business manager' is used instead.

If the field marshal of industry did manage to get together a crew of Chinese and train them to the point that they were letter-perfect in the theory of salesmanship, he would be in the position of the young man in the popular song who got all dressed up and had nowhere to go. To be more accurate, he would be in the position of having an expensive staff of young men all dressed up with very limited places to go, because neither in business nor social life in China are strangers welcome. The house-to-house canvasser who attempted to ply his trade would be beaten before he started. The Chinese servant considers that one of his most important duties is to protect his master and mistress from the intrusion of strangers, whom he naturally assumes must be intent upon some evil purpose. A full explanation of the reason for the visit is necessary before one gets past the watchman at the gate, and as soon as the servant learns that it is for the purpose of selling something, his suspicions as to the evil intent are confirmed. Besides, he knows that there is no need for this particular article in his household and saves the canvasser a lot of trouble by telling him so. Then he closes the gate and the interview is ended with no sale and no encouragement to make a second call.

The portals to the executive offices of the big shop, or the business offices of other concerns, were not quite so effectively closed as were the doors to the home, but the salesman would waste so much time slipping or bribing his way through them that it was hardly worth his while to make the attempt. In the business office, as in the home, the doors were open to friends but closed to strangers, and the assistants of the proprietor or manager guarded their employer from intrusion just as carefully as the servants did in his home. It is extremely difficult for an unknown Chinese to gain access to the office of another Chinese, no matter what his business may be, except through the introduction of a mutual friend. Even if he did succeed, the chances of his doing any business were very remote. It was not quite so difficult for a foreigner, but he was likely to run into barriers which were none the less real because they were invisible. It was not an unusual experience for a newly arrived foreigner to make a number of calls and spend hours in a Chinese business house trying to close some deal, only to find out eventually that the non-committal man he had been talking to was an assistant who had no authority to do anything more than talk, and had merely been shielding his superiors. But once the two parties to a deal, the salesman and the customer, were brought together by a mutual friend, the whole atmosphere was changed. The clouds of distrust and suspicion vanished and the two got down to the details of the transaction with the ease and security enjoyed by those who have been doing business together for a decade.

Very few foreigners, even including those who lived in China, realize the very important part that mutual trust and confidence plays in all Chinese business transactions. A Chinese wants, first, to do business with members of his own family, next, with his friends, arid will not have any dealings with strangers if it is possible to avoid it. If two strangers are parties to a business deal then it is absolutely essential that there be a go-between, a mutual friend who will conduct the negotiations, compose differences of opinion and, when the deal is concluded, act as joint guarantor for both parties, making himself personally responsible that the contract will be carried out and the money paid. When a Chinese whom I did not know came to see' me on business, he was almost invariably accompanied by a mutual friend who introduced him and took part in tire negotiation. Sometimes the circles of our friendship did not overlap and then it was necessary to bridge the gap by means of a mutual friend of a mutual friend, which was a little more complicated but answered the same purpose. I did exactly the same thing if I Lad any business to discuss with a Chinese with whom I was not personally acquainted and had no business connections. It did not matter if each was well known to the other by reputation. The friendly relationship must be established in the orthodox manner. In many ways, it was a nice, and very useful custom. Business relationships were established at once on a basis of mutual trust and confidence and, if there should be any difficulties later on, the go-between was always available to straighten them out. If you were a seller instead of a buyer it had one disadvantage when you were called upon to manifest your friendship by a reduction in price, but the wise business man knew that this request was inevitable and had prepared for it in his 'first asking price.' But this custom of doing business only with friends did not fit in with high pressure or mass salesmanship, as the salesman's contacts were limited to the number of mutual friends he could locate. This complicated the routine of selling to such an extent that it became impractical.

I was once very much surprised to receive a postal remittance for $20 from a retail merchant in remote Kansu, with a letter asking me to invest that amount in the toilet soap we were advertising and ship the cargo to him. Hardly a month went by after that that I did not receive similar requests of this sort. What happened in the case of the Kansu dealer was typical. He read one of our advertisements and was interested in selling the soap. But as the manufacturers were unknown to him, he called on his friend the publisher of the paper, to secure an introduction. The manufacturer was also unknown to the publisher, as all his dealings regarding advertising matter were with me. So he introduced the retailer to me and I introduced him to the manufacturer. A mutual friend of a mutual friend bridged the thousand miles between Kansu and Shanghai and established business relationships between a small retail dealer and the biggest of British soap manufacturers. If business developed to proportions of any importance I was usually asked to act as guarantor for this British firm, which listed its assets in terms of millions of pounds sterling. On several occasions I acted as guarantor for world famous British and American companies, binding myself to meet their obligations if they should fail; but I never said anything about it to the companies concerned for they would probably not be flattered.

There were, of course, a great many Chinese whose business was to turn in daily orders for goods, and who performed that function very successfully, but this was not because of their abilities as salesmen but because of their friendship and acquaintance with a number of individuals in one particular classification of dealers. In other countries, there is a theory that the volume of business a salesman turns in will depend on the number of calls he makes. If ten calls a day will produce x sales, then twenty calls a day will produce 2x sales. It is a favorite theory of sales managers and they can prove its correctness to everyone except some of the salesmen who have to make the calls. In China, the number of calls a salesman made did not have to be taken into account and he did not mention them in whatever reports he made.

He takes a rickshaw to the tea house

Usually he made but one call a day and that was to the tea house which served as a sort of informal club room and meeting place for the dealers interested in the line of goods he was supposed to sell. He did not have to worry about the heat of the pavement or the -weight of the sample cases, because he took a ricksha to the tea house and, if he had any samples, they were stowed under the table where he sat to drink tea, nibble watermelon seeds, and gossip about the market with his cronies. But the volume of business he did depended entirely on the number of friends, acquaintances, and relatives he had. Of course, he had to know something about the goods he was selling, but it was not because of any abilities he has as a salesman that he enjoyed any degree of success and prosperity. He might be the most successful hardware salesman in China, but would starve to death if he changed his line to soap or handkerchiefs, because he would have no friends dealing in those lines.

There are a great many export managers who, on reading this, would feel quite justified in rising up to accuse me of bearing false witness and, to prove their charge, would only need to point to the record of the sales they made while on a brief visit to Shanghai. The export manager, on coming there, naturally visited the dealers, escorted by his local agent, and, in order to show the agent how things should be done, booked as many orders as possible. He found the dealers surprisingly easy to sell, and, when he left Shanghai, it was with the satisfaction of knowing that he had not only secured a record-breaking lot of orders, but that he had shown the local agent what could be done and had put him on his toes, which was one of the principal objects of his visit to China. The local agent did not share this happiness and satisfaction. If I was handling the advertising of the product I did not share it either. We knew that the increased orders were given solely because of face. If the agent should call on a dealer with his export manager and no business resulted there would be a loss of face all round, for the agent, for the export manager and for the dealer. The agent would lose face because he introduced his superior and no business resulted. The export manager would lose face because he came all the way front New York or London to get tin's business and was sent away empty-handed. The dealer would lose face because he did not place an order—his shop was not prosperous enough to do so.

Orders were placed and so the amenities were observed and everyone's face had been saved. But the agent knew that long before the transaction was finally closed one after another of the fat orders the export manager had secured would, for one good reason or another, be canceled or cut down and that in the end the volume of business would probably be about the same as it would have been if the export manager had remained at home. And he also knew that it would be a difficult matter to explain.

It is because of this desire to confine one's business transactions -to the circle of family and friends that residents of certain provinces or of certain localities within a province tend to monopolize certain lines of business. Nearly all the silk dealers in the country were Soochow men, while the tea dealers came from Anhwei. The sundry goods shops, which sold odds and ends of foreign goods such as thermos bottles and aluminum ware were largely dominated by Cantonese, who also ran most of the bake-shops of the country. Until the turn of the century practically all the banking business was done by men from Shensi, and all the scriveners came from Shaoshing.

We were once given the handling of a fair-sized chewing gum campaign, and as the manufacturer thought it might be possible to teach all China this picturesque habit, we were more than usually anxious that the advertising should produce results. According to the program which had been mapped out by the manufacturer, the distributor was to do his part by getting the gum I put on sale in every possible shop in Shanghai before the advertising started, and we were to hold up the campaign until we had a favorable report from him. When the report finally came, it was too good to be convincing, for he said the gum was on sale in 90% of all potential retail outlets. We did some investigating of our own and found that his figure was just double - what it should have been. We also made the very interesting discovery that while the gum was on sale in every

Cantonese sweetmeat shop in town, it was not on sale in any but Cantonese shops. The Chinese staff of the foreign distributor were all Cantonese and they hadn't bothered trying to sell to anyone but their fellow provincials who, of course, were the easiest to approach.

The office boy consolidates his position

6. Getting a Job and Keeping It

For a good many reasons Chinese liked to work for foreign firms. The pay was usually better than that of Chinese firms, there were shorter hours, more frequent holidays, and greater opportunities for advancement. Although the observance of Sunday as a day of rest was growing as a business rather than as a religious custom, and was practically universal in Chinese banks and big-concerns in Shanghai, it was by no means common; more than nine-tenths of the business houses of China never closed their doors except for the annual New Year holiday, and in many of them the ten or twelve hours' day was the general rule. On the other hand, foreign concerns in Shanghai took two hours off for the midday *tiffin*, closed their doors at noon on Saturdays, and observed Sunday and many national holidays in addition to a two weeks' summer vacation. A computation of the working hours of foreign and Chinese firms which I made in 1934 showed that the former aggregated less than 1,800 a year, while the latter was more than 3,000. Short hours, however, did not provide the most compelling- attraction. In a Chinese concern, the relatives of the owner or manager had first opportunities for promotion and the richer rewards of labor, and they were usually so numerous that, by the time they were served, there was little or nothing left for the other employees. In a foreign company the ability of an office boy to sharpen pencils and answer the telephone intelligently might lead to promotion, without the aid of powerful family influence. Also, there was a strong and popular belief that the biggest and easiest of fortunes were to be made in foreign trade and that the ambitious boy should learn the import and export business. The result was that

Chinese boys in Shanghai tried to break into offices of foreign firms just as ardently as American boys in Los Angeles try to break into the Hollywood studios.

The ability to read, write and speak a little English, and to peck on the keys of a typewriter were prerequisites to employment in a foreign office, and every purposeful lad in Shanghai made himself proficient in these lines as early as possible. He did not expect to become letter perfect in his knowledge of English by the school or text-book method. His mastery of, the language would come later, if it ever did, by the trial and error method, when he was comfortably established on the pay roll of the foreign firm which would not only employ him but educate him as well. His immediate linguistic requirements embraced nothing more than the mastery of enough words to make a good enough showing to get the coveted job, so he took all the short cuts possible, and limited his vocabulary to words which would be of some practical value. Soon after he learned to identify and to form the letters of the alphabet, he acquired a second-hand copy of an English ready-letter writer[1] and was then fully equipped to carry on the most complicated correspondence in the most correct English.

There must have been many of the old Mid-Victorian letter writing manuals still knocking about in the second-hand bookshops of China, a quarter of a century ago, for their presence was unmistakably revealed by the atmosphere of great respectability which surrounded an occasional letter. Although, from the point of view of present-day social and business requirements, these old manuals of correspondence were sadly deficient, they were quite adequate for their time and period and, in fact, appear

---

[1] A number of Chinese publishers brought out local editions of letter-writing manuals, with footnotes in Chinese explaining the difficult passages and with many useful suggestions as to how a Chinese youth should behave in the presence of his foreign employer.

to have taken into consideration, and dealt with, almost every circumstance of life in which a letter might come in useful. It was to the branch of correspondence dealing with applications for a position that Chinese boys paid the most attention, laboriously copying such complicated words as 'diligence,' 'faithfulness,' 'integrity,' and winding up with the stately old flourish:

'I beg to remain, Sir, your ob'd't and f'th'fl servant.'

I dare say a great many of them wondered what an 'ob'd't and f'thf'l' servant is, for they could not find the words in any English-Chinese dictionary.

Sometimes they hit the wrong page in the letter book, and it is said that one liverish old English gentleman of Hongkong, with married daughters of his own, was some years ago shocked to receive a letter kindly but sternly telling him that he must mend his wild and dissolute ways if he hoped to be allowed to pay attentions to the fair young daughter of the subscriber. The 'subscriber' in this instance was an ambitious Chinese school-boy looking for employment in the old gentleman's firm. He had copied the wrong letter. There must be a very old and well authenticated tradition that many young men have obtained employment, and so become wealthy, through the simple expedient of writing a letter. Nothing less than this would account for the zeal with which hundreds went through the telephone book for names and addresses and copied out letters, which were usually in a legible hand, and remarkably free from errors, considering the fact that, in a great many cases, the writer had a very hazy idea of the meaning of the sentences he was transcribing. I suppose I received more of these letters than Smith or Jones, for my name came near the front part of the list of telephone subscribers, and they wrote to me in the vigor of their first enthusiasm.

When I took the trouble to interview any of these applicants, I usually found that the fluent letter writer was

73

so timorous about his vocal English that he had brought a friend along to help him over the rough places. The friend explained that the applicant's knowledge of English was practically perfect in theory, but that he has not had very much practice in speaking it, with the inference that as soon as he had accustomed himself to his surroundings, and learned the kind of English you were accustomed to, he would amaze you with his fluency. I also learned that the amount of pay he was to receive was a matter of indifference to him, and that he was willing to start at no salary at all, so as to give me an opportunity to observe his abilities. If he was really a smart lad, he would prefer a low wage to a high one. He would like his place on the payroll to be so unobtrusive that no one would think it worth while to, discharge him. What he really wanted was to be taken on as an apprentice, where he could learn the mysteries of foreign trade—could start by carrying messages and sharpening pencils and so work up to the dignity and emoluments which go with the decoding of cables or making out consular invoices. He would usually be content to work for years at a wage which was little more than rice money, and would make no attempt to better his position by securing a place in another company. Very few Chinese will change from one employer to another if they can avoid doing so, as with all of them, permanence and security of employment is of much greater importance than the amount of the monthly wage.

While the young Chinese employee sticks resolutely to a job, that does not mean that he may not have had one or more additional jobs on the side. The short hours observed by the foreign firms made this easily possible.

In spite of the apparently widespread theory to the contrary, I doubt if these many letters asking for employment ever accomplished very much. Whenever there was a vacancy in any office, there were innumerable cousins, nephews, or younger brothers of members of the staff who, it appeared, were just fitted for the work in hand

and were temporarily unemployed. Of course, if the writer of a letter should secure an interview with the foreign manager, find favor in his eyes, and be approved by the cashier and be employed, and it should transpire months or years later that he was the younger brother of the cashier and a nephew of the chief accountant and a cousin of three or four of the clerks, that was something everyone would set down as a fortunate coincidence, one of those turns of fate which should be accepted with gratitude and not inquired into. If, on the other hand, the choice of the manager should light on an applicant who was a stranger to older members of the staff and, further, if he came from a remote part of the country with no fellow provincials on the payroll, that would neither be a coincidence nor would there be anything fortunate about it. This lone employee might possibly hold out for a time and, with the support of the manager, gain what appeared to be a permanent place on the payroll, but the chances were very much against it. Outwardly, everything would be serene, and, if the manager asked the opinion of the staff, he would hear nothing but praise for the employee he had selected. But things would go wrong. An important letter missed the boat. The items in an invoice were wrongly totaled. A parcel of advertising material which should have been sent to Soerabaya was delivered to Singapore. Japanese copy was sent to a Chinese newspaper. The trail of these petty errors inevitably led directly to the lonely newcomer who was outside the clan. The pack was after him and there was no hope for him.

Boys who' were fortunate enough to have well-to-do parents with progressive ideas, did not go into offices and acquire their proficiency in English by the trial and error method. They were sent to school where they went through the pangs of learning grammar, which was especially obnoxious to them, because anyone can learn all there is to learn about Chinese grammar in one easy lesson, for all he has to learn is that there isn't any; there being no infinitives, no one has to worry about splitting- them. Formerly the only schools that taught English were mission establishments and the boys emerged from their training speaking with a distinct evangelical accent, which followed them through life, no matter how sinful their later occupations might be. Often it was the only available evidence that they had ever been under missionary influence. Just why the devoted old missionaries thought one could be a better Christian in the English language than in the Chinese I do not know. Probably the poor expatriates were lonely and homesick and just wanted someone to talk to. Of recent years, a great many secular government and private schools have been established-in many parts of China; here the boys learned a lot of text-book English, which was understandable enough in print, but, when it was vocalized, sounded surprisingly like a strange tongue.

My wife and I were on one of our trips through the waterways of Kiangsu province and, in the late afternoon, had anchored the houseboat and gone for a stroll through a picturesque Chinese village. As had been our good fortune on many similar occasions, we were soon joined by a group of small boys who showed us about the place, and, behind our backs, giggled luxuriously at our strange and comic appearance. It was rather unusual in one of these villages to find anyone who spoke English, so we were very much surprised when the most handsome and best dressed lad of the crowd came forward and said:

'Good morning. You are from Shanghai?'

'Good morning,' I replied, although it was late afternoon. 'We are from Shanghai.' I knew what his next question would be, so anticipated it by adding: 'We are Americans.'

'Thank you.'

It was now my turn to make polite inquiries, so I said:

'This is your native place?'

'This is my native place. My school is Soochow, I am now resting from my studies.'

The conversation which had started with such fluency flourished for a quarter of an hour. On seeing various objects come into view, we mutually confirmed the fact that a dog was a dog, a cat a cat, a tree a tree, until we began to run out of things to talk about. The other small boys, in the meantime, were simply goggle-eyed with astonishment that one of their gang could carry on a long and involved conversation in this strange barbarous tongue. They were so impressed that they forgot to giggle at us. About the time we appeared to have exhausted the conversation we came to the school grounds, where there was, an obviously new basketball held. The boys were very proud of this, even though most of them were too small to play, and we had been lured around first one corner, and then another, so that we might admire this monument to the progress and prosperity of the village. It was heart warming to see the pride and joy the lads took in their school and the basketball field they could play on when they were a few years older, so there was no insincerity about the way my wife and I admired and talked about it to each other. Even our polyglot guide couldn't follow this, and he began to lose a bit of prestige with his colleagues. He had had nothing to say for a full two minutes. Then a set look came on his face. He was in the throes of literary composition. At length he looked me squarely in the eye and said slowly and deliberately:

'I love to indulge in athletic exercises.'

This was his most ambitious linguistic effort, and his' companions looked at him with some scepticism until my wife and I both assured him that we enjoyed similar tastes. So two bonds of fellowship were established— sportsmanship as well as scholarship. It now being about time for tea, we all adjourned to the houseboat, some twelve or fifteen of us, and had a most enjoyable party, cleaning out the entire ship's stores of cake and sweetmeats. When the boys left, the spokesman knew something was demanded of him. There was the right thing to say, if he could only remember what it was. We wanted to help him but were as tongue-tied as he, knowing that the more we said without his being-able to reply, the more face he would lose. He thought of the right remark when he was half-way down the gangway. He said:

'I am glad to make your acquaintance.'

This established a third bond of fellowship between us. I knew then that there was a strong American influence in his school. An Englishman might ardently desire to make your acquaintance, and it might prove very profitable and agreeable to him to do so, but he would never tell you that he was glad or even faintly pleased. So far as I was concerned this schoolboy's knowledge of English, though incomplete, was well rounded.

As soon as he gets on the payroll, a Chinese starts in to consolidate his position. If he has written a letter of application, he is certain to have promised to be diligent and faithful and, in the case of almost every employee I have ever had, he works diligently and faithfully. That is about the point where the ambitious employee of other nationalities stops, but it is where the Chinese begins. He takes those virtues more or less for granted and then learns and practices a thousand different ways to make himself indispensable to you. The best and most striking example of that is supplied by the personal servant, who pursues the same policy, but on a more intensive scale. Though I lived in the East for a quarter of a century, during which time I always had one or more personal servants at hand, ready to tie my shoelaces, put on my slippers or light my cigarette, the tradition of my birth persisted and I liked to fend for myself, or at any rate feel that I was still competent to do so and that I would not be entirely helpless if compelled to live in some servantless land. But if I should decide to change my clothes without the aid of my houseboy, I would have a sorry time of it. The. shirt buttons, studs, collar or socks would be missing — not exactly missing but located somewhere out of my easy finding. Before I got very far, I would have to ring the bell for Ghing. If I tried to enjoy a bottle of beer by the conventional American method of going to the ice box and getting it myself, the strong probabilities are that the opener would be so carefully concealed that again I would have to ring the bell. The Chinese servant does not care how often you ring the bell. It is his job to take care of you, and he does this gladly and cheerfully no matter how unreasonable or cantankerous you may be. The more he does for you, the more secure is his position. What worries him is when you stop ringing the bell and start doing things for yourself. That lessens his value to you.

The office employee had no opportunity to conceal collar buttons or beer openers, but he made himself indispensable in many other and more important ways. I remember that in one of the few success books I have read, there was some sapient advice to the effect that one method of mounting the ladder to success was to teach the man under you how to do your work, as that would pave the way for you to climb a step higher. I lost two jobs before I found out the sophistry of this advice, but with the Chinese it would not hold water for a moment. Their theory is: 'Teach friend, friend take job.' The employee will learn his particular duties as thoroughly as he can, but if anyone learns anything about them from him, it must be by stealth. There was something else I once read, or was told by a big business man, and that was that the written records of an office should be so complete that if anything should happen to anyone — such as sudden death or imprisonment— the affairs of the office could be carried on without a hitch. It was one of my pet adopted ideas, and I spent a lot of time impressing it on members of my staff, in groups and individually. They all agreed that it was a fine theory — for me — and encouraged me in every way to carry it out. But not for them. In fact, the idea of a Chinese was that an office should be so organized chat if he should leave it the whole place would be thrown into the utmost confusion and remain that way until he was called back to straighten it out. The result is that I could go away on long vacations and everything seemed to run as well or better than it did when I was present, but when a Chinese executive was kept away from the office for a few days by illness, we usually had to send someone to his sick bed to check up on some matters that should be clear in the correspondence files. Very rarely can a Chinese be induced to take a lioliday, because that would mean turning over to someone else too much detailed information as to how he does his work and so make his position precarious. He is afraid that by the time he gets back, someone else will have replaced him or will have learned so much about his work that he is no longer indispensable. This is also why it is so difficult to acid to the payroll anyone who is not a member of one of the clans already securely established in the office. The cashier, if his duties grow so arduous that he has to have an assistant, makes sure that the new employee is a nephew, or a younger brother, or some relative whose dangerous ambitions can be kept in bounds by means of family discipline.

Just after the close of the First World War, we had a lot of strange American visitors in Shanghai. They were the new millionaires who had been created by the War, and most of them gave me the impression that they were taking a trip around the world to see whether or not they wanted to buy it. One of these millionaires spent a good deal of time in my office, because he had once been in the advertising business and liked to talk shop, and as I was just getting my business started, he gave me a lot of advice. For one thing, he told me that an advertising agency, in order to function efficiently, should be 'highly departmentalized.' As I had only about a dozen employees, including coolies, at the time, I couldn't do very much about following his advice, as there were already more departments than there were men on the staff. But as the business grew, and I learned what little encouragement a payroll needs to climb clear over the fence, I kept his advice in mind. But I soon found out that in China you did not have to employ experts to help you to departmentalize your business. If you just employed enough people, and let nature take its course, pretty soon you would find that while one office boy licked the stamps on domestic mail, another was required for the more exacting and important duty of computing and affixing the postage on overseas letters. We never attained to that high degree of departmentalization of duties, because we never had enough office boys to go around; one member of our staff was supposed to know when different mails closed and no one else ever ventured to express an opinion on the subject.

The division of work in a commercial art studio afforded an interesting example of the way in which Chinese apportioned work between themselves so as not who specialized in painting pretty faces, and they charged a rather fancy price per face. Once an artist had painted in the faces, he would have nothing further to do with the job; a second artist had to be employed to paint in the figures. This one considered himself too important a personage to put in the background of foliage or furniture, so a third artist did that. There was often a conventional border design and this final work was done by a fourth artist. The result was that the finished job usually showed not only several qualities of art work, but several different styles. It was the trade union system worked out according to different grades of skill.

We always redraw the picture in China

Because he is always an individualist it is not easy to step into each other's spheres of influence and to give employment to as many as possible. A great many colored hangers or calendars were used for advertising in China, and there was a good deal of rivalry between foreign concerns to see which could produce the most attractive ones. It goes without saying that the picture of a pretty girl, or of several pretty girls, always appeared on the design; there were a number of Chinese artists for a Chinese to fit comfortably into a big business organization. He feels at home in a small one, for that is more or less of a family affair, and that relationship is one with which he is familiar. But when an organization numbers hundreds or thousands of employees, the individual cogs do not fit accurately into the giant wheel and there is some trouble keeping the machine going efficiently. The Chinese employee may give the most complete loyalty to a small and personally conducted business, like mine was, but the idea of any sort of loyalty to a corporation whose owners are merely names to him, is something that comes outside the scope of his philosophy. He does not understand why lie should suffer unnecessary fatigue building up profits for people who are neither friends nor relatives. The first important employers of Chinese labor were foreigners, who erected cotton mills and cigarette factories, established shipping companies, and built up big organizations for the sale and distribution of kerosene oil. These concerns had never leaned very heavily on the loyalty of their Chinese employees. They did not occupy any important positions for each one was under more or less direct control of some foreigner. These companies gave their employees, as far as it was possible to do so, security of employment, reasonable opportunities for promotion and liberal retirement pensions. In that way the older companies have built up a remarkable esprit de corps. Chinese were proud to be able to say that they worked for the Standard Oil Co., or for Jardine, Matheson and Co., but this was the result of years of fair dealing on the part of these concerns and cannot be easily duplicated by a newcomer.

The fact that Chinese are individualists, and do not readily submit to discipline, or conform to what appears to them to be artificial loyalty to a company, is one of the reasons, perhaps the principal reason, why there are so few big Chinese-owned companies and why most of those which are in existence suffer from frequent labor troubles. As a matter of fact, aside from a few semi-governmental concerns, there was no such thing as an important public company in China, though there were a few big family companies in which most of the stock was owned by members of the same clan, who also held the most important and lucrative positions. This made for a certain harmony in management, but this harmony was secured at considerable expense to the payroll and considerable loss of efficiency. Mr. Wong might be a stockholder and hope for a profitable year which would mean satisfactory dividends. But he was also an employee, and while waiting for problematical dividends, he saw no reason why he should not cash in on the opportunities afforded him by his connection with the organization. There were supplies to be bought, and why should they not be bought through the agency controlled by his wife's brother, in which he was a silent partner? His cousin, who held about the same position in the company and owned about the same amount of stock, had eight sons or nephews on the pay roll. Mr. Wong had only three. Why should there be this discrepancy? The next time there was a vacancy, he successfully presented his claim and another incompetent but deserving nephew was added to the payroll. These nephews never resigned and no one dared to discharge them, with the result that a Chinese company payroll soon resembled a family tree—a tree that was barren but not dead, for the roots sucked nutrition from the soil but produced no profitable fruit.

While the big opportunities to squeeze these indirect profits out of a company came to the stockholders and executives, there were many small but lucrative plums which might be picked up by the humble, and no plum ever rots on the ground in China. In those prosperous days just after the First World War we were buying a large amount of advertising posters, booklets, etc. My bank account had never before been so active; with the paying in of thousands of dollars on the part of our clients and the paying out of slightly smaller amounts to printers, the difference represented a satisfactory profit to ourselves. For one good reason and another, most of our printing business finally went to a shy but hard-working and dependable assistant manager representing one of the big Chinese jarinting companies. We had met each other only a few times before Mr. Yen told me his troubles. It appeared that he was the only man with a responsible position in this big company who was not related in any way to the family which controlled it. He had got on to the payroll more or less by reason of a lucky accident, and he was sure that sooner or later another accident, an unlucky one, would add him to the unemployed. He thought the only reason this had been delayed was because of the big orders he was getting from us.

One day, when we had just paid over to his company the biggest check it had ever been my privilege to sign, I remarked to him that I was very happy to be able to give him all this business and that I supposed his commissions must be piling up at a very satisfactory rate so that, if the worst did happen, he would have something to live on until he could find a new connection. He expressed his appreciation for the business, but said that so far as the commissions were concerned, he had a rather difficult time holding on to any reasonable proportion. Every employee in the place not only knew the commission he received, but also the amount of our contracts, and everyone who had anything to do with the production of our work insisted on a division. Lithographers, compositors, pressmen, all demanded a share. If he did not divide with them, our work would be delayed, and he would get no further orders. He didn't dare complain to the management, if he did so, the workmen would be sure to find out about it, our work would be still further delayed, besides which they would probably employ some toughs to beat him up. The result was that he was lucky if he managed to keep a fourth of the commissions which he earned. The worst of it was that before our work began coming in in such a big volume he had been getting a fair salary on which he could live. As his theoretical commissions began increasing, his salary had been cut and now he was actually making less money than before.

No one had seen such a wonderful display of firecrackers

7. Office Morale and the Casting Out of Devils

On the Saturday afternoons which I spent at home in Shanghai there was one household routine which the house coolie always followed—the polishing of one particular window. There were a number of windows he might have worked on for the combination of dampness and soft coal smoke made Shanghai windows perpetually dingy. But on Saturday afternoons he always devoted his attention to the window in the corner of the long veranda, where I would be sure to see him every time I looked up. If I should go out for a walk, he would leave his windows, but not to loaf, for he was cursed by some devil of energy which kept him busy from the time he got up at daybreak until he went to bed, sometimes very late at night. In my absence, he did some other work—followed some necessarily clandestine employment—such as scrubbing the kitchen floor. That was one thing he could not do publicly. When I returned he would resume polishing windows or dust the veranda furniture which had been thoroughly dusted that morning. If it was impossible for him to find anything to do, which I would see him doing, he started to work chopping- kindling wood. That operation was performed in the privacy of the kitchen yard, but he always made so much noise about it that I could not help hearing- him. In fact the whole

86

neighborhood heard him and knew that the Crows had kindling- wood and that it was being-chopped.

When I left the house to go to the office in the morning, he would be at the front gate polishing the brass door knob. In a competition for well polished door knobs I would have backed this one against all comers. There were several other brass door knobs around the place, but they received attention only on the regular brass polishing day, which, I believe, was Thursday. He was busily happy during the winter months, for there were two fireplaces in the living-room and that gave him an opportunity to bustle in every quarter of an hour or so to put some fresh coal on the fire. My ash-tray used to give him some well advertised employment, for every time as much as a match end appeared, his hawk's eye would see it and ■the ash-tray would be cleaned and polished. It was the constant emptying of ash-trays that finally led to his banishment from the room when I was writing and reduced him to the necessity of polishing windows, dusting furniture, and splitting kindling wood.

He was not a new coolie who was on trial and was attempting to make an impression so that he would get a permanent job. His job was about as permanent as any employment could be. He had been with us so long that we couldn't get along without him, and he couldn't get along without us, and he knew it as well as we did. His ancestors held the universal belief that the laborer is worthy of his hire, but they learned that he would have much less difficulty about getting it, and that it would be paid much more cheerfully if the labor was performed out in the open where it could be observed. So long as work had to be done, why not do it in the full blaze of publicity and get all the credit possible for it?

Any time anyone dropped into my office he could, as soon as he entered the door, tell whether or not we were shipping any advertising material; for the parcels, ready for mailing, would be piled up in the reception hall. He could also tell whether or not we were doing any direct mail advertising, for the circulars or booklets would be stacked up on the counter. If we had recently received a case of electrotypes or matrices from London or New York, he would see that also, for the case will be halt opened and some of the contents, with careless care, displayed on the top, so that any visitor could see the identity and be impressed by the importance of the clients we served. A part of this evidence of activity was intended for my benefit, but most for the benefit of our clients — to show that we were on the job. We did not conceal our activities except through urgent necessity.

When we were mailing a quantity of circulars, we usually posted them 10,000 at a time, dividing them into two batches and posting half in the morning and half in the afternoon. What we would have preferred to do would have been to mail the whole lot at one time — a whole truck load. We used to do this until the postal clerks complained at piling so much work on them. When we started mailing in lots of 10,000 daily, thereby making the biggest display possible, we got another complaint. Why should we load so much work on one shift of sorting clerks and give the other shift nothing to do? That reduced us to mailing lots of 5,000, which was a great disappointment, because the quantity is not at all impressive to anyone, and would indicate that we were doing a very small business. However, we made the best of it. We did not mail one lot until a second was ready, so that the reception hall was always piled high. It would have been more convenient to send the mail to the post office before office hours in the morning or late in the afternoon. The streets were less crowded then, but we liked to do the work in crowded streets. If some important client was coming to see me, it almost invariably happened that the coolies were, with great noise and bustle, going out of the doorway staggering under loads of outgoing mail just as the visitor arrived. When they got to the ground floor, the big hall leading to the street door gave them a convenient place to rest. It also afforded, to all who were passing, an opportunity to observe that while business in other lines might be slowing up a bit the advertising business as represented by our concern was showing some very healthy activity.

The circulars were usually piled into a ricksha for transportation to the post office, and this was an event comparable only to the loading of an ocean liner. Everyone in the immediate neighborhood took a hand in it, either by actively helping or giving advice. Chinese all like to appear to be associated with obvious prosperity. The ricksha coolie did not care how high the parcels were piled, the higher they were the louder he yelled as he threaded his way through traffic. From his tone and manner one might think that he was shouting: 'Gangway! Valuable cargo here!' 'Gangway! Gangway for big business!'

When we moved into new office quarters, I thought the change gave me an opportunity to put into effect some much needed reforms in office procedure. It was the first office we had ever occupied which was equipped with a freight elevator and that equipment provided the text for my business sermon. We were now going into new quarters with this modern improvement and so we should keep in step with the times. We should give up the good old-fashioned Chinese custom of hauling parcels up and down the stairs and use the freight elevator which was provided for us and which could be used without one cent of additional cost. I also told them that on my recent visit to advertising agencies in New York, London, Paris, and Berlin, I had not found a single place where the reception room was used for the storage of advertising material. There the reception rooms were fitted up with handsome furniture, rugs on the floor and pictures on the walls. I had not seen outgoing mail piled up in any of them. We were now going to follow their example. Everyone thought it was a good idea. Then I bought for the reception hall some blackwood furniture which any New York agency would envy, put linoleum on the floor and some Hogarth prints on the walls. We also fixed up a store-room and mailing-room so secluded that a visitor would never suspect that we had one.

That was as far as our great reform movement ever went. When the blackwood furniture was delivered it was not brought up the freight elevator, but through the main entrance of the building and up four flights of stairs, with leisurely but noisy halts at each of the landings. The only thing that could have made the arrival of the furniture any more public would have been a fife and drum corps. Tenants on each of the four floors had plenty of opportunity to admire the tables and chairs and speculate on their cost. The new reception room, in all its glory, had not been completed a week before I came in one afternoon and found half a dozen clerks addressing envelopes or wrapping up parcels of advertising stereos. They said the light was bad in the mailing room. It was bad because they had removed the electric light bulbs. I finally gave up and our reception room soon resumed its natural appearance, looking just like all the others in China. In it the visitor again found visual evidence of all our current activities. The only way I could ever hope to make it otherwise would have been to build a reception room so small that no one could get into it. We did draw the line at putting teapots on the table and storing electros on the chairs.

The first time the typewriter service men came into our new office to perform their monthly duties, they picked on the blackwood table in the reception room as the logical and proper place to do their work. Everyone around the place apparently agreed with them, because they kept on working there merrily and noisily until I caught them at it. As the result of strong executive pressure on my part the service men were induced to oil and repair the typewriters in the middle of the large office which housed all the clerks and coolies. Through my idiosyncrasies they were denied the more select audiences provided by the reception room, but they had the satisfaction of working in full view and hearing of most of our staff. So far as I knew, these service men did their work very well, the typewriters were kept in good condition, and of one other thing I am certain. Many obscure advertising agencies in other cities might have had more typewriters titan we had, but none could make more noise with them than we when we were going full blast.

Chinese love noise and bustle and a display of activity, and usually see to it that there is just as much display as there is activity. They also hold in high regard the credit which is reflected on all concerned when an office is obviously busy. If it is not busy, they will do their best to make it appear so, and even do a lot of unnecessary work in order to accomplish this purpose. They do not in the least mind working overtime, especially if employees of less prosperous offices who go home at five o'clock can see that they are still hard at it. In fact, they appear to enjoy occasional overtime work. During the first few days of every month, there was in our office the usual extra labor of getting out the statements and invoices. We had in Shanghai a two-hour luncheon interval, a survival of the leisurely old sailing ship days when there wasn't very much to do except when a ship was in port. As most of the staff had their midday meal brought into the office from a restaurant it would have been an easy matter for them to get on with the extra work as soon as they finished eating. But they never did. Until 'Big Ching,' the customs clock, struck the hour of two, when work was supposed to be resumed by all hands, they read the newspapers, gossiped with friends in other offices, played checkers or looked out of the windows. When five o'clock came they stayed on a few hours longer. They boasted to their friends:

'Pretty busy in our place just now. We didn't get away until almost eight o'clock last night.'

We once started a chain letter scheme for the distribution of samples. It was very successful and grew to such proportions that, for a month or more after we began trying to kill it, the clerks had to work until very late opening letters and addressing packages of samples. No one complained about the late hours and extra work, but soon I heard from outside sources a peculiar story to the effect that the landlord was going to raise our rent because we were using too much electricity, keeping the lights going unreasonably late at night. When the story-was traced to its source, it transpired that some of my employees had been boasting to the employees of a competitor.

This hustle and bustle and pleasant pretensions of activity give the Chinese employees confidence in themselves and in the firm they are working for. They create this atmosphere for themselves, but if they are to have complete confidence in the office they need to be assured that the influences surrounding it are not malignant. They know, as their ancestors have known for forty centuries, that one course of action sometimes results in success, that at other times exactly the same course of action, under what appears to be the same or similar circumstances, leads to failure. There can be but one reason for this, and that is the presence of malignant or benevolent spirits. Thousands of years ago, this gave the philosophers of the day a great deal of anxious thought, and they came to the conclusion that while it was perhaps impossible and certainly difficult to change the fates, their influences could be measured and foretold and one's actions governed thereby. So they set up an elaborate system by which those who master its secrets can calculate to a nicety the element of luck which may aid or thwart them. The element of good or evil chance enters into every human activity. There are lucky and unlucky offices, houses and days, even suspicious days for burial.

Everyone in my office thought that our organization was a very lucky one, because not only had it never been touched by death, but no one belonging to it had suffered a serious illness. We were very much saddened a few years later by the sudden death of a Russian artist, who, in spite of the fact that Chinese as a rule, do not like Russians, was a general favorite with the Chinese staff. After the sadness over his death had been somewhat softened, the matter was discussed at length, and it was finally decided that, as he had been with us only a few years, his death had not been the result of any evil influences emanating from our organization and that our charmed circle remained unbroken. We got a good deal of satisfaction out of this, though we did not tempt fate by talking about it to outsiders.

Not only was our organization lucky, but our office quarters were also lucky. This is not boasting or guesswork, but a plain statement of fact, for the good influences were surveyed, determined and appraised by the best talent the Chinese staff could obtain. This was done by a geomancer who, I suppose, would be called in other countries an 'engineer of psychic influences.' I met hint quite by accident, because he was supposed to get his work done during my absence. The Chinese members of my staff were somewhat embarrassed when I came in unexpectedly and demanded to know what a stranger was doing in my private office. His profession was such a peculiar one that I did my best to get acquainted with him. Though engaged in a very strange occupation, there was nothing unusual about him. He was middle-aged, soberly dressed, and looked and talked like a high school teacher. It took him several hours to go over our new office, with his compass and footrule, but when he got through his verdict was favorable. You probably think this is a lot of nonsense, anyway, so I will not bore you with the details but mention only the most essential features. Facing the front door was the biggest bank in China. On the south was an American bank, which was presumed to be very prosperous, and in the opposite direction was the office of a British land company ol great wealth. There were a lot of other good influences, such as the Dollar Company boats on the river and the British Consulate in the neighborhood, but the two banks and the land company, with their substantial assets, provided enough prosperous influences to satisfy anyone. He changed the location of a few desks and paid a good deal of attention to mine, for it presented some extraordinary difficulties. The correct orthodox position for my desk would have left me facing a window, which was obviously impractical for one with weak eyes, accordingly a compromise was worked out so that the lines of the desk ran clue east and west. This placed it at an awkward angle to the wall, but that was a matter of small importance considering the fact that the geomentic influences were correct.

The depression caused a drop in club bar receipts

Not very many months had passed before we began to feel that we would need all the beneficent influences we could get, for hard times surrounded us with the relentlessness of a cholera epidemic. Shanghai's artificial real estate boom collapsed, local stocks dropped to a fraction of their former value, the banks demanded the payment of old loans and refused to make new ones, and for the first time in my experience there were vacant shops on our principal business street, Nanking Road. It was a fine time for everyone to get panicky and a great many people availed themselves of the opportunity. Every club in town lost a lot of members because they couldn't pay their bills and the bar receipts of the Shanghai Club declined, providing most conclusive indication that the British and American communities were feeling the pinch of hard times. It often seemed to me that my office was the only cheerful spot in town. Nothing could daunt the confidence of my Chinese staff that, while less favored concerns might go to the wall, we were surrounded by such an aura of good fortune that nothing could seriously affect us. And strangely enough they proved to be correct. Very few prospered in Shanghai during that period of depression and we are not numbered among them, but we had nothing to complain about. We collected accounts we thought we would have to write off, all our clients continued to advertise, and a few new accounts which we never solicited walked into the office and made themselves at home.

On the rare occasions that I did more than look at the profit and/or loss items on our balance sheet, I noted that among our assets was an imponderable something known as 'Good Will.' As I understand it, this represented an attempt to appraise in terms of dollars the value of the reputation we might have acquired for honesty and efficiency and the resulting confidence reposed on us by our clients. It was a very flattering item but, if the auditors would have let me do it, I would have replaced it with another item which would be identified by the Chinese pidgin English word 'joss.' This would represent the confidence of my Chinese staff, that, come what may, ill-luck could not harm us, that there was no occasion to worry, that we would be able to pay the rent and meet the payroll.

A few months after our local depression started I had, or thought I had, some reason to be disturbed regarding these very fine *geomentic* influences which were supposed to surround us. The big Chinese bank on the east moved into temporary quarters several blocks away and their old building was torn down. The big British land company on the north fell on evil days and was unable to pay its debenture interest. The American bank on the south failed under most dishonorable conditions and its president and manager were sent to prison. The British Consulate continued to function and the Dollar boats made their regular scheduled appearances on the river, but these, the geomancer had told me, provided influences of secondary importance. It appeared to me that so far as our joss was concerned, we might as well write it off as a total loss. I expected the Chinese to begin looking down in the mouth, but they were as cheerful as ever. Geomancy is a subtle and complicated science, but I have not followed it very far and am familiar with but few of its mysteries. It appeared that the removal of the good influences which had formerly surrounded us did not in any way affect us. Why this should be true I do not understand, but it was reassuring.

Mine was not the only office which was controlled by geomantic influences, though I am one of the very few who admit it. Most foreigners laugh at this sort of thing, and since derision is something no Chinese can stomach, his Chinese assistants and colleagues told him nothing about it, but in the arrangement of their desks and in the arrangement of his, they saw that the evil influences were guarded against and the good influences given every possible opportunity to show what they could do. An old English neighbor told me that for fifteen years he had occupied a poorly lighted and poorly ventilated office because his Chinese staff thought it was 'good joss.' His continued prosperity seemed to confirm this, and so he had quit fussing about it and come to a kind of a halfway belief in it himself. Until the real estate boom resulted in the razing of a lot of obsolete buildings, and so compelled them to move, some prosperous old concerns had been for years occupying cramped and uncomfortable quarters. Every time anyone suggested moving the Chinese staff put up such determined opposition that the project was dropped.

About the time I was beginning to have complete faith in the good influences which surrounded and protected us I learned that these influences were purely local in character.

One day we were visited by the headman of a village, ten or twelve miles from Shanghai. He was quite apologetic about his mission, which turned out to be of rather serious import. A year before this we had erected a large cigarette sign near the village and it appeared that soon afterward ill-luck descended on the vicinity. Crops had been bad, there had been an unusual amount of sickness and a few death. The elders of the village had consumed innumerable pots of tea discussing the matter and had finally called in an efficient geomancer to give them expert advice. He made a thorough survey of the situation and came to the conclusion that our cigarette sign was the trysting place for evil spirits who gathered there and then swooped down on the village. The elders had no desire to break my rice bowl, and the object of the headman's visit was to inquire what we would consider a reasonable compensation for removing this evil influence.

A great many diplomatic matters of this sort came up in my office and the problems were solved without my knowing anything about them. The Chinese said that they didn't want to bother me with such trivial matters, but the truth of the matter is that they thought that I, being a foreigner, must lack the finesse necessary to handle affairs of this sort and would make a mess of things. Purely by accident, I learned about the visit of the headman, and introduced myself into the negotiations. The situation was very complicated. All agreed that the village had a just cause for complaint. We were quite willing to take the offending sign down without any payment by them, but the sign was maintained for one of our golf-playing clients and he saw it every time he drove to the golf course. He had, in fact, selected the position himself, and for that reason thought it was a good deal more valuable and important than it really was. If we took the sign down, we would have a lot of trouble explaining matters to him. He hadn't been in China long and didn't know about the dangers of evil spirits. Furthermore, he would probably get some other concern to put up another sign in the same place, so we would lose business and the village be just as badly off as before.

Then I made a suggestion that met with general approval. Since that was the lurking place of devils, why not shoot off a lot of fireworks around the place and frighten the evil spirits away? The headman thought this was a fine idea but, like a sensible man, insisted on getting the opinion of his professional adviser, the geomancer. He came back a few days later to report that the geomancer agreed that this would solve the problem, though he was cautious enough to advise us that we might have to repeat the performance every year or so. The devils might muster up courage and come back again. At the same time, he picked out a lucky day for setting off the fireworks, which everyone hoped would be an unlucky day for the devils. It was thought that ten dollars' worth of fireworks would do the trick, but as it was my first experience in exorcising devils I was determined to make a thorough job of it, so I doubled that amount. You can buy an amazing amount of fireworks for twenty dollars. Some members of my staff went out to see that the job was clone properly, but I couldn't get away and so missed a corking good show.

All the villagers were out, with a few from neighboring villages. None of them had ever before seen such a wonderful display of fireworks and they marvelled at my lavish expenditure. The noise was terrific, and must have frightened the devils so thoroughly that they fled to another county. At any rate, they never came back, for the village prospered and we had no more complaints. The headman sent me annual presents of tea until the sign was torn down. Our golf-playing client gave up golf for yachting and so lost interest in this position and did not renew his contract. I have often thought what a pity it was that my New England forefathers did not know the use of fireworks. A few dollars' worth of them would have driven all the devils out of Salem and it would not have been necessary to burn the witches.

When I came home, I could not help noticing that there are few houses in America, from the White House downwards, that are built so as to ward off evil spirits and receive the benefit of the best geomantic influences. Nothing short of a pagoda could correct the evil influence around the White House lawn, and the position of the president's office desk is nothing more than an invitation to evil spirits to come in and do their worst. Buckingham Palace is a little better, thanks to the monuments which face the entrance, but there should be a running stream in St. James's Park, and a pagoda in the neighborhood would be of tremendous value. Some of my Chinese friends would be horrified if they knew the way my sisters in Washington and St. Louis leave my charming young nephews and niece exposed to any evil spirit that may be loitering about the neighborhood. Among the new buildings the New Yorker hotel was, from a geomantic point of view designed along correct lines, but the architecture of the Empire State Building was perfectly harrowing. No Chinese in his right senses would ever occupy an office in any of the upper floors.

The barrage cut us off from the motor-car

8. Tremble and Obey!

During the centuries that China was a monarchy, almost all official orders were issued in the form of 'Imperial Mandates,' that is, either as a direct order from the emperor himself, or an order from some subsidiary official who spoke with delegated authority from the Son of Heaven. The mandates issued in a single busy day might range from such important matters as a command to a viceroy to contribute a few million dollars and raise an army for the defense of the country against a threatened invasion, to such comparatively trivial matters as an order to the headman of a village to repair a dyke or a canal. The edicts were very often verbose compositions which might lead anyone to wonder how the august Son of Heaven could take time to exercise such circumspection. Often the edicts contained detailed instructions as to just how the work was to be done, details shrouded in language as beautiful as it was vague, but there was never any doubt as to the final results the official who received the mandate was supposed to accomplish. No matter what the mandate was about, the text almost invariably concluded with the exhortation: 'Tremble and obey.' Then, if the matter was one of some urgency or importance, there was a second admonition: 'Do not try to avoid responsibility!'

To the Occidental this conjunction of the two phrases may seem illogical. It would appear that any official who received and read the edict and then trembled and obeyed was not trying to avoid responsibility. But that did not necessarily follow. The ancient Chinese statesman who put this, formula into imperial edicts many centuries ago had a very thorough understanding of the idiosyncrasies of his fellow-countrymen. The only time that obedience is pleasant to him is when it carries with it the concomitant and mitigating circumstance of freedom from responsibility. What he would like to do would be to tremble, and obey specific orders, so that if the job he is supposed to do is hopelessly bungled he would be able to say that he did what he was told and is in no way to blame for the failure which resulted. It was to circumvent this desire on his part that the mandate was complicated by the inclusion of two commands. In plain, blunt language, the purport of the injunction from the Son of Heaven was:

'Get busy! Do your job! No alibis!

As a part of my everyday work, I attended a lot of sales and advertising conferences. Having taken a prominent and sometimes very vocal part in them in New York, London, Paris, Berlin, to say nothing of Osaka, I think I may be allowed to say that although they are necessary institutions, one can seldom leave one without the mental reflection that there has been as much talk and cigarette smoke as results accomplished. Advertising conferences, like committee meetings, have a tendency to reduce each individual to the lowest common denominator of intelligence. The more people there are at the conference, the more difficult it is to accomplish anything and, when more than one nationality is involved, the smoke and the talk are prodigiously increased without in any way speeding up the work or adding to the volume of accomplishment.

When the conference was held in China and a prominent part in it was taken by Chinese, it was usually productive of even more than the usual amount of talk and even less than the usual results. In fact, it required a lot of careful steering and diplomatic maneuvering to accomplish anything at all. In nine out of ten conferences I attended the two principal parties consisted of a foreign manufacturer who wanted to promote the sale of his goods, and a foreign advertising agent (myself), whose duty it was to assist in this laudable ambition. We talked the matter over and got as far as we could, with the Chinese listening and saying nothing, or perhaps not even listening, and soon we floundered about in what we believed to be our imperfect knowledge of Chinese psychology, taste, and everything else connected with the problem of selling to the Chinese. In a good many cases, each of us was suffering from an inferiority complex, because the observant and intelligent foreigner who had lived in China for a long time had, with his detached point of view, a better knowledge of the Chinese than they have of themselves. This is no reflection on the Chinese mentality. But if I wanted to find out something about the psychology of, let us say, the Latvians, I would much prefer to ask an American who had lived in that little half-pint size country than to take the opinion of a native Latvian. In fact, asking the native of any country about the tastes and the psychology of his own countrymen is like asking an orange tree how an orange blossom smells. The tree doesn't know because it has no basis of comparison.

In any event, we have no particular confidence in our individual or collective knowledge and opinions, so we ask our Chinese colleagues for their help. It should be easy for them to put us on the right track and keep us from blundering. So long as it is a matter of getting' information and advice on minor and unimportant details they are honestly and sincerely helpful. And if we have already decided on the main features of the scheme, and only want their reassurance before going ahead with it, we find that it has their enthusiastic endorsement. If we were not disillusioned hands at the game we might be flattered. But being what we are, sly and crafty, we discount the unanimous approval, talk all around the subject and eventually come to our own conclusions as to which way the wind is blowing. We know that no one could be so supremely impolite as to say that a scheme was impractical, no matter how sincerely he might think so. But if you give him time enough, he may be able to convey that idea to you in some indirect way that will save face all around.

Sometimes it comes to a question of whether we shall do this or do that, and when the Chinese members of a conference are confronted with a definite issue like this, they will invariably and instinctively run to cover. They will talk about everything under the sun, drag in innumerable side issues, hope for something that will break up the conference, anything to avoid being compelled to come to a definite decision. Each one may have a fair idea of what he thinks should be done. Mr. Chang may be convinced in his own mind that the this' policy is the right one, but he reflects that if he should come out openly and enthusiastically in its favor and it should I prove later a failure, he would have to bear the responsibility. All the others feel the same way. Each one is evasive and non-committal, though full of talk, and so the conference drags on. In order to stir things up, the manufacturer and myself become violently controversial and take issue with each other. Finally someone cautiously advances an idea, leaving himself plenty of room for retreat if he should find himself in hostile territory. Someone else makes an equally cautious suggestion. Mr. Wong and Mr. Chang find themselves in apparent agreement, and Mr. Ling also says something in approval of their plans. The bogy of individual responsibility is broken. We find that we are all agreed as to what should be done and set to work with enthusiasm planning the details.

Of course Chinese are at a disadvantage at a sales and advertising conference. They do not think in merchandising terms, even those who are engaged in merchandising. Their approach to any problem is always objective, and they find it impossible to detach themselves from their surroundings and visualize the sales possibilities in a city a hundred miles away. Statistics bore them to the point of resentment. Figures will either confirm the fact that they are right, which is unnecessary, or prove that they are wrong, which is unwelcome. Furthermore, a Chinese mind has distinct feminine traits. He comes to a conclusion by instinct or personal preferences, especially if it be regarding something imponderable such as a sales or advertising plan. He may be perfectly sure that he is right, but it is very disconcerting to him to be called upon to give reasons for his conclusions, for that is something he has not thought about. When reasons are demanded, he tries to produce them, but he gets excited and flounders about and often ends up by advancing the silliest reason possible under the circumstances. The Japanese mind follows the same feminine mental processes, the only difference being that, in its application to modern problems, the Japanese mind is more sophisticated. Innumerable examples of this are to be found in the diplomacy of Japan. The militarists, who rule the country, decide what they want to do and do it, and then the diplomats have the job of justifying and explaining what has been done. In the end it comes back to the old idea of cause and effect, but with this important difference, that, in Japanese diplomacy, the sequence is reversed, and the effect is accomplished before anyone has bothered to see just what the cause was. That is why Japanese diplomacy is so disconcerting to those whose minds run in logical channels.

Every foreigner who lived in China was annoyed almost daily by what appeared to him to be the inexcusable dilatoriness of the Chinese with whom he came in contact. Except in matters of great emergency, it seemed impossible to get one of them to act with any reasonable degree of promptness. A cardinal rule of conduct appeared to be: 'Do not do anything to-day if you can possibly put off doing it until to-morrow or the day after.' This is not the philosophy of a lazy man, for, whatever else their critics may say against them, no one can accuse the Chinese of laziness. In my opinion, it is solely because of their timorous avoidance of responsibility. They know that they may fail in any task they are given to do, and, before undertaking it, they wish to have themselves fortified against that contingency with a sound and unassailable excuse. My theory may be wrong, but I know from experience that no matter how stupidly a Chinese has blundered, no matter how ignominiously he has failed, his excuse will be a perfect one. Indeed I have often marvelled that the same brain could produce such a stupid blunder and such an amazingly brilliant alibi. It is because of Chinese aversion to accepting any responsibility that so many foreigners are employed in China, doing work the Chinese themselves are quite capable of doing, but will not do because they have not the courage to make decisions. In any business house in Shanghai, the Chinese were quite willing to do all the work, in fact they insisted on it, but the foreigner had to make the decisions and bear the responsibility, even in the most trivial matter. In big Chinese companies where no foreigners were employed, there was seldom a single individual who decided important questions. They were always family decisions. There are, of course, exceptions, and that is why the rare Chinese who will accept responsibility and make decisions often achieve such a meteoric success.

Chinese have always made a very fine distinction between abstract and concrete truth, that is, truth as to facts and figures, and truth as to ideas and opinions. If you ask him how may bales of cargo have been delivered, what the price of a certain commodity is, or any other question whose answer can be computed on the abacus and set clown in figures, you may be sure that his answer is not only truthful but, what is more important, accurate. But if you ask him a question about some abstract thing, such as his idea as to whether or not a certain article will sell in the Chinese market or if it would be advisable to change the packaging of an old established brand, the truth is very difficult to find. Having no fixed or well-thought-out opinions on theoretical matters which are of no practical interest to himself, he looks on it as an encroachment on his rights when he is asked to make up his mind and express an opinion on matters which are of no personal concern or responsibility. The result is that when he is asked a question of this sort, his first concern is to give you an answer which he thinks will be pleasing to you, and thereby get the matter over with as quickly and easily as possible. The surest way to escape arguments is to agree. I dare say that if some educational mission from England were to ask ten thousand Chinese schoolboys where they would like to go to school if given the opportunity of an overseas education, the response would be 100% for England, unless some schoolboy was stupid enough to get his nationalities mixed up. The same tiling would be true of inquiries by a similar commission from America, France, Germany, and almost any other country, even Japan. It would be excessively impolite and troublesome to give any other answer.

Chinese are like a good many other people in their aversion to violent mental exercise, and it is their habit of thought to avoid issues and delay decisions so far as it is possible to do so. For that reason, we foreigners who have to deal with them are constantly complaining of their lack of initiative. There is a good deal of justice in this criticism, and it is not until a Chinese gets himself into an embarrassing situation, which is so complicated and desperate that there does not appear to be any way out, that he concentrates on the problem. He then shows an amount

106

of initiative and ingenuity that is amazing. Like an Englishman, he frequently doesn't know what he is going to do until he does it, so that his decisions are all in the past tense.

One Sunday, during the period of Chinese civil wars, I took a couple of tourist ladies out to show them what a Chinese battle was really like. Two local war lords were manifesting their hatred of each other on the shores of the Yangtsze about thirty miles away, and several friends who had been out to see the battle said it was more than usually thrilling. We drove through the war-ravaged countryside, where a terrified population was fleeing to safety, and had just got settled in a comfortable and fairly safe position, when the attacking troops decided to try a little diversion by putting down a barrage. It was so placed as to cut us off from my motor-car, and so close to us that we moved away as fast as it was possible for ladies with high-heeled shoes to move through muddy roads. A dead shell fell with a big splash in a filthy pool near by and irritated one of my tourists because it muddied her dress. An old farmer tried to convince us that we should seek safety inside his thatched hut. We turned a corner and saw the body of a little girl who had been killed only a few minutes before.

We had seen all the war we wanted to see, and what had started out as an exciting excursion was turning into terrifying and ghastly experience; all we wanted to do was to get as far away from it as possible. As there was no let-up in the barrage we tramped several miles. Night was falling and the ladies were getting rather frightened, when we were picked up and taken back to town by a British military observer. He said the barrage was having its effect and had been followed by an attack and that he thought the defenders would retreat as soon as daylight broke. He thought my chauffeur had very probably been killed, for the fighting had been very heavy round the spot where my car was parked. As for the car, it was a foregone conclusion that it had been, or soon would be, confiscated by the retreating troops.

While I was eating my breakfast the following morning, the chauffeur drove into the yard with the car. We must have looked at each other rather foolishly, for each of us was certain that the other was dead. It transpired that when the barrage cut us off from the car he started in search of me and dodged bullets for several hours until he came to the conclusion that I had been killed, a fate which I certainly deserved for having been so foolhardy. He asked some of the soldiers to help look for me, but they were busy with their own affairs. When he came to the conclusion that there was no sense in looking for me any further, his one idea was to get back to Shanghai as soon as possible and tell my friends, so that the corpse could be rescued, and given a decent burial. What happened to the two ladies did not interest him in the least.

I couldn't imagine how he had managed to get the car back, but he said it had been rather easy. As soon as daylight came he had one more look for me, then piled a couple of wounded soldiers into the car and started for Shanghai. Every time he was questioned, he explained that he was driving an official ambulance car, so had no trouble. As soon as he got past the last sentries he left his wounded soldiers by the side of the road, where someone else could pick them up, and drove to my house as fast as he could. There were three bullet holes in the car, and he spent all his spare time for several weeks showing the car to his friends and was a little disappointed when I had the car repaired and the holes were covered. There was gossip around the office that he had charged the wounded soldiers a dollar apiece.

On an average once a year there was an emotional wave which hit some part of China and gave the foreign importer or manufacturer some rather serious worries, because the object of this wave was to boycott foreign goods and thereby break the foreigners' rice bowl. Sometimes these movements were directed against some particular nationality, the Japanese receiving especial and persistent attention in this regard. Since the Japanese militarists provided new reasons for Chinese animosity with almost every move they made, there was a general Japanese boycott going on all the time, but other boycotts were spasmodic, regional, and often confined to one particular line of goods. In a great many cases they were promoted by some group of Chinese manufacturers who had been hard hit by foreign competition and were pursuing the course of self-preservation that they thought would prove most effective. They seldom accomplished anything of benefit to themselves, for, though it was a fairly easy matter to stir up the mob spirit and arouse a lot of animosity against the brands manufactured for a foreign competitor, it was quite a different matter to turn the mob into customers for another brand. They were usually very noisy affairs, but we 'old China hands' did not take them very seriously, for we had seen too many of them fizzle out. A Chinese, like most other people, has too much common sense to buy inferior goods or pay a higher price just because the goods happen to be made by a fellow-countryman. He may make up his mind that he is going to do it, but his resolution weakens when he comes to make the purchase, when he compares the goods, and counts out the purchase price to the shopkeeper. As a matter of fact, there were in China what might be called two schools of advertising thought on this subject. Some believed that it was an advantage to be able to advertise that an article was made in China and so appeal to the patriotism of the people; others were equally insistent that it was good merchandising to advertise an article as made in America or England, with the inference that it was therefore superior. Since most advertisers are timid creatures and have an almost Chinese aversion to making up their minds on controversial questions, most of them maintain a discreet silence on this point.

When a group of young hot-heads set out to injure foreign trade and promote the sale of Chinese goods, one of the first things they thought about doing was to go out and tear down all the foreign advertising signs in town. That sounded like a feasible and spectacular thing to do, but if the signs had been properly constructed and the different units scattered at strategic points over the city, as they should be, the job was not an easy one. Even if the police did not interfere, the patriotic youths usually succeeded in smashing up a few of them; they then got tired and called it a day and went home to bed. We had our outdoor advertising-plants in various cities condemned to destruction so many times that I couldn't even guess at the number, but nothing really serious ever happened, except when Communist soldiers got busy and did a job of destruction which was almost perfect. They carried away enough of my good galvanized iron to make all the water pails the Communist army could use for years.

In 1925 the anti-foreign stew pot in Ningpo was boiling and we were, in a way, a contributing cause. A brand of American cigarettes which we were advertising had built up such a good volume of business that Chinese competitors were hit and a boycott against foreign cigarettes was worked up. The movement culminated in a mass meeting at which a lot of red-hot speeches were made, and it was decided to adjourn the meeting at once and destroy all our cigarette signs. Our Ningpo manager had attended the meeting and contributed to the oratory. He had not seen the agenda, and for that reason was under a very serious misapprehension. He knew that the purpose of the meeting was to work up a cigarette boycott, but it never occurred to him that it was to be directed against the brand we were advertising. There had been innumerable boycotts against the cigarettes of a big British competitor and he assumed that this new movement was following the old conventional anti-British lines. Up to this time, the sale of American cigarettes in China had been so small that no one, including the consumers, had paid much attention to them, and it had certainly not been worth while to promote an agitation against them.

Our Ningpo manager made a speech

It wasn't until the meeting was practically over that our Ningpo manager found that the sign-destroying program was aimed at our brand. This was a situation which an experienced diplomat would have a difficult time getting out of, with or without honor. Our man apparently made things worse in a second speech. He didn't retract anything he had previously said, in fact, he added a few new points he had just thought of, and then offered a very practical suggestion. He was, he admitted, an employee of the foreign firm which had put up these offending signs. He had been compelled to do this work in order to fill his rice bowl, but now he was anxious to make amends by helping to destroy the signs. He offered his expert advice and pointed out that to go out in the dark and tear down a few hundred advertising signs

111

presented a lot of difficulties. He exaggerated generously in giving the number of signs, he pointed out that it would be hard to find them, and furthermore than if they started ripping them down in the dead of night, when everyone was asleep, there would be a lot of trouble from the citizens, who would complain to the police. His suggestion was that they all go home as soon as the business of the evening had been completed and get up at daybreak to destroy the signs. He would meet them, supply a list of the positions and superintend the work; with his help they could make a very thorough job of it.

As everyone was pretty well talked out by that time, they endorsed his proposal, listened to a little more oratory, and then drifted home. Since all Chinese, who are not inordinately purse-proud, and sleep late as a matter of principle, get up at dawn anyway, a fair proportion of the enthusiasts were on hand at daybreak the following morning armed with such wrecking tools as they could find and ready to put in a hard morning's work destroying all of our advertising. They waited in vain for our Ningpo manager, so they started out on their own. They walked around for hours looking for the signs which had been sticking up over the city the night before. But they had mysteriously disappeared. Not one was to be found.

The first news we had of this occurrence came in the form of a perfectly accurate report of the speeches our Ningpo manager had made at the mass meeting, and, without my knowledge, some of our bullies had taken the five o'clock boat to Ningpo to execute their own personal, as well as the company's vengeance on the traitor. They didn't find him, for by the time they got to Ningpo he was back in Shanghai. And then we learned what had really happened. At the time he made his first speech at the mass meeting he thought they were talking about the British company, and as he had his private grudge against the bill-posters in that concern he was quite enthusiastic about the idea. When he found it was our posters they intended to destroy he offered to help them so as to prevent immediate action. He then thought and worked very fast. After the mass meeting adjourned he went to see a friend and colleague who had charge of putting up the posters for the Chinese company which had inspired the boycott, and presented to him in a very convincing way the community of interest which exists between billposters. It was obvious that once people started tearing down advertising signs there would be unemployment among the bill-posting fraternity of Ningpo, and no one could tell how far this might go. Having made an ally of his friend, the two of them collected their pots of paste, some of each crew, and worked all night covering our posters with the posters of the Chinese competitor. That was the reason that when the Don Quixotes of Ningpo went out the following morning to attack the windmills of foreign trade they could find no windmills.

A few days later the whole furore died out. A technical victory had been won by the Chinese company because our posters had disappeared. In a week or so we started putting them back again and within a month we had a complete showing. That was the last I ever heard of the matter. The Ningpo manager had a wonderful opportunity to put in an expense account which, even if exorbitant, could not very well be questioned. He paid for his own trip to Shanghai, stayed around the office for a few days, boasting about what he had done, and then paid his own way back to Ningpo and started to work again. The face he had made by out-witting these Ningpo college boys and saving my rice bowl was worth a great deal more to him than any profit he might get from a padded expense account. He would spend the money, but his grandchildren would hear about how smart he was and perhaps tell their grandchildren.

Chinese dogs always bark at a foreigner

9. Hark! Hark! The Dogs Do Bark!'

Every now and then we were visited in Shanghai by an export manager, usually a new one, who appeared to be spending his company's money on an expensive trip around the world for the sole purpose of discovering how many points of superiority he and others of his nationality enjoyed over the people of the country he was visiting. This was an old subject with those of us who lived in China. We had argued about it, and threshed it all out from several national angles so many times that we had entirely exhausted its conversational possibilities. Most of us had lived in China so long that the ricksha coolies had given us nicknames, so we could, in a way, qualify as experts on questions of Anglo-Saxon superiority and the shortcomings of the Oriental. It is extremely irritating to an expert in any line to have to listen to ex cathedra opinions of a man who doesn't know what he is talking about, no matter whether the subject be an old or a new one, and the; visitor to China who insisted on bringing up comparisons with life as it is lived in the old home town caused us more mental suffering than any other species of bore we had to endure. Local opinion was rather evenly divided as to whether Englishmen or Americans were the worst, but all agreed that most residents of California were in a class by themselves.

Whenever I had a visitor of this sort on my hands, whether he was an important export manager or an

114

unimportant tourist, I never overlooked an opportunity to lure him into a motor-car trip through the countryside, followed by a stroll through a Chinese village, for the chastening and enlightening influence that the barking dogs would bring to him. The dogs of the village always started a chorus of protest as soon as we got near them, and the boldest of them would come yapping around our heels, while the cowardly and the lazy, who vastly outnumbered the others, barked away at us from a distance. As every Chinese village was equipped with a great many more dogs than could be justified on any grounds, we usually managed to raise a terrific hubbub, which kept up persistently, for as we strolled out of the orbit of one neighborhood of dogs we came into the orbit of another.

The visitor was invariably annoyed,-as I anticipated he would be, and almost as invariably asked why we should be the cause of this canine chorus. I explained that it was because we were foreigners, and then awaited results. As most people take a certain satisfaction in putting two and two together and confirming the fact that the total is four, it usually didn't take him very long to figure it out and say:

'Of course! The dogs notice our clothes,' thereby proving that he knew nothing about dogs.

'No,' I would reply sadly, but as convincingly as possible. 'That is not the reason. It is because they don't like the way we smell. They think that we are a fox or that one of us has the uncured pelt of a skunk in his pocket.'

It was usually possible to prove that his theory about clothing was wrong by pointing out that there were, in the neighborhood, a number of Chinese dressed just as we were, and that the dogs were paying no attention to them. If his pride appeared to have been hurt, and it usually was, I shouldered my share of the responsibility by saying that, in spite of my membership of the China Kennel Cub and my naturally kindly feeling toward dogs, to say nothing of the ownership of the champion Scottie of China, the dogs of

China resented my scent and barked at me over a period of a quarter of a century. I also explained that, as a matter of choice, and not with any idea of catering to the finical tastes of Chinese dogs, I used in my bath a world-famous soap which is presumed to banish all body odors, but which never fooled the dogs. .In fact I have, on many occasions, stepped from a houseboat bathed, shaved, redolent of the odor of soap, as immaculate as a male.can be, and, in a few minutes, every dog to the windward of me has registered an anguished protest. Those who could not, by any possibility, get a whiff of me, knew, from the noise their colleagues were making, that some strange animal was prowling about the neighborhood, and added their noisy note of protest. This little psychological experiment always hail one of two results. It either had the effect I hoped for and brought the visitor's self-esteem down to reasonable proportions, or augmented his hatred for dogs.

Physicians, anthropologists and others, who know, or should know, what they are talking about, say that there is no inherent reason why the dogs should find the scent of Chinese so tolerable and the scent of foreigners so objectionable. They say that we white folks, were not born that way and that we cannot blame evolution as we do for most of our imperfections, but that we have acquired our peculiar and irritating aroma through years of meat eating augmented, perhaps, by whisky and gin chinking, while the Chinese are either odorless or more delicately scented because of their diet of rice, bailey, cabbage and fish with only an occasional least of pork.

That theory may be correct in the main, but there is something wrong with it. We must have inherited something from our more thoroughly carnivorous ancestors, for a Chinese dog will bark at a vegetarian foreigner and pay no attention to a wealthy Chinese with degraded tastes who eats a big meal of pork every day and empties many bottles of Mattel's brandy.

It is difficult to get a Chinese to tell you anything that is even indirectly uncomplimentary to yourself, but some, who have known me so long that they look on me as they would on a Chinese book in a foreign binding, have admitted to me that we do smell, not only peculiar, but rather nauseating, though they have hastened to add that I was an exception, a flattering statement which any dog knows to be untrue. All Chinese readily account for the Englishman's traditional daily bath by the very simple explanation that he is by nature such a dirty beast that he must bathe frequently. In the market survey covering the use of soap in China, we did discover the very interesting fact that in Northern China a daily bath is the rule, even in the below zero weather, while in the comparatively warmer climate south of the Yangtsze such a prodigal use of soap and water is looked on as unnecessary, the more virile Northerners, who, as a rule, conquer China every 800 years, eat noodles instead of rice, have no dependable supplies of fish and eat a great deal more meat than the small-statured Southerners.

Perhaps the surest method of increasing soap sales in China would be to convert all the vegetarian Buddhists and make meat-eating Christians or Mohammedans out of them. Efforts to make them drinkers of gin and Scotch have, so far, proved entirely futile, though for some curious reason they do drink port and brandy. On my infrequent trips to America I always encountered a lot of nasal evidence of the way my fellow Nordics smell when assembled in generous numbers. The first time for many years that I was in a crowd of non-Chinese was in the New York subway, and at once I was conscious of the presence of that overpowering body odor which, according to the advertisements, wrecks romance, prevents happy marriages and proves an insuperable handicap to business success. After many years in China, I had forgotten that human beings smelled that way. It was the same in London, Paris, Berlin and Moscow. No, not quite the same in Moscow, for there the body odor encountered on trains and in railway waiting-rooms reached a height of perfection which would indicate some conscious striving toward an ideal, the following of a cult, a determination to excel.

There are famous smells in China, many of them of nauseating intensity. If you are foolish enough to get up for a stroll through a Chinese city before breakfast, your route will inevitably lead you through u good many spots where the garbage coolies are quite frankly at work. You can only pass through them with a fair degree of comfort in a cloud of tobacco smoke, and with an averted gaze. Also there are other smells confined to certain geographical divisions. Once you cross the Yangtsze, on a trip from Shanghai to Peiping, you enter the great garlic belt. There the atmosphere is so thoroughly impregnated that, some old residents say, un-acclimatized mosquitoes from Shanghai who happen to be on the train drop dead in their tracks the moment the car window is opened and bedbugs survive only because of their less venturesome habits of life. Even here the local dogs will detect my (and your) animal scent through the thick fog of garlic and start on an impromptu fox hunt as soon as we get into the country.

I have often wondered what would happen if someone brought a pack of American bloodhounds to China and tried them out on a few escaped Chinese criminals. I don't believe they would bother about such a scent of rice and cabbage. I feel sure they wouldn't if they had previously nosed their way over many trails in the Union of Soviet Republics and learned what a real communist scent smells like.

While I might attempt to lower his Kiplingesque pride as a white man by taking a visitor on a tour of a Chinese village so that the dogs may note his offensive smell and bark at him, i always steered him clear of a herd of water buffaloes and even avoided the proximity of the individual buffalo unless, as was customary, he was securely tethered by means of a rope and a ring through his nose. The water buffalo is the most useful beast of burden the Chinese possess, and is almost indispensable in rice growing. Although his hooves do not, from my inexpert and cautious observation, appear to be unusually large for an animal of his weight, he will slog unconcernedly through a muddy rice paddy in which a horse or a mule would bog down—will travel securely through footing the smart labor-shirking camel would not even undertake. When he had ploughed a decade or more of rice fields and was too old for further work, he was slaughtered, and his flesh provided tough steaks, but passable beef stews, for Shanghai foreigners who usually thought they were eating the flesh from another and more aristocratic member of the cow family.

Although the conventional two sexes are represented in the water buffalo family in the usual proportions, it is customary to refer to all of them as males, because it seems an outrage to the romantic English language to use the feminine gender in referring to a beast which is so outrageously- ugly. He looks as if he had been fabricated by collecting on one chassis all the discarded parts from one of the assembly lines set up during some immature period of evolution. But as a machine he is, in one respect at least, mechanically perfect. His one joy in life is to submerge himself in water, and he can without effort do this so completely that only his eyes, nostrils and the tips of his horns are visible. No other quadruped except the hippopotamus can do anything like this. When submerged in this fashion the part of him that is visible looks like nothing so much as an alligator with horns. That is what I thought he was when I first came to China, fresh from the bayous of Texas.

He is normally one of the most docile of beasts, and in every farm household it is the duty of the smallest of the small boys to take him to and from the fields and watch him while he grazes under the trees or on the narrow strip of grassland along the canal. One of the most familiar sights in

China is that of a six-year-old boy perched on the back of this lumbering beast. This has been a favorite subject of Chinese artists, who find some intriguing charm in this association of the puny infant and the powerful beast. He accepts the small Chinese boy with a maternal kindness, but beneath that ugly and placid exterior there lurks a savage primordial hate against some ancient enemy.

Unfortunately, we foreigners appear to smell like these old foes, perhaps some ancient and odorous ape who lived in the buffalo's ancestral home in Africa. Whatever old enemy we remind the buffalo of, we should be proud of him. He must have been good with fang and claw, because today the buffalo is the one beast the tiger will not tackle and the lion respects. The fact that small boys in the country are almost invariably seated on the backs of buffaloes may be the survival of an ancient custom. 'When China was covered with dense forests, and there were many ferocious tigers about, the safest place for a small boy was on the back of the buffalo. No tiger would ever try to get past those menacing horns. Indian tiger hunters like to trail their game through wandering herds of buffalo, because with these neighbors they feel secure against any treacherous attack. But the Nordic is never permanently sale in the buffalo's vicinity. Occasionally some neolithic odor arouses him and he starts in to pay off an ancient grudge which has survived at least one geological period.

When British troops carried out maneuvers on the mainland near the British crown colony of Hongkong, the precaution was always taken to remove all water buffaloes from the neighborhood so as to avoid conflict with a foe whose tactics are governed by no accredited code. During the Philippine insurrection a company of American troops, which was otherwise victorious, was compelled to retreat in undignified and un-soldierly haste when a herd of buffalo decided to aid the Insurrectionists. In this battle between man and beast, one American soldier was gored in the rear and it took the War Department seven years to decide whether or not to classify this as 'wounded in action.' Fortunately for the soldier, they stretched a point in his favor and thus enabled him to collect an extra pension. No Chinese, not even an unfumigated soldier, who is covered with lice, have that wrath-provoking smell, because' any Son of Han can wander through a herd of buffalo as carelessly and as free from danger as through a chicken yard.

Fortunately for foreigners who lived in China, when we went tramping through the countryside, most of the buffaloes were so busy with their present tasks, or so exhausted from tasks they had just performed, that thev wouldn't pay an attention to a saber-toothed tiger unless he came up and bit them. If a buffalo has any leisure, his one idea is to submerge himself in a nice muddy pool and get so covered with mud that the flies can't get through his ugly thick hide and sting him. He may bitterly resent our provocative smell, but is usually cither too busy, or too tired to make an issue out of it. Sometimes he gets a different point of view and new ambitions dominate him. In the early morning, when he has had an unexpectedly satisfying bellyfull of coarse grass and a good night's rest in his stall, where he has slept in his own dung and urine, he feels differently about things. The ancient hate surges through his tiny brain and motivates his powerful body. The first odorous white man whose scent assails him drives him into action. His rice-field gait is about two miles an hour, but when his rage throws him into high gear, he travels over the ground with amazing speed. Fortunately there is always a warning signal, for ugly and ungainly as he is, the buffalo is a gentleman, and challenges his foes not once, but twice. The first challenge comes when he sniffs the air, looks in your direction, and manifests his profound distaste with a snort. His second challenge comes when he puts his silly tail in the air and paws the ground. I don't think anyone knows whether he paws the ground just once or a number of times, because no one ever stayed around long enough to find out. The first paw is the signal to get elsewhere with all possible speed.

All smell bad to the camel

The buffalo is often the stable mate of horses and what you might call orthodox cows, and they get along-together with chummy indifference. Chinese dogs and buffaloes are mutually contemptuous and pay no attention to each other. The city-bred Shanghai dog who was taken into the country and there saw his first vulnerable buffalo usually had a wonderful time for a few minutes, barking and snapping- at heels, but as soon as he found out that he might just as well be barking at a piece of mud, he gave up. The only animal the buffalo wants to attack is the white man. Why should our odor be so offensive and provocative to him? In China, he has not been menaced by wild beasts for many centuries and, even when the forests of China were full of enemies, they were not two-legged beasts. What is there about the scent of the Nordic that recalls an old foe and arouses this instinct for vengeance?

The camel, who is to be met in the streets of Peiping and other places near the Great Wall of China, has probably had more experience with human smells than any other animal, wild or domestic. He has for months on end associated with Chinese, Mongols and Thibetans without benefit of or desire for a bath. In Peiping, he had an opportunity to sample the odors of the diplomatic body, composed of representatives of all the great powers and of a few who hope to become great.

A more versatile experience could not be imagined, but the camel has never learned to distinguish between an ambassador extraordinary, a third secretary, a dowager and a Mongol sheep herder. No one except a tourist ever tries to pet a camel and he seldom tries it more than once. Sophisticated dowagers and third secretaries never pet a camel or go near one except through necessity. When a foreigner in Peiping walked by a camel train, some camel was likely to take a nip at him, or, what is worse, to cough at him. When a camel coughs at you with any degree of accuracy the only thing you can do is to go back to the hotel, have a bath, and change your clothes. There is no narrow national, racial or personal animus about the camel's attitude as in the case with the water buffalo and the Chinese dog. All human beings look and smell alike to him and he hates them all with equal intensity.

Having gone so far in an indelicate exposure of Nordic body odors, I may as well be even more shameless and go a little farther, and say that the domestic animals of China do not make any differentiation as regards sex; the dogs bark at dainty ladies with just as much noise and cowardly enthusiasm as at fat and perspiring gentlemen. On every occasion I have had an opportunity to do so, I have escorted a young lady, of Dresden-doll charm and daintiness, about the Chinese countryside or any other place she wanted to go, because I liked to look at her and be patronizingly paternal. I thought she would fool the dogs but she didn't. There was a lot of difference between the appearance of the two of us, but we smelled just the same to the dogs. I never tried her on a buffalo or a camel, but I am sure the result would have been equally disillusioning.

Chair coolies complain about my increasing weight

10. Fish and String and Melon Seeds

Business deals in China were always lull of surprises, because, until the transaction was finally concluded and the goods or service paid for and consumed or performed, no one could ever be quite sure that all the details of the transaction had been settled, and that there would be no misunderstandings. Many authorities contend that the Chinese have a genius for misunderstanding which works to their advantage in many lines and that it is especially advantageous to them in matters connected with travel or in bargains with the in-experienced. In fact, in most of the deals undertaken by the stranger, the one thing that he can be certain of is that, when the time comes to pay, the price which has been definitely agreed upon has for one very plausible reason or another been increased. It appears to be impossible to foresee all the twists and turns that force majeure or the acts of God. may take, and they invariably turn to the disadvantage of the party to the contract whose function is to pay the money. Chair bearers who carry you over hilly or mountainous roads arc notoriously skillful at wangling extra money in this way and many travelers have suffered at their hands. Of course, if one jumped into a chair as into a licensed taxicab and started on a journey without having a definite understanding as to how many coolies were to be employed for each chair, the route to be taken,

125

the number of stops to be made, the time to be spent at each stop, the amount to be paid per chair, whether or not the lunch basket and other light luggage was to be carried in a separate chair, and the wine money allowance for each coolie, he had made a very careless contract in which there were plenty of loopholes for honest differences of opinion to say nothing of dishonest ones.

After long experiences, I became, I think, fairly expert at arranging these matters, but I never succeeded in making a deal for chairs in which every contingency was provided for so thoroughly that there was no room for argument at the end of the journey. It has rained, and thus the trip has been made over muddy roads which the bearers had not anticipated. Or the sun has come out and made the bearers lose a lot of sweat. Or I have walked a large part of the way, loitering and looking at the wild flowers and taking photographs and thus delaying the journey, or they didn't notice that I was carrying a camera and thereby adding to their burdens. In later years my increasing weight formed the basis of many disputes. I knew that I was fat and must pay for it. They knew pretty much what I weighed at first glance, because it was their business to estimate the weight of a passenger and they were expert at it. But they always insisted at the end of a journey that my appearance was very deceptive and that they would certainly have added something to the price before agreeing on it if I had not, in a way, deceived them. When we were in Chungking with a party of friends one summer, my wife and all the other members of the party paid 12 large coppers for the regulation chair journey from waterside to hill top on which this Specimen city is situated. It cost me 16 coppers. I don't know how the coolies arrived at that exact figure, but during the two weeks we were there I could never get taken for any less, though, as a matter of principle, I tried to beat them down by one copper. When we took chairs for a trip in the country in any part of China, I was always conscious of the fact that every ounce of my superfluous flesh was being tallied up and taken into consideration. But when we got to the end of the trip the coolies were unanimous in expressing surprise and astonishment at my excessive weight. They would shout to each other about it, demanding to know if anyone had ever heard of a fellow that could weigh so much as I did. They all agreed that no one had. A foreigner like me, they said, must be filled with rocks instead of flesh and blood.

All this, of course, was intended to be very polite and delicately flattering to me. The Chinese theory is that anyone who has money to pay for food will eat his fill and therefore, when you get near the age of fifty, you should be comfortably fat unless you have been a wastrel and therefore unable to keep your rice bowl filled. Fatness also denotes a philosophic calm that comes with a study of the sages, so that in China you can spot a prosperous scholar across the street. When these rascals went into ecstasies over my rotundness, they were really paying me very sincere flattery and hoping to get me in such good humor that they could gouge a few extra coins out of me.

A crowd always gathers, for these squabbles are more fun than a lawsuit. The coolies have their say and we have our say. The lie is passed freely and cheerfully by both parties and with no hard feelings on either side. As soon as tire neighboring crowds learn the gist of the matter, they step into the argument, inquire about the facts, and eventually decide how' the matter should be settled. So far as I know this rough and ready jury decision is usually as just as one has any reason to expect, and I never had any reason to believe that there was any prejudice against me because of the fact that f was a foreigner. There was the assumption that anyone who idled his time away riding around in chairs and looking at the scenery must be a rather prosperous individual, and therefore should be liberal, but that would apply to a Chinese as well as to a foreigner. Ol course, if I had been foolish enough to start out without a definite and thorough understanding as to the amount to be paid, then it was obvious that no one could do anything for a fool like that, and so the villager would leave me to pay for my own folly. But if the chair bearers, on the other hand, tried to wriggle out of a lair and definite agreement, then the crowd was against them. Of course, the jury must be a fair one. If the place was packed with chair coolies then the passenger had no chance, so I always made it a point to discharge the coolies in some neutral territory where there were no other chair coolies hanging about. And no matter what the decision is, everyone's face must be saved. Even if the coolies have completely failed to establish their case, it would be too bad to let them put up all this argument and get nothing for it. Also it would prove us to be stingy, mean-natured people who do not deserve to enjoy the hospitality of the countryside. So they are given an extra wine money allowance whether they deserve it or not. Everyone has had a glorious time over the argument and everyone is satisfied.

Of the many pleasant excursions my wife and I enjoyed in China, one of the finest was a houseboat trip with three friends on the Chien Tang River, the beautiful stream that flows into Hangchow Bay. It has been visited by few foreigners, but if more accessible it would be one of the famed beauty spots of the world. We intended to do a little fishing on this trip and had brought a variety of equipment with us from Shanghai. When we got comfortably settled on the houseboat the environment appeared to be appropriate for our enterprise. All about us were successful Chinese fishermen who would go by in their little boats and proudly exhibit beautiful strings of fish. And at dusk we would hear the thrilling splash of fish leaping out of the water, the pleasantest sounds a man can listen to, except the solemn honk of a wild goose. The Chine-c on this river fish with cormorants, nets, traps, hook and line, and every device known to fishermen and, what is more important, they catch fish, beautiful freshwater fish, born and brought up in clear mountain streams and without the muddy taste of those caught around Shanghai. I can't yet understand why we were so completely unsuccessful. There were many opportunities, many pools which appeared to provide an ideal rendezvous for fish! There was nothing wrong with the technical equipment and the bait was such as should have tempted am fish. In fact, we tried any number el different kinds of bait, grasshoppers, angle worms, grubs, bacon and rice balls. But it finally became apparent that if we were going to eat any of the Chien Tang River fish we would have to use more simple and direct methods of securing one.

Magnificent string of fish

Very soon after we had reached this rather mortifying conclusion a professional fisherman came along with a large and very beautiful fish whose points were strange to me. The cook and the crew were unanimous that it was a fish of exceptional fine quality. We opened negotiations for its purchase, and this proved to be a long drawn-out affair. The first asking price was a dollar, countered by an offer of twenty cents. For bargaining purposes the cook mentioned that a former master of his had once bought a fish like this and that it turned out to be so bony that no one could eat it.

The crew, who came from a different part of the river, said publicly that no really fine fish were to be found here and urged me to wait until the following day, when we would not only find fish that any gentleman of my standing could eat, but also be able to deal with fishermen who were imbued with some ideas of decency and honesty. This went on for some time with the *laodah* and everyone else taking part in the bargaining and having a very noisy and joyful time until I, after a conference, took executive action and closed the deal by paying sixty cents, thereby, in all probability, setting a new high level in the local fish market.

As soon as I had paid over the money and we started to take delivery of the fish, a new and complicated situation arose. The fish was very much alive and was secured by a string about twelve or fifteen feet long, tied through its gills. Having lived long in China I should have known better, but I assumed that when I bought the fish I bought all the gear and equipment appertaining thereto; but that had not been the understanding of the fisherman. The string had not been mentioned in the negotiations and according to the vendor, was not included in the sale. Fie was quite right about this, for the urgent need of the string had not occurred to anyone. Ordinarily a string can be dug up out of the immediate neighborhood, but we didn't nave a foot of string on the boat. Furthermore, it transpired that, except for the bathtub, the only vessel we had big enough to hold the fish was a water bucket which was in frequent and urgent use in bailing. The fish was not to be eaten until the following day, and the only way it could be kept alive and fresh was to put it on a string and anchor it in the water alongside the boat.

The negotiations for the purchase of the string were even more difficult than the deal for the fish. As I had already paid for the fish, the fisherman was in a very advantageous position, for he knew that we were like a man who has bought a horse and has no halter to lead it home. But while he had this advantage on his side, we outnumbered him ten to one and could make more noise. He soon weakened. The price of ten coppers was finally agreed on, and then it transpired that, with all of our smartness and browbeating, the deal had not been specific enough. We all had thought that the ten coppers were for the entire string. The vendor insisted that when he accepted this ridiculously low price he assumed, and in fact definitely understood, that we were only purchasing string sufficient for our immediate needs, that is string enough to string the fish. He tried, unsuccessfully, to shame us by saying that it was grasping and ungentlemanly to expect more string. He didn't make any remarks about foreigners, but he did comment to the cook on the well-known iniquities of Shanghai people. During a lull in the proceedings he got out his knife and started to cut the string a scant four feet from the fish. While his knife was in the air the *laodah* yanked the string so as to give us an additional foot, and so we won. But it was an empty victory. That night the fish got away—and all we had was the string.

Now if I have given the impression that the Chinese are a nation of hagglers and higglers whose main business in life is to snare extra coppers from the unwary, I must correct that impression, for it certainly is a wrong one. They love to bargain for the fun of it as well as for the profit, but they are quite willing at any time to stop the most absorbing negotiations and toss a coin to determine whether you get a fish free or pay for a fish and get nothing. As might be expected from that sporting, happy-go-lucky point of view on life, they are very kindly and hospitable. Usually all the country people have to offer a visitor is a cup of tea, and not very good tea at that, but the pot and the cups are always brought out and if there happen to be a few tea leaves of extra good quality in the house, an extra pot of tea will be brewed for the guest.

The day after the fish got away we anchored near a temple which for some reason was occupied by soldiers, so moved a mile or two further up stream, for soldiers in any country, whether at peace or war, are usually not good neighbors. At this new anchorage I found something I had been curious about for years, and that was a patch of watermelons of the variety grown for their seeds. These edible seeds have a delicate nutty flavor and are served at all restaurants and tea houses; dishes of them are on the table at every Chinese feast. They are supposed to have a slightly aphrodisiac effect and so are not offered to ladies. A great many tourist ladies insist on eating- them and probably wonder why every Chinese around the place has suddenly found something so irresistibly amusing.

One of the surest ways to make friends with a Chinese farmer is to give him an empty beer bottle, which they appear to value above all other bottles. I don't know just why it is, but an empty beer bottle seems to carry with it some of the friendly and hospitable traditions of its former alcoholic contents. It can always be offered and accepted with propriety and always calls for a return of the compliment. I admired the farmer's melons, gave him the bottle, and he asked me to help myself to the melons, which I did to the extent of picking out one, which was all that I needed for my amateur scientific investigations.

The transaction should have ended there, but while I was, as the saying goes, fanning the breeze with the farmer, a boatman who followed me filled his apron with melons, picking out the finest and biggest in the patch. I didn't see him until he had pulled off all the melons he could carry in his skirt, and as it was too late to do anything else about it, I tried to square matters by paying the farmer, but he refused to accept anything. I thought he was being excessively polite, so I slipped two twenty-cent pieces into his jacket pocket and walked back to the boat. Now these silver coins represented a good deal of wealth in that part of the country. An able-bodied man would work hard all day to earn them, and as this old man was no longer able-bodied it would be difficult to translate the money into terms of his earning power. It was either a princely gift or a very generous payment for the melons.

I was back in the boat showing the melons to my shipmates and we were marvelling at the vast quantity of seeds and the inedible quality of the flesh, when there was a terrific rumpus at the foot of the gang plank. The old farmer had found the two coins in his pocket and had walked a half-mile to return them and to tell his troubles. He put the two coins on the gang plank with a dramatic gesture and then recounted his grievances to all and sundry. Boiled down, it was something like this. I had called on him, had admired his miserable melons and had presented him with the most magnificent beer bottle he had ever seen. He was not one to whom beer bottles were a new experience, for he had owned several tens of them during his lifetime, but the one I gave him was twice as large as any he had ever seen before. He was well aware of the hospitality one owes to strangers and had turned his insignificant melon patch over to me, had not ever bothered to count what was taken. He did not at the present moment know and did not care. This far it had been a transaction between two gentlemen, but I had not been content to let it remain so, but had turned it into a base commercial transaction by slipping these two coins into his jacket pocket. Fortunately he had found them and had come back to return them.

It is never difficult to start an argument in China and here the situation was ideal. The old man's friends and neighbors were all on his side and my boat crew all on mine. The rascal who had started all the trouble by filching the melons led off. The old gentleman, he said, was not familiar with the large and generous way in which foreigners did things. It was quite obvious that I was a very wealthy man for here I was, for some foolish reason understandable only to foreigners, renting this boat for the sole purpose of idling about in it, paying out money every day and making no attempt to get anything back. I had even lost my temper and threatened to fire the whole crew when they had been caught trying to smuggle a cargo of odorous hams to Hangchow. For me to chuck twenty-cent pieces about was mere child play, and as for beer bottles, he would not dare tell how many my party emptied in-a day, because no one would believe him. This was a very timely and convincing remark, for several quart bottles of beer were being emptied at that very moment, within plain view of the crowd on the river bank. As a crowning example of my foolish and almost unbelievable extravagance, other members of the crew told of what had happened only a few nights previously, when we were anchored near a sandy beach. I had paid an entire dollar for bundles of firewood and then, when darkness fell, had piled it up and burned it for no apparent reason except to amuse the little girl who was a member of the party. The ways of foreigners were past understanding.

Others added their testimony. The reputation for prodigal generosity which the ship's crew was building up for me was very amusing, because only the day before we had had a serious argument over their claim for an extra wine money allowance, in which I had come out completely victorious, and I knew that they privately thought me to be the most close-fisted foreign devil they had ever come in contact with. However, they seemed to have the best of the argument. Some of the villagers were loud in their denunciation of my conduct, but the old man, having had his say, let matters go at that and declined to be drawn into any side issues. He stuck around until the argument fizzled out and no one was paying any more attention to him. He went back to his melon patch, leaving the two coins on the gangway. Later when it occurred to me to do so, I went down to retrieve the money, but it had disappeared. I am morally certain that the boatman who got the old man's melons also stole the two coins, but as I had no definite proof I said nothing about the matter.

"Off with his head, and no nonsense about it"

11. The Few Who Read the Papers

When I first went to China the Manchus were ruling the country, the boy emperor who later became the adult but powerless ruler of Manchukuo was seated on the dragon throne, Sun Yat Sen was a political refugee and the revolutionary movement which was soon to upset the monarchy was so obscure and so timorously concealed that few of us knew that it existed. But the Manchus knew about the activities of the revolutionists and took no chances with them. A revolution cannot thrive and prosper without publicity and the cheapest and most efficient vehicle of publicity is the newspaper. Therefore the members of the ruling clan were against all newspapers, and none was published except in the foreign concessions and settlements where no heads were chopped off and no one even sentenced to jail without some regard for the processes of law. Even with this protection the zeal and efficiency with which the Manchus sought out and beheaded the publishers of newspapers made it a very hazardous undertaking.

In this connection, I recall of one Chinese I knew whose life insurance policy proved to be real insurance against loss of life. This man happened to be the first Chinese newspaperman I ever met. He was an ardent revolutionist, and when he decided to start a newspaper in one of the foreign concessions in Hankow he was well aware of the high percentage of publishers who parted with their heads. He took out an insurance policy with a British company so that if he were decapitated he would not leave his family destitute. He had not been publishing his paper very long before something he wrote offended the dignitaries. He was seized while on a reckless visit outside the foreign concession, was thrown into prison by orders of the local mandarin, who ordered the publisher into his presence to inform him that his head was about to be chopped off, and no nonsense about it. While languishing in prison, the publisher had plenty of time to think over his troubles and try to devise a way out of them. He thought of something that might be effective. As he had nothing to lose in any event he decided to try the appeal he had worked out.

'Excellency,' he cried, pounding his head on the floor, 'you can, of course, cut off my insignificant head, but if you do so you will be offering a grave affront to the King of England and the consequences may be very serious for your excellency.'

The idea that the King of England would be annoyed by the execution of a louse of a Chinese revolutionist, and that the long arm of British vengeance would reach him, intrigued the curiosity of the mandarin, and he forgot his dignity long enough to inquire how such a remote and trivial cause could have such a far reaching and important effect. With much head knocking the publisher explained. His insurance policy with a British company bound him to pay to the company certain quarterly sums as long as he lived and, on the other hand, the company was bound to pay to his heirs a surprisingly large sum of money in the event of his death. If he lived, it would be distinctly profitable for the British company, but if he died it would be distinctly unprofitable. If he died from natural causes the company would have no reason for complaint, but if his head was chopped off by official orders, thereby cutting off their revenue and putting them to this extraordinary expense, they might be expected to complain very bitterly about it.

The British lion roared a good deal louder and more I frequently then than it did a few decades later, and it roared louder around Hankow, than in other parts of China, for the Yangtsze Valley was presumed to be a British 'sphere of influence.' The local consular officials had made things hot for the mandarin on numerous occasions when Chinese merchants failed to take delivery of cargo they had ordered, or when the mandarin had been caught levying illegal taxes on British goods.

He decided there might be something in what the publisher said and postponed the execution until he could inquire into matters. A dispatch was sent to the capital I in Peking and the Wai Chao Pu, or Chinese Foreign Office, drafted a note to the British Minister inquiring whether or not the publisher could be executed without causing diplomatic complications. No one will ever know just what the British official attitude on this problem would have been, for, before a reply could be sent, the Republican revolution had broken out; the prisons were thrown open and the publisher escaped to start a paper in Shanghai, where he told me how his life had been saved. Incidentally, there was a local boom in the life-insurance business. With the establishment of the Republic, the danger of editors getting their heads chopped off did not entirely disappear, but was minimized to such an extent that the publishing business became almost as safe as any other and enjoyed a mushroom prosperity. Just as in other countries, almost every Chinese who had the equivalent of a grammar school education thought that he could edit a newspaper or a magazine, and enough of them tried it to keep the country well supplied with a lot of useless publications and a few really good ones.

When a new or prospective client asked me how many Chinese were able to read and write and I gave him the melancholy statistical information that not more than one out of ten could either put the queer Chinese characters on paper or know what the characters meant when written by others, the market for newspaper advertising always took a very decided slump. If such a small proportion were able to read, it appeared obvious that any appeal that advertising could make must be extremely limited. Our stock reply to any pessimism of this sort was that the people who could read were the only ones with money enough to be good customers. This reply was not only fairly truthful, but, in most cases, convincing, so that the advertising appropriation was saved, but the advertiser lost a good deal of his enthusiasm regarding the possibilities of the China market.

Partly for the benefit of our clients, and partly in order to satisfy a natural curiosity on such statistical matters, we went to a good deal of trouble to arrive at a reasonable conjecture as to the number of newspaper readers there were in China. Since there was no audited circulation, figures and the claims made by publishers reflected future hopes rather than past performances. It was by no means easy to determine the circulation of one publication, and when it came to arriving at a figure which would represent the circulation of all the daily papers in the country the problem became very complicated. However, we had a fair idea as to the circulation of the leading papers (less than a hundred) with which we did business. The statistics of the Chinese customs showed how many tons of newsprint were imported into the country each year. Since the domestic production of newsprint was so small as to be negligible, it was rather an easy matter to figure out the maximum number of average-sized newspapers it would be possible to produce from this newsprint supply.

Then we had accurate figures as to the number of newspapers and other periodicals that were transmitted through the Chinese Post Office. This figure, of course, represented only a liberal fraction of the total number of papers circulated, since most of them were delivered by the publishers, but it served as a check on our other calculations. We also had fairly complete information as to the press equipment of the papers, knew which ones could not possibly print more than 2,000 copies daily, which ones were limited to 10,000, and so on up to the select few with equipment to print more than 100,000. We placed a lot of advertising containing coupons which people could send in to us with a few cents in stamps and receive in return samples of tooth paste, pen nibs, toilet soap or lip-sticks. We received thousands of these every month and compiled them very carefully. We calculated that if an advertisement in a newspaper with a known circulation of 10,000 pulls 100 coupons and the same advertisement, in another newspaper of unknown circulation brought in 50 coupons, we were fairly safe in setting down the circulation of the latter paper at 5,000. From these four sources of information, which we knew to have an element of inaccuracy, and by a method of calculation which we knew to be haphazard, we arrived at the conclusion that the total number of purchasers of daily newspapers in China was approximately 3,000,000. This included innumerable small 'mosquito' papers which earned a precarious livelihood by blackmail. Smart auditors who figure circulation so closely that they leave out nothing but the decimal points will probably observe this figure with very little respect. If any one of them thinks he can arrive at a more accurate figure he is perfectly welcome to make the attempt.

The figure of a circulation of 3,000,000 daily newspapers indicates that less than 1% of the population of the country were newspaper readers, but that figure presents an inaccurate picture. Every important newspaper enjoyed what we called a 'secondary' circulation. Many newsboys in Shanghai sold their papers on what might be properly called a rental basis. The paper was first delivered to Mr. Wong who worked for a foreign firm and therefore had to appear at the office at nine o'clock. When he left his home the paper was collected by the newsboy and delivered to a reader of more leisurely habits, and this procedure was carried on until, a week later, the same paper might be in the hands of a provincial reader a hundred miles away.

This penny-saving device of renting a paper instead of buying one was, of course, scorned by the well-to-do, but in many cases their servants saw to it that the value of a morning newspaper was not destroyed with the advent of the midday sun and they sold the paper to some less prosperous neighbor. No one could make more than a blind guess as to how much this secondary circulation amounted to. It may have meant that the total number of newspaper readers was three or four times the total of 3,000,000 daily papers printed, but with the most optimistic guess, the fact remained that the total number of daily newspaper readers in China was a good deal less than 5% of the total population. That may present a very gloomy picture, but there is a brighter side to it. Using in part the same methods by which we arrived at the figures regarding existing circulation figures, we reconstructed the newspaper history of the past and found that although the existing number of Chinese newspaper readers was discouragingly small, it was more than twice as large as it was fifteen years previously.

When any figures regarding the illiteracy of China are quoted, the mental picture presented to the average person is a very black one. Most of us have known of one or more persons who were too stupid to learn to read, and the natural assumption is that China's vast population must be made up of many millions of people who are much below the human average in intelligence. Of course that is all wrong.

Very few Chinese are illiterate because of the fact that they are too stupid to learn to read and to write, but many are so because they were given no opportunity to learn, or found themselves engulfed in more pressing duties. It has rarely been because of lack of energy, of desire, ability, or ambition. From the earliest period of China's long authentic history, the Confucian tradition of honor to scholarship has prevailed. It has made prime ministers and field marshals out of inefficient men who were clever word carpenters, and accounts in great measure for the dilettantism which resulted in the country's weakness. For several centuries they tried to solve serious diplomatic and domestic problems by writing clever essays. Only since the present generation came into power-have more practical methods of administration and diplomacy been adopted. This has not been done by discounting scholarship, but by giving it a more practical application. Except for a very early period of Chinese history there has never been a scholarly caste in China nor even a scholarly class. Any boy who had the inclination and opportunity to study might attain to very high honors.

Men and women who are blind or deaf develop compensating faculties which are very noticeable in the individual, and the generations of illiterate Chinese have enjoyed a similar development. In many ways they are more intelligent than their literate brethren. The man who gets through life successfully without the mental labor-saving devices of pencil and paper has to use his brain a great deal more than the man who has these aids. One of the most intelligent men I ever knew was an illiterate Chinese carpentry contractor who, as a routine of his everyday work, performed mental feats few college professors could equal. He could compute quickly and accurately the cost of any job of work and, if you were curious about such details, could tell you exactly how many nails would be required, the size of each kind of nail and the number of pounds needed for the total job. With the help of a re-write man he would have made a corking good newspaper reporter, for his powers of observation were almost uncanny. With one glance at a roomful of people he seemed to mentally photograph each individual, and a month later could either name them all or describe those he did not know. I am not mentioning him because he was in any sense a prodigy, for he was not. He did not think there was anything remarkable about his mental abilities, and neither did any of his Chinese friends. His family were poor country people who could not send him to school. As he had no opportunity to learn to read and write he had to learn how to accomplish things in other ways. There are millions of Chinese who are just like him.

Newcomers to China with little or no knowledge of the Chinese language were usually surprised at how easily they got along with no language at all. Chinese seemed to know instinctively just what the needs of the traveler were, and would guide him to the inn or show him where the boat landing was, and generally see to it that he was helped on his way.

The automobile was still quite a novelty in China when most of the Chinese living along the new motor highway began to familiarize themselves with the needs of the traveling motorist. Many foreigners who drove their own cars through the remote countryside were surprised to find that the villagers were aware that the traveling motorist needed water for his radiator, gasoline for his tank and might be looking for a place to spend the night. Without the exchange of any words that were mutually intelligible all those things were provided. There is nothing psychic about this. It is a natural development of conditions peculiar to China. There are innumerable dialects spoken in China, and for generations the Chinese have been accustomed to meeting and dealing with fellow-countrymen who could not make themselves understood, so they have learned to appraise and satisfy a traveler's needs without the aid of conversation.

The fact that such a large proportion of the people could not read led us to adopt a very simple technique in the preparation of advertising copy, and that was to make every advertisement as complete as possible without the use of a word of text, in other words, to resort to the old device of picture-writing. We knew, in spite of our sales argument to advertisers that anyone who can buy advertised goods could read a newspaper, that the statement was slightly inaccurate. There were a great many illiterates who, like my carpenter friend, owned motor-cars and smoked expensive cigarettes. There were even more wives of prosperous men who could not read, because female education had only recently become a popular movement. The Chinese wife who spends the money in the family usually cannot read the paper her husband subscribes for, but she will look at the pictures and, if our advertising showed a good picture of the package with an illustration showing what the article was used for, we felt that it had probably accomplished something, had presented a message to the reader who could not read.

Because many Chinese are illiterate does not mean that they do not enjoy good literature, for they do. The professional story-teller was to be found everywhere, and his repertoire was rich and varied. Some were itinerants who set up shop on any street corner where a crowd might collect and garnered enough coppers to keep their rice bowls filled. Others, the aristocrats of the profession, were employed on the small canal boats, where every passenger, as a matter of course, paid the copper which old custom established as the fee for the story-teller. One did not need to understand a word of Chinese to appreciate the talents of these troubadours. The histrionic, though restrained, gestures, the carefully-modulated voice, the dramatic pause, the occasional burst into snatches of song, the rapt attention of passengers, all showed that the narrative, in any language, would be a work of art. He held them for hours with ancient fairy stories or narratives of famous sieges or battles, the popular classics of the country. In a more modest and restricted way, the Chinese nurse who cannot write her own name knows by heart the famous old romances of the country. The result is that many who cannot read or write have a solid background of knowledge and appreciation of Chinese literature.

During the early mushroom growth of Chinese newspapers it was much easier for the Chinese publisher to get a subsidy from some individual, or a group of politicians, than it was to secure a paid circulation and sell advertising, and most of the papers were started in that easy way. A few of them outgrew that political genesis, but the numbers of newspapers in China, both foreign and Chinese, which enjoyed independent ownership and derived their sole revenue from circulation and advertising could be counted on the fingers of two pairs of hands. With almost all the small provincial papers, and some of the fairly important ones, this subsidy system led to a rather curious situation as regards advertising. With his expenses already paid by means of the subsidy, the publisher did not have to take into account his cost of production when figuring what he would charge for advertising. Anything he could get for the space was just so much net gain. The result was that we placed a great deal of advertising in some of these small papers, at rates which we knew did not meet more than a fraction of the cost of the white paper on which the advertisement was printed. We never asked these small publishers anything about their rates. If we did, it would have taken weeks or months to get down to a reasonable and mutually satisfactory basis on which we could do business. If we had any business to place, we figured out about what we thought space in this particular paper should be worth, sent along the order on that basis, and usually it was accepted without any further correspondence.

All of Yunnan would learn of our rascally tricks

Although their rates might be satisfactorily low, that was about the only thing about business relationships with these subsidized papers that was satisfactory. The small provincial publishers were not interested in any advertising except that which was scheduled to appear every day. We once sent to a newspaper in Yunnan an order for a small advertisement which was to appear-twice a week, on Wednesdays and Sundays, without having come to any definite understanding as to what the rate was to be and, through an oversight, failed to specify in our order the rate we were prepared to pay. We finally received an invoice charging us, for these infrequent insertions, twice as much as had been previously charged for a daily insertion of the same size. We wrote the publisher a letter in polite Chinese, pointing out that, as we were using the space in his paper only two days out of the seven, the very most we would expect to pay would be about half the charge for publishing the advertisement daily. In conclusion, we said that in any event we wouldn't pay the invoice he had sent us.

The publishers' letter in reply was just as polite as ours, but, between the courteous phrases, it bristled with indignation, and he made his point of view perfectly clear. When people ordered advertising which was to appear daily, at a certain monthly charge, he could take care of the business with no particular trouble, because the advertisement was put in the forms and stayed there permanently. But since we ordered the advertisement for Wednesdays and Sundays only, he had to check up and see that it appeared on those days, and did not appear on others, and if we insisted on putting him to all that extra trouble there was no reason why we should not pay for it. In conclusion, he said that if we didn't pay the bill, all Yunnan would learn of our rascally tricks.

We were not convinced by his argument, and as to his threat, we had heard the wind blow before without tearing oil" any thatched roofs. So we wrote and told him, not too politely, that he had better put himself in line with modern advertising- practice and concluded with a remark to the effect that unless he sent us an amended and reasonable bill he would never get a cent out of us, and that there was no need to write us any more letters on the subject. The next development came a week or so later in the form of an anguished call from the client for whom we had placed the advertising. The publisher had written his own account of our controversy, naming the client as well as myself, and published it on the principal news page o£ his paper with a warning to all his fellow-Yunnanists to beware of us both, and advising them that, if they did any business with us, to be sure to get the cash in advance, because if they did not take that precaution they would probably never get it all. He also said that this was only the first of a series of articles he intended to write on this subject and that they would be continued from time to time until I paid him what was justly due him. Of course, with this wind knocking over thatched roofs, we forgot about teaching this publisher any ideas of correct advertising practice, and paid the bill. In fact, our client insisted that we remit by telegraph so that the money would reach him before he had time to write any more articles. I regret to say this was the first, but not the last, experience of this sort. Trouble usually broke out when we refused to pay for an advertisement, perhaps because it had been so poorly printed that no one can identify it, or for some other good reason. Then we found ourselves 'posted' again, like a club member who has not paid his bill, and our iniquities are heralded to all who read the paper. We did not waste any sleep over this, but it invariably put our client in a blue funk, especially if it was the first time he had met blackmail face to face. I may say that this was a rather common practice among small Chinese papers and, as a method of collecting debts, was very successful. When the publisher was in need of cash and found that he has a sizeable amount of outstandings, he compiled and published a list of debtors with the amounts they owed him, reprinting the list every day, but he was fair enough to keep it up-to-date by deleting the names of those who paid up.

Any advertising man who made a collection of the rate cards of the Chinese newspapers of Shanghai would doubtless have been surprised to note that, of the dozen standard sized dailies, the rates were exactly the same.

Even to one who had had no experience as a space buyer, it must appear rather peculiar that a newspaper with a circulation of less than 10,000 could ask as high a rate for its space as the paper with a circulation of more than 100,000. The answer to this curious situation was found in the extremely flexible scale of discounts. The publisher of the newest and most clandestine of papers would feel that he had suffered a serious loss of face if he published a rate card quoting rates any lower than that of his biggest competitor, as it would be a virtual admission that his paper was inferior. The result was that the rate cards are all the same, but the discounts ranged from 5% to 90%. The same thing was true in every large city in China. When we had a rate card from one paper, our rate file for that city was complete except for the all-important figures showing the discount and commissions each paper would allow us.

One of the cardinal tenets of the British and American advertiser is that his advertising shall not appear alongside, or on the same page with, that of a competitive product. Almost every order we received from America contained a clause about competitive advertising, printed in bold type, and sometimes accompanied by the stern warning that payment for the advertising would be denied unless this injunction was complied with.

We did everything possible to carry out the wishes of the advertiser. By devious inquiries through friends on the papers, we learned the dates when competitive advertising was appearing, and scheduled our advertising for different days so far as that was possible. As comparatively few Chinese observe Sunday, and all the days bear numbers rather than names, there was no particular difference between the days and, for advertising purposes, one was just about the same as another. We wrote the newspapers strong letters on the subject and cultivated friendly relations with the Chinese foremen in charge of make-up, but invariably, sooner or later, one of our tooth paste or lip-stick or cereal advertisements would appear alongside that of a hated competitor. We always tried to get a free re-run of the advertisement, but whether we succeeded or not did not depend on the justice of our claim but on whether tire publisher was in need of more advertising and was therefore inclined to keep us in a good humor, or already had so much business that he could afford to be independent.

When the highly-efficient auditors in New York or London got the voucher copies of newspapers containing these offending advertisements, they wrote us letters which were very difficult to answer, because it was impossible for them to believe that any newspaper could be run with the divided authority and lack of discipline that existed on a Chinese paper. The truth of the matter was that the printers considered it their privilege to make up the advertising pages to suit their own convenience, so they shifted the advertisements about in any way that they saw fit. It was the advertising manager's business to turn in the copy, and it was the printer's business to put it into type and print it, and they would brook no interference. We actually received fewer complaints than were justified regarding Chinese, Japanese and Russian advertising, because the auditor could not read these languages: his advertising might be completely surrounded by competitive advertising and he would never know anything about it. But quite frequently one of our advertisements appeared alongside a competitive advertisement in one of the English language dailies of Shanghai, Hongkong, Tientsin or Hankow, and that was a very difficult matter to explain to the auditor. He might understand why, in a Chinese newspaper, specified advertising positions might go awry, because even he himself couldn't be certain of the makeup in these newspapers, but he found it very difficult to understand how this could happen in a paper published in the good, old, thoroughly understandable English language.

The explanation, which was quite simple, but not very convincing, was that the linotype operators, makeup men and all the other mechanics who were responsible for the production of an English language newspaper jn China were practically all Chinese who, in most cases, neither spoke nor understood a hundred words of English outside the technical terms of their own craft. Unless the illustration gave them some hint, they did not know whether a given advertisement exploited a tooth paste or a cure for Hongkong Foot or Shanghai Throat. The text meant no more to them than the text of a Chinese advertisement meant to the foreign auditor. It is difficult to imagine an illiterate printer, but they were thoroughly illiterate so far as the English language was concerned. They set up many columns on the linotype every day, but they had no idea what the text meant. In spite of the fact that they worked blindly in a language they did not understand they were remarkably efficient compositors. The Chinese linotype operator has always been a marvel to me, as he must be to anyone with any understanding of his difficulties and his handicaps. Without the faintest idea of the meaning of the text, without the ability to carry a sentence or a phrase in his memory, without knowing when a word in the typewritten text contains a ludicrous typographical error, he clatters rapidly over the keyboard and produces proofs which, while remarkably clean, will accurately reproduce all the misspelled words and typographical errors contained in the typescript.

There were English, French, German and Russian linotype keyboards in Shanghai, as well as a good many special alphabets, which printers and publishers found indispensable in this most cosmopolitan and polyglot of cities. I don't suppose any American linoytpe operator would think of trying to operate a Russian linotype machine unless he had at least taken a correspondence school course in the Russian language and had learned what some of the more important words and phrases mean, and that is not an easy accomplishment. During the early months of the First World War, I made a two weeks' train trip through Siberia, and having nothing to do but watch the dreary Siberian landscapes and smoke the thoroughly unsatisfactory Russian cigarettes, I spent my time trying to learn the Russian written language, but when the train finally pulled into Petro-grad, I was still a little hazy about some of the letters of the alphabet. These language handicaps which affect one with an English education do not bother the Chinese operator. The thirty-two letters of the peculiar Russian alphabet are so simple, as compared to the thousands of characters of his own language, that he soon masters them and in a couple of weeks can operate a Russian linotype as well as an English language machine. It takes him even less time to learn to operate a French or German machine.

This ignorance of English on the part of the printers sometimes led to ludicrous mistakes, and we occasionally enjoyed some very rich typographical errors in the Shanghai papers. The wonder is that there were not more of them. In 1911, when I was night editor of the local American owned paper, I was giving a proof of the front page a final glance before calling it a day and going to bed, when I happened to see a curious-looking paragraph which, on examination, proved to be a flippant and slightly ribald note I had written to another member of the staff earlier in the evening. He had left it lying on his desk and some boy had put it on the copy hook. I still shudder when I think what the consequences might have been if I had not caught this paragraph in time and it had appeared in the following morning's paper. One of the results would undoubtedly have been the termination of my career on the paper, and the end of my life in China, for I had made some unnecessary and entirely unjustified remarks about the editor and the business manager for whom I was working. They sounded innocent and playful when I typed them out on a piece of copy paper, but they were shocking when I read them in cold type on the page proof. I can't imagine how supremely ghastly these silly sentences .would have appeared if I had read them for the first time the following morning, after the papers had all been printed and delivered. It is very probable that I would not now be writing about a quarter of a century of life in China, because I would certainly have been fired and would probably never have come back.

Another Shanghai journalist, editor of the leading British newspaper, was not so fortunate in discovering and deleting his flippant remarks which crept into print. His paper published an annual city directory which was the standard publication of its kind in Shanghai. He had nothing to do with its compilation but, as a matter of routine, the corrected page proofs were always submitted to him for final approval before being sent to press. One year he was glancing through the proof sheets, when he happened to see the name of a man he detested and who had died a few months previously. In reproof to the compiler of the directory he inked in a black border around the name of the deceased and wrote on the margin of the proof: 'This silly ass is dead.'

A few days later the annual edition of the directory came out, with the black border around the name of the dead man and the editor's comment. The subsequent developments proved very conclusively what transient and changeable factors affect and degrade honest reputations. This English editor was one of the most brilliant of the many who have contributed to the fame of British journalism in China, but he is famous, not for his accomplishments, but because of his silly, unconsidered comment on the proof of a page of what, after all, was not a very important publication.

They learned poker according to Texas rules

12. Straights and Flushes

There was one period of several months when anyone who visited my office in Shanghai would have found, in one of the inner rooms, a round, cloth-covered table with chairs, cigarettes and ash-trays, a pack of playing-cards, and some piles of neatly stacked poker chips. It looked very much like a layout for a friendly poker game, and that is exactly what it was. If the visitor had remained for any length of time he would, in all probability, have seen one of my Chinese staff come in and consult with me, and we would have gone to the table, shuffled the cards, counted out the chips and played a few hands of poker with a good deal of Anglo-Chinese conversation. Then he would have seen us, apparently, go back to work again. The spectacle would have impressed any visitor as a very singular way for a reputable business office to be conducted.

As a matter of fact, we were hard at work on a very important commission when we were playing the few hands of poker, for we were preparing the Chinese rules for that great American game. We had just been employed to do this by an American manufacturer, for, by a curious coincidence, poker playing became popular in China about the same time that Americans went through a mild Mah Jongg craze. I am not sure which was published first, poker rules in Chinese or Mah Jongg rules in English, but both appeared about the same time.

We had just completed the work of translating the United States Pharmacopoeia into Chinese, a task which had occupied several men for more than a year; beside that monumental undertaking the translation of the rules of poker appeared to be very simple. I told the manufacturer we would complete the work in a week and quoted a correspondingly low price for it. He was going to be in Shanghai for a fortnight and the plan was to have the translation completed and in the hands of the printer before he left. At the end of the week, I realized that we were confronted by a very difficult task—much more difficult than I had anticipated. There were no Chinese equivalents for what might be called the technical terms used in poker and we had to adapt old characters to new uses and then explain what they meant. By the time the manufacturer left Shanghai we had made such little progress that we couldn't even guarantee when we would finish the work. He couldn't understand why there should be so much pother and delay about a matter which was as simple as a, b, c, to him, as poker is to most Americans, including myself. I am sure he would have turned the work over to someone else if he had had time to make the arrangements, but he couldn't delay his sailing and so left us to muddle along with it.

Eventually our amateur poker players finished the translation and we followed the usual custom of giving the Chinese text to an outside translator to be put back into English for the purposes of checking. When retranslated into what is the mother tongue of poker, no one could make head or tail of the rules. They would have applied to Mah Jongg or Parcheesi as readily as to poker. It was then that I set up the poker table as a laboratory and school room, and became a teacher of the art of poker playing. We played as a part of our regular daily work, taking up one rule at a time and making sure that it was not only understood by the Chinese staff, but put into understandable Chinese before we went on to the next one. Naturally there was no money at stake, but I tried my best to win so as to give my pupils confidence that they were being taught by a master and so stir them up to put their hearts into the work. We went through straight poker and show down first, and gradually progressed through jack pot, stud, seven-toed Pete, whisky poker, and all the other ramifications of the game. Our efforts to put poker rules into Chinese aroused the sympathetic interest of some of my fellow-Americans and they gave a lot of help. One of them insisted that the introduction of poker into China and its general adoption as an indoor sport would be a great civilizing influence, would serve to break down the provincialism of the people and provide them with a common interest. My volunteer helpers got so enthusiastic about the work that, towards the end, I was able to turn it all over to them and so maintain my usual decorum in my own private office. Six weeks after we had started the work, they announced that the compilation was complete. A re-translation proved understandable and, with a few slight exceptions, entirely accurate. Then, as a final test, we selected five non-poker-playing Chinese for a laboratory experiment. We sat them at our poker table, gave them chips, cards and copies of the rules, and, watched anxiously while they struggled with the rules and put them into action. In-order to make the test as effective- and realistic as possible, I supplied them with chips, which had a small cash value. We found a few obscure points which required straightening out, but at length we were able to call the job complete and send the copy to the printers.

Few books ever published in China had such a wide distribution as these rules of poker. The translation of President Wilson's speeches during the First World War had proved very popular, but never had anything like the popularity of these poker rules. The first edition consisted of

100,000 copies, and I don't know how many times it was reprinted, for we sent the plates to the manufacturer in Ohio and he printed subsequent editions there to be packed in cases of cards shipped to China. I understand, however, that the printings ran to well over a million. My name and address appeared on the first edition and, over a period of more than fifteen years I received letters enclosing postage stamps in payment for copies of the book. They came from all parts of the Far East, from Peru, Jamaica and Mauritius. One came from a town on the edge of Thibet, giving the address of a Lama monastery. The compilation of this book took so much time that we didn't make any money on it, so I must take a little credit to myself. I learned to play poker in Fort Worth and have always played the orthodox game. Like others of my generation, it has grieved me to see the debasement of the game which has been brought about through the influence of women players, such perversions as 'spit in the ocean,' 'railroad,' 'one-eyed jack,' and other games which allow the use of wild cards. My colleagues felt as I did, that a poker hand which might contain five aces was an abomination, and so we not only framed the rules so as to prevent anything of this sort, but incorporated a solemn warning against it. Our rules constitute the standard authority in China, and, as a result, Chinese play orthodox poker as it was played in Texas forty years ago.

It was this attempt to put more life and action into a game which needed no improvement that killed Mah Jongg, which was, for a year or two, so popular in America and England. Like poker, Mah Jongg is a game into which an infinite variety of changes may be introduced. But, as in poker, when new values are given to the tiles, the game becomes more one of chance and less one of skill, and human nature is such that people soon tire of a game in which, when they win, they must give the credit to luck and cannot enjoy the secret satisfaction of a belief that they have Avon by clever playing. Mah Jongg is a comparatively new game in China, having been invented by a Ningpo fisherman only 300 years ago, but it has always been popular because luck plays a very large part in the game, the competent player is the one who will eventually win.

The translation of the rules of poker was the most difficult job of that sort we ever undertook, but when we began advertising motor-cars, we found plenty of trouble expressing motor-car terms in the Chinese language. Naturally, there were no Chinese names for the parts of cars and, in order to define them, it was necessary to devise some arbitrary combination of existing Chinese words or to put old words to new uses. This had to be done with every new article introduced to China, and sometimes it has been very easy. For instance, a mortar is called a 'frog gun' and an electric light is called 'bottled moonlight,' two perfectly descriptive phrases. As between 'bottled moonlight' and 'incandescent bulb' I would choose the 'bottled moonlight' as one which at least has greater advertising possibilities and would lend itself to romance and to poetic phrases.

Motor-cars had been in use in China for some time before anyone gave a thought to what Chinese names should be given to the various parts; in fact, the whole problem was dumped on us when we took on the first motor-car account of any size and started to write and design Chinese press advertising and translate some catalogues. In our search for a glossary of Chinese automotive terminology, which we soon found did not exist, we ran across a very interesting argot which had been developed by Shanghai chauffeurs. Many of them had started in life as carriage drivers, for it was perfectly natural that when the master replaced his carriage by a motor-car, he should give the driver of his carriage an opportunity to learn to drive the new vehicle. As the art of driving cars was entirely unknown in China, a horse carriage driver was as well prepared as anyone to learn it. In fact, he had one distinct advantage over others, because he did know the names of streets and the situation of the master's club, and was familiar with the two or three traffic rules which were adequate for sedan chairs, carriages and rickshas. The new chauffeurs brought their stable language with them, with the result that various parts of the motor-car were referred to in rich horsey terms, some of which were quite suitable for the stable, but would not look well in public print. Then we found that the motor-car mechanics had an entirely different set of terms, which were also curious, but at any rate were printable and gave us some-I thing we could start with. Their terminology smacked of the sea, because a lot of them had been recruited from the ranks of marine engineers because of their ability to effect repairs. We felt quite encouraged over this, until a new complexity presented itself. The mechanics in different garages had each adopted their own Chinese terms, so before we could make any progress we had to make a collection of all the different terms in use in Shanghai, then select those which appeared to be the most suitable or had the widest currency.

Grooms speak a horsey language of their own

Those first catalogues we got out were fairly intelligible in Shanghai, but when copies were sent to Hong-kong, Tientsin and Hankow, the people there hadn't any idea what the text was about, and wouldn't have I known that it was a motor-car catalogue if it had not been for the illustrations. To give some idea of the confusion, we referred to gasoline as 'steam oil,' but in Tientsin it was known as 'electric oil.' We called a tire a 'rubber tube,' but in Peking it was called a 'rubber band.' There was some similarity in these terms, but when we came to such complicated matters as carburetors and gear shifts and differential, there was absolutely no similarity in the terms used in different places. In each place, the chauffeurs and mechanics had picked out names which were entirely different from those in use in Shanghai, and worse than that, the Chinese names of the cars we were advertising were different in every city where they were sold. Obviously, if we were going to do any business advertising cars to Chinese, which we eventually did, we would have to manage in some way to make the advertising message intelligible. With that idea in view, we set to work on the compilation of a complete glossary, collecting from each center all the terms which were used locally. From these we threw out those which were ribald or obviously absurd, and then printed a glossary which contained a wide selection of terms.

Copies of this were sent to everyone who was in any way interested in cars, and everyone who manifested the least interest in our project and their opinion solicited as to the terms which were most suitable. When we had collected all the opinions we could get, there being no one else to assume the responsibility, we made a final selection of the terms to be used and published a glossary which we referred to as 'standard', and cajoled an indifferent association of car dealers into giving it their official endorsement. No one ever questioned this glossary, which was soon adopted by common consent, and so it became the standard. The terms we selected are now found in all Chinese technical dictionaries.

In Peking the size of your card is important

The chauffeurs were not the only Chinese who developed an occupational *argot* of their own; in fact, almost every occupation has an argot which cannot be understood by the uninitiated. Each craft thus becomes a kind of a masonic mystery with symbols and signs which enable fellow-craftsmen to communicate with each other without divulging to outsiders any hint of the subject under discussion. The hundreds of stable boys and *mafoos* employed around the Shanghai Race Club spoke a language which no one else understood and used this as a means of levying tribute on the newcomer. When the foreign horse owner employed a new stable boy the latter was unable to perform his duties satisfactorily until he mastered the argot of the other stable boys, and they charged him for the privilege, taking a percentage of his wages for the first few months. It was, in effect, an initiation fee which he must pay before he was admitted to the full privilege of the guild. Shopkeepers and their assistants have their own system of signs and slang which they find very useful. By a gesture or by the use of words which are meaningless to others the shopkeeper can tell his assistant to accept the price offered by the customer or to hold out for a higher figure.

Every foreigner who lives in China for any length of time must get a Chinese name for himself if he wants to have an identity among the Chinese, as he must have if he intends to do any business with them or meet them socially. It is probably unnecessary to explain that the Chinese is not an alphabetic language in which words are formed by a combination of letters, but that, each word is a separate character in itself. The foreigner's business card is just as unintelligible to the average Chinese as the hieroglyphic on a Chinese business card would be to him. As there is no Chinese alphabet and as it is impossible to do more than approximate the sound of a foreign name by the use of Chinese characters, the foreigner's name is usually an arbitrary selection. His name may be a simple one such as Smith or Jones, but his Chinese will be something quite different. Furthermore, a hundred Smiths may, and probably will, have a hundred different names, for it is impossible to express the sound of that name with Chinese characters. The name selected depends on the caprice of the Chinese who selects it, and my experience is that when it comes to giving names to foreigners they are extremely capricious, not to say waggish. If you are fortunate enough to be named Lee or Washington, the sound of your name can be expressed perfectly, but in the case of most names the sound gives little hint of the original. For example, my official Chinese name is 'Ko Lo' which is as close as they can get to Carl Crow. My name could be translated, but it was not expedient to do so because a crow is a bird of evil habits and ill repute. My simple four letter Chinese name, which means 'untiring energy,' was given to me by a Chinese clerk in the American Consulate in Shanghai during the days of the Manchus. I suspected him at the time of saddling me with a humorous name and often thought I saw suppressed smiles when I was introduced to Chinese, but it wasn't until I had worn the name for ten years or more that I found out how good the joke was. In my vanity I had assumed that the untiring energy referred to was that dynamic, driving energy that characterized captains of industry and makes millionaires out of poor boys. My conscience hurt me a little when I reflected that I had never tried to live up to such a grand name, and then I found that in my own mind, I had been living under an alias. My name does not refer to that kind of energy at all, but to the muscular energy necessary to push a wheelbarrow or pull a ricksha.

However, I am not so badly misnamed as some of my friends, who are simply top heavy with such names as 'Perpetual Virtue,' 'Ancient Sage,' 'Quiet and Discreet,' 'Always Temperate' and 'Admired by Sages.' These are really semblances of the titles formerly bestowed on deceased rulers. I prefer my name with its humble implications, for I would rather be a live ricksha coolie than a dead duke.

Not only the names of foreigners but the names of all foreign cities have to undergo these transformations and be christened anew in Chinese. In most cases the Chinese name is only an approximation of the sound of the 'foreign' name, but in other cases it is descriptive. London is known simply as 'British Capital.' San Francisco is 'Old Gold Hill,' Honolulu as 'Sandalwood Island.' San Francisco was the focal point for early Chinese immigration to America, and the name was given it by the Chinese gold hunters. At about that same period the Hawaiian Islands provided China's supply of sandalwood. In Chinese songs San Francisco is known by the poetical name of 'Market of the Three Barbarian Tribes,' referring to the Americans, British and Spanish who made up the greater part of the population of California in the Gold Rush days. Filipinos, on whom Chinese traders have waxed fat for several centuries, are known simply as 'Luzon-Kwei' or Devils from the Island of Luzon. Every time we undertook the advertising of a new brand our first task was to select a suitable Chinese name, and it was not an easy one. But no client ever understood either its importance or its difficulties. In fact, we usually had a troublesome time explaining to him that his brand, which was well known in many countries, had to be rechristened in China, so that it could be identified by the millions who knew no language but Chinese. The Chinese brand name must be simple, easily read and yet so distinctive that it cannot be easily imitated or confused with other names. When we selected a name which met these requirements we had to make a test for ribaldry. China is the paradise of punsters, and the most sedate phrase may, by a simple change in tone, be turned into a ribald quip which will make the vulgar roar. This is something we had to guard against as we would the plague. We almost slipped once or twice.

Foreigners, except for the very few who are able to speak the language, find Chinese personal names very confusing and difficult to remember, and few bother to learn them. I don't suppose there is one foreigner out of fifty who has the faintest idea of the names of their personal servants, who are called boy, cook, coolie, amah, or gardener, as the case may be. In offices the foreign manager will know the names of the principal Chinese employees, but all the others are known merely as boy, shroff or coolie. As there are more than one in each occupation they are given separate identities by means of numbers. The dean of the staff of office boys is known as No. 1 Boy and the next as No. 2 Boy and so on down the line. This method of ranking people by number is so convenient that it has been generally adopted. Instead of referring to a man as general manager or president of a company we called him the company's 'number one.' If in a conversation anywhere on the China Coast someone referred to the King of England's 'No. 1 Boy,' the allusion might be in doubtful taste, but everyone would understand that the Prime Minister was the person referred to.

No matter what your official Chinese name may be, you will be known by one or more nicknames which will be given you by your servants and employees. Very few foreigners know what their servants call them, which is probably just as well. Chinese do not give nicknames to foreigners because they are foreigners, for it is a universal custom and almost every Chinese has a nickname. If a man with the family name of Wong should have survived the smallpox it is a foregone conclusion that he will be known as 'Pock Marked Wong,' a name which he does not resent, because the good luck which is supposed to follow a recovery from smallpox more than compensates for any facial disfigurement which results. Any physical disability or disfigurement will form the basis for a nickname and, in the absence of these, any peculiar mental characteristic. Chinese servants find it difficult to remember and to pronounce the names of foreigners and resort, to the simple expedient of referring to them by their street addresses. Thus my boy, when sending a message to one of my friends through another houseboy, does not refer to me by either my foreign or Chinese name, but as 'No. 883 Connaught Road Master.' This was all very simple before there were any apartment houses in Shanghai, but the latter brought complications, for two or more of your friends might have the same address. Thus, when my wife was. told that while she was out 'Broadway Mansions missie' has telephoned her, she had to inquire which 'missie' was referred to, and the boy explained that it was the 'old missie.' In point of years the old 'missie' was by far the youngest, but she had been a resident of Broadway Mansions longer than the other,, and therefore took the more honorable rank. The other nicknames which were given us were not so colorless. I happen to know only one of my Chinese nicknames. When I came out of the American Club in Shanghai, the doorman called out:

'Co Co.'

The chauffeurs who were waiting for other lingering club members to go home repeated the call until my chauffeur heard it. It was not very dignified for an old and more or less respected resident to be hailed by the frivolous comic opera name of 'Co Co,' and I could have put a stop to it, but if I had, the only result would be that I would spend a lot of time waiting for my car. When it arrived, the doorman opened the door respectfully, I stepped into the car with dignity and the chauffeur drove away. The doorman had only done his best to pronounce my name and improved it by making its accoustical properties simpler and easier to recognize above the street noises.

Even in what you might call my 'garage name,' I did not fare so badly either, when it came to a matter of dignity. One of the editors of the leading English language paper was known to all the printers in the place as 'Fat Rascal.' He was undoubtedly fat, but his rascality appealed to consist only in his insistence on clean proofs. One of our most illustrious citizens, for many years the chairman of the Shanghai Municipal Council, was known by every ricksha coolie and taxicab driver in Shanghai as 'Young Jelly Belly.' The reason this venerable old gentleman's name was prefixed by the qualifying 'Young' was because a predecessor was given the original name of 'Jelly Belly,' and, when the second pear-shaped man came along, the only logical thing to do was to give him junior rank. Another old gentleman was known among the ricksha fraternity as 'Twenty Cents,' because no matter how long, or how short his ricksha ride was, that was the amount he paid. The ricksha men understood and enjoyed this, for it introduced into his patronage a delightful element of chance. He might use the ricksha for only a few blocks and the puller was happy over the rich reward for his labor. On the other hand, the coolie might pull up tired and perspiring at the end of a trip from the Bund to the Race Club, and still get the conventional twenty cents. He was not happy about it, nor was he unhappy. It was just a turn of fate which had been against him and to-morrow he might have a luckier break, such as getting an American tourist who would pay him in U. S. currency, which, when exchanged for Chinese currency, always proved to be of fabulous value. .

The sick man gambles on the choice of a doctor

13. Pills for the Ills of China

I don't suppose there is a proprietary medicine manufacturer of importance in any part of the world who has not, at one time or another, encouraged his imagination to play with the idea of the prosperous business he might build up, and the wealth he might accumulate, if he could, by some means, convince a reasonable number of Chinese of the efficiency of his remedies. The less the manufacturer knows about China, apart from the population figure, the less restricted are his day-dreams, and, as he usually knows nothing about the country, his fancy is in most cases free to wander into distant and prosperous fields. He knows from his own practical experience as a vendor of remedies that no one is going to eat an apple a day in order to avoid contracting debts to the doctor. So secure does the normally healthy person feel regarding the continuance of his good health that he will not even eat a prune or a raisin a day. Everyone will buy remedies, but few will bother to take a prophylactic, even if it costs nothing. Everyone knows, or should know, that a glass of hot water before breakfast provides a fairly reliable guarantee against certain common ailments, but not one in a thousand will bother to drink the water. But the medicine man knows that when a man gets a

168

bellyache, or a backache, or a headache, or any of the numerous aches this flesh is heir to, he almost invariably takes some medicine which will relieve his pain and make him feel like a normal human being again. When he computes the number of China's millions who must, according to the laws of average, be suffering from some kind of an ache at any given moment and reflects on the efficacy with which his pills would cure them or give them relief, it is easy for him to conjure up rosy day-dreams in which a private yacht occupies the foreground and a country estate can be seen in the middle distance.

He knows that the problem of advertising a medicine is a very simple one. You never have to worry about the interest of the reader, and do not have to resort to expensive art work and tricky layouts in order to attract his attention. If, for example, you are advertising pills which will take the misery out of a backache, you may be sure that no one who is unconscious of the existence of his back will do more than glance at the display lines, but that everyone with an aching back will read the advertisement through from beginning to end, tally up the symptoms and convince himself that his is no ordinary run-of-the-mill backache, which any Tom, Dick or Harry might suffer, but one with a perversity of its own and superior on many counts to all others. The most satisfactory and enjoyable hours a sick person spends are devoted to talking to others who are suffering from the same ailment, comparing symptoms and boasting about them. If he can't talk about symptoms, the most pleasurable alternative is to read about them. Backaches make the whole world kin, because a Chinese coolie's back can ache just as painfully between the shafts of his ricksha as a millionaire's back can ache on the seat of his limousine.

Since the 'confession' type of magazines have had such a success in America, I wonder why someone doesn't start a .similar periodical in which invalids and the casually sick could express themselves, and feel that by doing so they had gained a sympathy as broad and all-embracing as the audited circulation of the magazine. If anyone ever starts a publication of this sort, I can give him a corking confession on 'Hongkong foot' and a fairly good one on gastritis.

From the theoretical, or what one might call consular report point of view, the assumption that China should provide a big and profitable market for proprietary medicines is a perfectly sound one. Here is a huge population, comparatively ignorant of the blessings of liver and kidney pills, cold cures, blood purifiers, tonics and all the other remedies which find such a large sale in other countries. It would appear reasonable to suppose that there would be a great quantity and variety of diseases and an urgent demand for anything which would cure them. If the manufacturer takes the trouble to investigate the matter by reading the reports of the medical missionaries, who should be, and are, honest and reliable sources of information, he will find plenty of reason for encouragement. Every report from these honest, hard-working and self-sacrificing Christian missionaries will tell of crowded surgeries and dispensaries and of the urgent need for more hospitals and for increased funds for the support of the medical missions. To the pill manufacturer, it looks like an opportunity to serve suffering humanity and make a fortune while doing so.

I used to be enthusiastic myself about the possibilities of this business until I learned better through the process, expensive to my clients and discouraging to me, of helping some of them to spend money in advertising-new remedies which never found a market of profitable proportions. In this way I learned, first, that the Chinese are a very healthy race. Many of them live in poorly ventilated houses, amid filthy surroundings and take no exercise. By rights, they should be very sickly. Why they are not I will not attempt to explain except to say that the high infant mortality may mean that only the strong survive to middle age and so can put up a stubborn resistance to disease. Whatever the reason may be, the fact remains that a dozen or more big life insurance companies are glad to insure the lives of Chinese, and at no increase over the rates charged to men of other nationalities in other parts of the world where people live under presumably much healthier conditions. As a matter of fact, since Chinese will bargain over life insurance premiums as over anything else, many of them actually paid (in some companies) less for insurance than we foreigners paid, or received greater benefits for the same premium payment.

The second thing I found out about the Chinese as potential consumers of medicines was that, when a Chinese falls ill, he does not, like other people, send for a doctor or run to the family medicine chest. It wouldn't do him any good to run to the medicine chest, because he hasn't any, though a few medicinal herbs may be hanging up in the kitchen. In a good many cases, he just goes to bed and, as he has no appetite for food, undergoes a fast which involves no hardship. That is what he does if he has a cold, and he usually gets well just as quickly as he would if thoroughly dosed with medicines. I believe the-American doctors-say to each other, but do not confide the fact to laymen, that a cold should be cured in two weeks with proper treatment by a physician and in a fortnight with no treatment at all. The Chinese learned this centuries ago. They do not even delude themselves with the idea that a good hot alcoholic drink will do them any good.

The third thing I learned about the sale of pills in China was that, when a Chinese does get sick enough to feel the urgent need for medicines, the chances are a good deal more than ten to one that he will go to an old-fashioned Chinese doctor or else buy herbal remedies from an old-fashioned Chinese apothecary shop, or entrust himself to the ministrations of some old man of the neighborhood who is famed for his skill in taking care of the sick. This preference for remedies, which have been hallowed by centuries of use in his own country is not confined to the poor and the ignorant. I know at least three graduates of American universities who depend on Chinese doctors and Chinese medicines to cure them, and there are doubtless many other university graduates who hold the same views.

At first glance-this would appear to prove the mission doctors guilty of gross exaggeration or willful perversions of facts, but this conclusion would be unjust. Their reports are quite correct when they tell of crowded dispensaries, but they do not explain that the mission dispensaries are usually so small that a couple of sick families would crowd them. In few cities are the dispensaries large enough to take care of more than one per cent of the population who may be sick, so that a very moderate acceptance of 'foreign medicine' will provide more patients than the dispensary can accommodate.

Although, in the inexperience and youthful enthusiasm of my early forties, I aided and even encouraged some of my clients in the spending of advertising appropriations to establish new remedies which remarkably few people ever bought, I later shied away from a business which I knew had little or no chance of success. In fact, if I had only a portion of the money I have saved manufacturers of several nationalities by talking them out of going into the medicine business in China, it would provide a lot of interior decoration for my bank account. One of the unfortunate circumstances connected with the business of an advertising agent is that the most valuable service he can render to a manufacturer is to keep him from throwing his money away on a vain enterprise, but it is a service for which he seldom gets paid.

In spite of the more or less open contempt in which the Chinese doctor and the Chinese materia medica is held by almost all foreign doctors, the fact remains that crude and imperfect as their methods may be, they have held the faith of millions of their fellow countrymen for a staggering number of centuries. And though American doctors hold Chinese medical practice in very low esteem, it should be remembered that there are a lot of different kinds of medical practitioners in America, that each has a certain amount of contempt and disdain for the others and vice versa. Though working along different technical lines, the Chinese medical profession has not been without its heroes, its practitioners of great fame and its patient searches after scientific facts. In 1848, the decade which saw the opening of China to foreign trade and to the residence of foreign missionaries, there was published in China a monumental work: 'Researches into the Names and Virtues of Plants.' This set of books consisted of 60 volumes and contained almost 2,000 accurate botanical drawings. Although there was some new material in this encyclopaedic compilation, a very large part of it was a resume of ancient medical works. More than a thousand years before the birth of Christ, the medical profession was well established in China and doctors were writing-down case histories and arguing with each other about the values of different herbs.

Although I am fortunate enough to be a very poor customer so far as doctors are concerned, and know much less about doctors and hospitals than the average layman of my age, I have a very decided, though entirely amateur and theoretical opinion about Chinese doctors. I do not believe that a hundred generations of them, carefully observing the effects of the administrations of various herbs on their patients, could have failed to learn a great deal about the art of healing.

That is the way the Chinese feel about it, and, on the few occasions in China when I was really sick, my Chinese friends implored me to call in a Chinese doctor or to take some of the Chinese medicine which had cured the ills of their forbears for many generations. Of course, my theory doesn't go that far, and when there was anything the matter with me I listened to, and sometimes followed, the advice of my old friend, Dr. Tom Dunn.

The practice of Chinese medicine was never put on a formalized or scientific basis, and was taught by the apprenticeship system. Each doctor taught his craft to one or more of his sons or other younger relatives, just as doctors did in other countries until a comparatively recent period. Until 1858, any number of schools and other institutions in Great Britain laid down their rules and granted licenses to practice medicine without any state supervision. In China, it has not been necessary to secure a license or diploma from any organization, and anyone who cares to do so Can set himself up as a physician, a privilege which many quacks take advantage of. In the eyes of the law all varieties of medical practice stand on an equal footing in China, but in all public health services, Western medical practice was adopted. No doubt, a great many of the Chinese officials who are responsible for carrying out quarantine and other public health measures secretly believe in the superiority of the old-fashioned Chinese doctor. But there being no system, standards of practice or code of ethics, it is a much easier matter to adopt foreign medicine en bloc than to reform and standardize the old medical practice, and this is what has been done, just as it was done by Japan under almost identical conditions.

A large number of foreign manufacturers sold their remedies in China, some as 'ethical' preparations which are prescribed by doctors, and others as household remedies which make the employment of a doctor unnecessary. The pages of the Chinese newspapers are full of medical advertising. There are a number of preparations which enjoy a world-wide sale and all of them arc to be found in China. We handled the advertising for several of them. All have been sold for a generation or more and have built up sound reputations and a profitable following. These remedies appear to satisfy the existing demand completely and so leave little room for the introduction of any new competing nostrums. Since the Chinese are so reluctant to change old brands for new, it is not surprising that they should be conservative about a matter of such personal importance as, let us say, a kidney pill. The present generation wants the pill that cured grandfather's backache and will take no other. That is all very fine for the brand which cured grandfather, but discouraging for the man who is trying to put a new pill on the market. About the best he can hope to do is to get a few satisfied customers now and wait for the grandchildren to grow up before expecting any great and dependable volume of business. Even after waiting three generations for it, the volume may not be very large. The total amount of business done by anyone of the manufacturers in the field is really absurdly small as compared to the theoretical volume that can be built up without" doing violence to a healthy imagination. The total consumption of foreign pills probably does not average much more than one pill per annum per person.

One of the many old sailor yarns about China and the Chinese is to the effect that the Chinese pay their doctors to keep them well, and stop their pay when illness invades the family circle. About all that this interesting bit of misinformation amounts to is that many centuries ago a few Chinese established the system of paying the doctor a regular annual or monthly fee for which he was supposed to look after the ills of the entire household. It is a very sensible system and has in recent years been put into effect in progressive communities in many countries. It assures the doctor of a steady income and insures the head of the household against the extraordinarily heavy expenses which a long period of illness might involve. This employment of doctors on a monthly or annual basis is by no means universal, is in fact confined to a very small number of the thrifty well-to-do classes. It is probably no more common in

China than sickness and accident insurance in its various forms is in America.

A great many people never consult a doctor until some member of the family is really ill. Then there is a serious problem to be solved—which of the neighboring doctors to call. Good Chinese doctors, like their ethical foreign brethren, do not advertise, and their reputations are established and their practice built up through the uncertain medium of common gossip which, as every doctor knows, may bring fame, practice and profits to a quack or ruin the reputation of an honest man who has made an unfortunate diagnosis. In these circumstances, the head of a Chinese household who has to employ a doctor for a son, wife, daughter or other ailing relative feels on his shoulders the weight of a very heavy responsibility. If he selects the right physician, the loved one may soon be hale and hearty again. If he picks the wrong one, there may be another mound on the family burial plot. The heads of a great many families in other countries have been confronted by the same problem, but few of them have ever put it up to themselves in the definitive and fatalistic way of the Chinese. Although the problem is one of tragic seriousness, the Chinese have what they consider to be a very sensible way of solving it. There are, perhaps, a dozen local physicians of good reputation, any one of whom would be as acceptable as any other. In order to make sure that fortune favors the selection of the doctor, the names of all those who are under consideration are written on individual slips of paper and the sick person draws one. The designated doctor is employed and everyone feels very optimistic about it. They all know that there is, in sickness and doctoring, a very important element of luck and that, by allowing the sick person to make a blind selection of his doctor they have in a way circumvented the bad luck which might have attended the selection made by some more logical method. Very important is the fact that the sick man, having drawn the name of the doctor himself, feels a complete confidence in him and is prepared to get well.

While we could not work up any enthusiasm in our agency over the idea of selling a new foreign nostrum to the Chinese, we would have welcomed the opportunity to advertise a Chinese patent medicine in some country such as Australia or India, the greatest patent medicine countries in the world. What interesting copy would be written, without serious deviations from the compass point of truth! We advertised one famous children's remedy for so long that, during the period of our stewardship, the slogan changed. It formerly boasted a reputation covering a period of half a century, but later that was extended to sixty years. That sounds like a very respectable age for a patent medicine, but suppose you were confronted in your morning newspaper with an advertisement of some remedy which had been curing this or that illness from the time of Nebuchadnezzar! Suppose we could tell you that the Samson-like strength of some living Chinese athlete was due to the use of the same tonic that, many centuries-ago, helped Genghis Khan to become the ruler of the world! Wouldn't that be convincing? Of course, there are a great many sceptical people who would scoff at good advertising copy like this, but I am sure that in the main it would be effective. It would certainly be as truthful as most patent medicine advertising.

A tonic for Genghis Khan

The preparation of patent medicine copy is not difficult anywhere, but it is less difficult in China than in most other countries. The securing of genuine testimonials there is a rather easy matter, and no one expects to be paid for them. If you can induce a Chinese to take your remedy and he finds that it gives him relief from pain or cures him, he has no objection to writing a letter about it which can be used in advertising. In fact, sometimes we received testimonials when we were definitely not looking for them. We once carried out a fairly big campaign for a British cocoa manufacturer who wanted to make the Chinese a nation of cocoa drinkers. As cocoa is a drink with which the Chinese were entirely unfamiliar, we put all our effort into getting people to send in 30 cents for a sample can big-enough to make a dozen cups and we were able to dispose of a surprising number of samples in this way. Full directions as to how to prepare the cocoa were enclosed with each can we posted. But in. order to make sure that there were no misunderstandings or mistakes regarding this important detail, we sent a second copy of the directions a few days later, with a letter in which we politely expressed the hope that the recipient had tried the cocoa and liked it. We had not expected a reply to this letter, but soon they began to arrive in surprising volume.

The first response came from a railway official at Hangchow. He said that he had been suffering from sleeplessness and indigestion for years and that he drank tremendous quantities of tea in order to keep himself going and get through his daily work. After trying out our samples of cocoa, he had bought a full-size can, discontinued drinking tea, had been drinking cocoa instead, and now, after a fortnight's change in diet, he was sleeping soundly, his digestion was improving, and he felt better than he had felt for years.

For an advertising agent to find a letter like that in his morning's mail is like finding an unexpected gold piece in a pocketful of coppers. In the next week or so we found more gold pieces, because we received other letters along the same line. It seemed to me that here was the basis for an entirely new advertising appeal in which we would stress the health-giving properties of cocoa. But it sounded too good to be true. In order to make sure that I was right in what I proposed to do, I called on an old missionary doctor who had been treating ailing Chinese for a generation, and showed him the letters. He said they did not surprise him in the least. Although Chinese tea is very weak, it will, if consumed in intemperate quantities, produce nervous disorders which would cause sleeplessness and indigestion. A change from tea to cocoa would naturally serve to correct these conditions, and cocoa provided some food elements which were lacking in the Chinese diet.

There didn't seem to us to be any further doubt as j to what we should do. We changed the whole campaign j into a health appeal, got photographs of some of the people who had been benefited by drinking our cocoa and printed these with their testimonials. We were rather" proud of ourselves when we wrote to the British manufacturer telling him what we had done. Unfortunately for us, the manufacturer did not share our enthusiasm. He did not approve of anything we had done. Though he wrote to us with some Quakerish restraint, his words were biting enough as they were, and much could be read between the lines. The reputation of his old and respectable firm had been dragged in the mire by our blatant unethical advertising. He took no more chances with us and turned the advertising over to another agency who could be trusted to maintain the respectability of the firm no matter how much that high estate might cost in the loss of sales opportunities. Fifteen years after this unhappy incident I noted that many manufacturers were advertising cocoa as a relief from sleeplessness.

Rice, shark's fins, and bird's nest soup

14. Shark's Fins and Ancient Eggs

Although the vision of selling an apple a day to th Chinese remains nothing more than a statistical extravagance, a great many foreign manufacturers have by persistent advertising, built up a good sale for certain foreign foods in China. Canned milk was the first to be introduced and gradually found acceptable as baby food As it was both the duty as well as the desire of every] wife to produce as many children as possible, the demand for wet nurses exceeded the supply and canned milk was welcomed as supplying an actual need. As there is little grazing land in this over-populated and intensely cultivated country, there are very few cows and the local supply of milk in all the communities of China wouldn't meet the demand that exists in a good-sized town in America. Canned milk and various milk powders were on sale in all parts of the country, but milk has never been looked on as a beverage. Its use was confined to children and invalids, and no Chinese drinks a glass of milk because he likes it.

We did go far towards making the Chinese a nation of raisin eaters. Before the First World War raisins were practically unknown in China. But a year or two after they were introduced the little red box which forms the packet of the world's most famous raisin is a familiar sight on the shop shelves of almost every city.

When we started promoting the consumption of raisins I suggested that we should conduct a cake-baking contest, offering cash prizes to those who would send in the best cakes in which raisins formed a part of the ingredients. It was my first experience with anything of this sort, and it wasn't until the entries began piling in that I realized how strong the gambling instinct is with the Chinese and how eagerly they seize an opportunity to get something for nothing. The day the contest closed I went to see my client and found him completely surrounded by a sea of cakes.

'You got me into this mess,' he said, 'and now you can get me out of it. You have been nominated and unanimously elected as sole judge of the contest and, within an hour, all the cakes will be in your office and you need not bother to return them.'

I must admit that at the time I proposed the contest the question of how we were going to decide the winners had not occurred to me. When the cakes were all in my office on display and covering every available desk and table I looked at the display hoping for inspiration, but none came. My Chinese staff were of no help, though one of them did point out that we could disqualify a few [of the contenders who had entered puddings, three who had entered plain cakes, and a few others who had put in currants or prunes instead of raisins. With these thrown out there were still more than 500 cakes to be judged, and the only sensible way to judge them was by tasting them.

While I was worrying about the problem a ricksha coolie came into the office and sniffed the cakes like a hungry dog in a meatshop. When I told him to help himself he looked carefully over the whole collection land sniffed at several before selecting the one he wanted.

That solved my problem. After talking- the matter over with my Chinese staff I told the coolie to collect fifty of his friends and bring them to the office as soon after five o'clock as possible and that they could eat all the cakes they wanted. He promptly suggested that the party be postponed for twenty-four hours, as everyone had: already eaten something that day; if a feast of this sort was in progress they should have an opportunity to take full advantage of it by fasting for 24 hours, which is what most Chinese do when they are invited out to dinner, This seemed like a sensible suggestion and so the party was postponed.

Ricksha coolies decided who bakes the best cakes

Next day the coolies arrived. Most of them had been to the barber and put on their cleanest clothes. All of them acted like the first one. They did not fall on their food and gulp it but picked and chose with what appeared to be rare discrimination, and most of them nibbled at several before they decided which one they liked best. Under the most favorable of circumstances the merits of a cake cannot be determined with scientific accuracy, and my system worked as well as any other. It was easy to note which cakes appeared to be the most popular, and the prizes were awarded on that basis. When weak human flesh could do no more and the coolies voluntarily quit eating, I called the incident closed and let them take the remaining cakes home with them. For months alter that, when some ricksha coolie greeted me with a particularly joyous grin, I realized that he had been one of my guests at the cake feast.

I had said nothing to my client about how we judged the cake, and a week later he asked me about it.

'Why,' I said, 'I just ate a good big piece out of each one of the 500 entries. How else do you think I could judge them?'

When we promoted the sale of raisins we were not introducing any new food product to the Chinese. Arabian traders brought raisins to China about the time of Christ, and later, grapes were grown and dried in North China. These Chinese raisins were not produced in any quantity and did not become a household article until the California raisin growers put on the aggressive selling campaign in which we played a part. The marketing conditions were ideal for, although the Chinese, like all other people, like sugar in any form, they do not eat sweet dishes at their regular meals. There are, on the other hand, I believe, more candy shops per capita in China than in any other country in the world, and the Chinese are a race of between meal nibblers. It was a very easy matter to convince them that in raisins they found sugar in its purest and most economical form and that the iron in raisins was conducive to health.

But I do not. believe that any amount of advertising-will ever lead to any change in the Chinese diet. Indeed, I can't understand why any Chinese would ever wish to change the diet to which he has been accustomed for, with the exception of the very poor, Chinese enjoy a wider variety of food and better cooking than is the lot of the average American. So far as I am personally concerned, there is no meal I enjoy better than a good Chinese dinner and I would not anticipate an unhappy future if I knew that I would have nothing but Chinese food to eat all the rest of my life. I would miss the corned beef and cabbage, the beafsteak and kidney pudding, baked beans and hot corn bread, but there are compensations in sweet-and-sour pork, Peking cluck and Canton chicken cooked in vegetable marrow. I am not alone in this opinion, for it is shared by almost all foreigners who have lived in China for any length of time and are not still encased in their narrow national prejudices. As a matter of fact, I would greatly enjoy attacking this problem from the other angle and could with a great deal of confidence, put on a campaign to promote the adoption of a modified Chinese cuisine and diet in America. If it were adopted it would give to m fellow countrymen a diet healthier and more economical than the one they now enjoy and a cuisine full of culinary delights they never dreamed of. A few Chinese who have lived in foreign countries have picked up a taste for foreign dishes, but they eat them only as a novelty or a pose and not as a steady diet or because they like them. Of course there are exceptions. I knew one Chinese; who was passionately fond of buckwheat cakes and maple syrup, the American dish which Benjamin Franklin tried unsuccessfully to introduce in England. The dish never became popular there, nor is there the least chance that it will ever be popular in China. The only foreign food for which there is a steady demand in China; is oatmeal, but that is so much like the native congee, or rice gruel, that its use as a breakfast dish involves only a slight adaptation and not a change in taste.

A Chinese friend who has lived in many countries, and is something of a cosmopolitan, once told me that the conception of an ideal condition of life was to be an American citizen with a Japanese wife and be able to eat Chinese food. His explanation was this. As an American citizen he would have all the world could offer in the way of liberty and opportunity, a Japanese wife is the most loyal, devoted and uncomplaining of helpmates, and with Chinese food he would have at his disposal food unsurpassed by any other country. Of these three ideals he had to content himself with the last, which, he said, was after all the most important of the three.

When you mention Chinese food to the average American who has never lived in China, he either has no idea of what you are talking about or if he has that dangerous small learning, which leads him to think of shark's fins, bird's nest soup and ancient eggs. No one of these is calculated to excite the salivary gland of the unsophisticated Anglo-Saxon. I have eaten all of them and will do so again the next time I go to a dinner where they are served, not because I care for them especially, but I don't mind them and it would be noticeable and an offense to the host if I didn't dip my chop sticks into all the bowls on the table. When I can't avoid it, I eat parsnips for the same reason. The shark's fin soup may be very good unless it is too sharky, and I was never able to discover any particular taste in bird's nest soup, but I find the ancient eggs slightly queasy. I once ate them for breakfast but that was because I could get nothing else. These eggs, by the way, are put through a pickling process which hardens and preserves them and they are, in taste and appearance, more like a strong-cheese than anything else. The eggs are not really ancient, for the pickling process is completed in about a month and if they are kept more than a year it is only because no sale has been found for them. Great age does not make them more valuable; in fact, if they are kept too long they desiccate and cannot be eaten. That fiction about great age used to be an old sailors' yarn until it - was stolen by fiction and adventure writers who wanted to put exotic local color into their stories but were too lazy to look up the facts. I once made a sandwich out of slices of these eggs, put in a dash of mustard and fed them to a squeamish friend. He liked them until the top of the sandwich fell off and he saw what they were. As I said before, I don't care for these ancient eggs. The taste is not repulsive but strange. However, as I have, without suffering any hardship or going out of my way to do it, learned to like Limburger cheese, escargots, raw fish, Scotch whisky and Dutch gin, it would not be a difficult matter to become accustomed to the taste and possibly cultivate a liking for pickled eggs.

But these three, and many other items which uninformed tourists talk about, are not common in China, are expensive, and might almost be classed as novelties.

186

There are a great many Americans who have never eaten caviar, terrapin, or canvasback duck, yet these items are much more common in the United States and eaten by a greater proportion of consumers than are to be found for shark's fin or bird's nest soup. Ancient eggs are a little more common, but there are a million of Chinese who have never tasted them—probably as great as the proportion of Americans who have never eaten Roquefort cheese.

A so-called Chinese dish which most foreigners have heard of and a great many have eaten is chop suey. it has been called by some 'the national dish of China,' and is generally assumed to be the Chinese counterpart of the corned beef and cabbage of New England. Now, the truth of the matter is that chop suey, as we know it, is not only not the national dish of China, but it is not even a Chinese dish and so far as I know no Chinese ever eats it. The only chop suey which the Chinese know is a cheap kind of hash which is salvaged by Cantonese beggars. The beggars in Canton go from door to door carrying their capacious food bowls, into which housewives who are charitably inclined throw any odds and ends of food which may be left over from the family meal. As the beggar has to visit several homes in order to get his bowl satisfactorily filled, he usually collects quite an assortment of meats and vegetables before he retires to some shady corner, stirs the accumulation with his chop sticks and eats his meal. In spite of its humble origin there is no reason why this beggar's hash should not be wholesome and tasty. But there is naturally a prejudice against it in the minds of all Chinese.

Dr. Wu Ting Fang, the famous Chinese diplomat, told me the peculiar circumstances under which this beggar dish became the favorite exotic dish of foreigners in many lands. The discovery of gold in California brought thousands of Chinese to San Francisco, some to work in the gold fields, but more to earn their fortunes in slower but more certain ways by working at various trades. For a long time all the shoes and cigars in San Francisco were made by Chinese, who also did most of the carpenter work. Soon after the discovery of gold the Chinese colony in the city was large enough to support a couple of restaurants conducted by Cantonese cooks, who catered only to their fellow exiles from the Middle Kingdom. The white men had heard the usual sailor yarns about what these pig-tailed yellow men ate, and one night a crowd of miners decided they would try this strange fare, just to see what it was like.

They had been told that Chinese ate rats and they wanted to see whether or not it was true. When they got to the restaurant the regular customers had finished their suppers, and the proprietor was ready to close his doors. But the miners demanded food, so he did the best he could to avoid trouble and get them out of the way as soon as possible. He went out into the kitchen, dumped together all the food his Chinese patrons had left in their bowls, warmed it up, put a dash of Chinese sauce on top and served it to his unwelcome guests. As they didn't understand Cantonese slang they didn't know what he meant when he told them that they were eating chop suey or 'beggar hash.'

At any rate, they liked it so well that they came back for more and in that, chance way the great chop suey industry was established. Many more Chinese fortunes have been made from it than were ever made from gold mining, and thousands of Chinese have laughed for generations because every dish of chop suey served is a culinary joke at the expense of the foreigner. Chinese restaurants where chop suey is served are to be found in big cities all over the world except in China. Our Chinese cook in Shanghai knew how to make it only because my wife taught him, with the aid of a San Francisco cook book. He ate some of it once, but said he didn't like it. As he was from Yangtsze Valley, he didn't like anything that was remotely connected with Canton. There is an entirely absurd story that the dish was popularized in America by Lord Li Hung Chang, but it is safe to say that, with his great wealth and fastidious tastes, this powerful Chinese statesman never ate 'beggar hash.' It was served in San Francisco long before Lord Li made his famous trip round the world. Dr. Wu told me that he had served it at a legation dinner party in Washington, but that he did so only because the American public seemed to expect it of him. Knowing the old gentleman's flair for personal publicity, I strongly suspect that he knew the dinner would be featured on the front pages of the newspapers.

Experts disagree as to the relative skill of French and Chinese cooks, but all those who award first place to the French give second place to the Chinese, and there is a general agreement that if the comparison were carried to the logical conclusion some other nation would naturally have to be awarded third place. That humble position would have to go to cooks so far below the French \ or the Chinese that it is not worth while going to the trouble to find out who should have third place. Americans have been mentioned for this distinction, principally by themselves, but if kitchen economy is to be taken into account, they would be ruled out, because they are the most wasteful cooks in the world. A good-sized province of China could eat to satiety from the waste food of American kitchens. Englishmen are usually keen to uphold national prestige in every line, but I have noticed that one thing they will not argue about is the superiority of British cooking. Britons cheerfully admit that their cooking is bad and do nothing to improve it.

Long before the Christian era the Chinese, in their search for food, were experimenting with everything they could chew and swallow. They had no inherited prejudices and conventional or religious prohibitions. Buddhism forbids the killing of animals and, as a corollary, the eating of flesh, but Buddhism was brought to China from India long after the Chinese had perfected the art of cooking and had established their food habits. The Buddhist prohibitions, which affected a very large part of the population, gave the Chinese cooks a difficult problem to solve, to provide a people accustomed to meat with a purely vegetarian diet which would be acceptable to them. I really believe that if the Chinese cooks had not solved this problem so successfully we would not now see the magnificent Buddhist temples and monasteries which are to be found in all parts of the country as testimonials to the strength of the following of the gentle Mahatma.

The Chinese cooks made the vegetarian diet so palatable that it was no hardship to adopt it, and what might have been a perpetual Lent fast became a perpetual feast. Dr. Wu Ting Fang was a vegeterian, not because of Buddhist faith but because some lady food faddist in Washington convinced him that a vegetarian diet would prolong life. I ate my first vegetarian Chinese meals in his home and they were very good. But I never realized how skillfully vegetarian dishes could be given the taste and appearance of meat until my wife and I were entertained at a rather sumptuous dinner by the abbot of a Buddhist monastery where we were spending our Christmas holidays. If I had not known that nothing but vegetables can be brought into a monastery kitchen and that the pious old abbot would rather commit suicide than serve so much as a spoonful of chicken liver gravy at his table, I would have thought that this was just an especially good Chinese dinner. The various dishes had not only the appearance and the taste of meat but even the texture.

Since the eating of meat is considered to be so evil I wondered why it was not sinful to give this Buddhist banquet such an evil appearance, but the abbot didn't know what I was talking about when I brought this question up, because there is nothing in the Buddhist doctrine which says anything about the avoidance of evil appearances. There are a few Protestant Christian sects which have made vegetarianism an article of faith, but shamelessly serve false replicas of pork chops and other food of sinful and evil appearance. I would like to ask them how they justify this in the light of the Biblical injunction. I know in advance that the answer is sure to be a good one and will probably show me up in the light of a sinner who has asked a foolish question, but I am willing to take the chance because I would really like to know. Christian theologians are notoriously skillful at exegesis and the Buddhists are not far behind them. The abbot was explaining to me the Buddhist doctrine which forbids the taking of life and, in order to make the matter understandable to me, abandoned metaphysics and confined himself to describing the harmlessness of various creatures and the benefits they bestow on men, even without providing food for him. He made out a fine case for the ox and the horse, which was easy, and gave rats and mice good reputations they did not deserve, so I asked him about mosquitoes.

'Man should be very grateful to mosquitoes,' he said, 'for they save a great many lives. In the summer when i it is hot the workmen in the fields get very tired and they lie down in the shade to rest. Sometimes they go to sleep, and if they sleep a long time they will get chilled and become sick. But they do not sleep long because a mosquito, on an errand of mercy, stings them and wakes them.'

During our fortnight in this Buddhist monastery, we didn't have to exist on vegetarian food, for we had brought our provisions with us and they included all the usual solids and liquids which enliven the Christmas holidays. A spacious apartment of the monastery-had been turned over to us and in one of the many-rooms our cook set up a very serviceable kitchen. When we were about ready to return to Shanghai, and I could bring the matter up without fear of raising a dangerous issue, I asked the abbot why he had been so lenient and allowed us to bring meat, to say nothing of whisky and gin, into the monastery. His explanation was just as pleasing as his exposition of the virtues of the mosquito had been. He recalled that two years before I had come to the monastery more or less as a refugee, for I had been on a houseboat trip on the Ningpo Lakes when a typhoon struck and I had abandoned the boat and headed for the monastery as the only shelter in sight. He said he knew at the time that among the supplies my servants dragged in there was very probably some sinful meat and that he should have refused to allow them to bring it in, but I was a stranger and I sick and he was afraid that if he deprived me of my I regular food it might be injurious to my health. So he I had said nothing about the meat and there had been no dire results. On the contrary, the monastery had enjoyed an unusual prosperity. In the five hundred years history of the monastery, I was the first foreigner who had ever spent a night under its roof and they had come to the conclusion that a part of this good fortune had been due to their hospitality to me. Also, I had not behaved as they had been led to believe foreigners would behave, had been respectful at the ceremonies and had contributed liberally toward the rebuilding of the temple. He said they looked on me as a kind of lay brother, albeit a sinful one, and that I was always welcome, even with my roast turkey and boiled ham and Scotch whisky, but he warned me not to encourage any other foreigners to come to the place.

In their search for food, the Chinese explored the widely different climates that are to be found between sub-tropical Canton and semi-arctic Siberia. Here were to be found a wide variety of animals, fish, birds, insects, fruit, grain, nuts, roots and green vegetables, and the Chinese tried them all, cooking them in every way possible, flavoring them with every conceivable sauce. Periods of famine intensified the search and broadened its scope. History does not record the name or the nationality of the man who ate the first oyster, but I feel certain that he was a Chinese.

Although the Chinese searched the earth, the waters and the air for food, they never learned to use dairy products.

Neither milk, butter nor cheese formed any part of the Chinese diet until foreigners taught them the use of milk. That is now consumed in fairly liberal quantities by the very young or the very aged. They make a very acceptable substitute for milk by squeezing the juices from soya beans. It looks like milk, tastes something like it, has most of the food values, and sells at a very small fraction of the price. They are indifferent to butter, neither liking nor disliking it, and as they see no need for it they do not use it.

They detest cheese, and will not eat it under any circumstances. Even if they ate cheese, it would not be a popular food product, because a very simple and obvious pun on the Chinese name turns it into the name of a substance which is certainly unfit for human consumption. During one of the many civil wars which for a decade made life in Shanghai a more or less continual round of excitement, a crowd of more than 1,000 hungry and defeated soldiers threw down their arms and sought refuge in the International Settlement. During those hectic days, almost every able-bodied foreigner in Shanghai was serving as a volunteer soldier or policeman, and in the latter capacity I was put in charge of the refugee camp for one spell of duty. All I had to do was to see that the refugees didn't run away, which was very easy, because that was the last thing in the world they wanted to do. However, they had had nothing to eat for two days and were desperately hungry; I appealed for help to the first man who came along, who happened to be a British army captain. He got busy at once and in less than half an hour we had several hundred cans of cheese and biscuits which he had managed in some way to get from the British army stores. We opened up a few cans to show the refugees how it was done, and assumed that they would fall to at once. As soon as they saw and smelt the cheese they set up roars of anguish. They could not have been more disappointed if we had given them a can full of nice hard flints. It looked for a moment as if a British army captain and an amateur policeman were going to have a rather exciting morning. But we arranged a truce and I made a hasty and very unbusiness-like deal with a Chinese restaurant keeper in the neighborhood by giving him all the cheese in exchange for a few thousand steamed dumplings. After the transaction was finished and our charges were eating the dumplings, the army captain cheerfully remarked that he supposed I knew that I had been guilty of the high crime of trafficking in His Majesty's army stores; he said it was a good thing I was an amateur American policeman instead of a British soldier, as under the latter circumstances, he would have had to report me for court martial. In the meantime, he had held on to one tin of cheese and so, as we didn't see any other food near at hand, we ate it for breakfast, to the great amazement of the refugees, who couldn't understand why we should eat that disgusting food so long as the steamed dumplings were available.

In the spring of 1923, a group of bandits in Shanghai province put to shame all the previous exploits of Chinese bandits by wrecking the Shanghai-Peking express train and carrying away to their bandit lair the entire trainload of passengers—about thirty foreigners and several hundred Chinese. For almost a week after their capture, there was no news as to their whereabouts; in fact, all we knew about the captives was that they had no food except for the coarse fare that might be found in one of the most poverty-stricken and inhospitable parts of the country. As most of the foreign captives came from Shanghai and included well-known foreign residents of several nationalities, there was more excitement around the town than anyone would have previously thought possible.

I was looking for an excuse to get away from Shanghai for a holiday and, with all the excitement there was about the bandit raid, I found it an easy matter to talk my fellow-members of the American Red Cross Committee into sending me to the bandit area to try to establish contact with the foreign captives and get food, clothing and medicines to them. I had barely effected diplomatic relationships with the bandits and got supplies organized and going forward regularly to the foreign captives, when one of the local war lords sent his secretary to me with a roll of currency amounting to $3,000 and a request that I get some food and, clothing and medical supplies to the Chinese captives who had up to that time been existing on what scanty rations they could get from the bandits, who were themselves impoverished. The first contribution by the war lord was followed by others as often as I ran short of funds. A month later, as a cordon of Chinese troops was thrown around the entire bandit area, cutting off their supplies entirely, the Chinese government commissioned me to feed the 2,000 bandits as well, so that they would not be driven by hunger to confiscate the supplies intended for the captives. They had up to this time scrupulously observed the promises they had made to protect the relief supplies, and nothing had been stolen, though the temptation must have been strong. The work kept me in the bandit area for six weeks— one of the most interesting holidays it is possible to imagine. I learned a lot about the technique and ethics of banditry, which will probably never be of any practical value to me, and I also learned a good deal about the cost of living in China. .

With my expenditures for relief work as a basis, and through investigations as to the diet of local people and the cost of supplies, I came to the conclusion that it was easily possible for any Chinese to provide himself with food, clothing and shelter for five Chinese dollars a month and that I could live for that myself, though I wouldn't have much fun doing it. At that time five Chinese dollars was worth about two U. S. dollars. My figure was a more or less intelligent guess and I was later very much gratified to learn that Shantung Christian University, a mission school of very high standing, had made a rather exhaustive investigation of the same kind, and their figure confirmed my conclusions. Their estimate of the cost of food was 15 Chinese cents, or about six U. S. cents per day per person. That would leave only fifty cents per month for clothing and lodging, which is a rather narrow margin, but the university survey covered consumption by the rather well-to-do middle classes who did not have to stint themselves on the quantity of food consumed and who ate some expensive sauces which could be dispensed with.

The following table shows the percentage in weight of different kinds of foods consumed by Chinese in Shantung according to the university survey, with comparative percentages showing a typical English diet.

	China Percentage	British Percentage
Bread, cereals and beans	71.	10.14
Fruit and vegetables	23.	44.
Meat and fish	2.3	13.
Butter, fats, sugar	1.2	7.6
Eggs	.7	2.3
Milk and cheese	.0	22.
Other foods	1.8	.02

The first thing that will probably strike the observant reader is the fact that rice is not mentioned in this table. There is a widespread misapprehension that rice is the staff of life of all Chinese. The fact is that rice is the universal food south of the Yangtsze River, but with unimportant exceptions it is practically unknown in the north, which is not a rice-producing area. The list given above would appear to indicate a very limited variety of foods, but that is not the case. The wheat is not only baked into bread, but also provides an infinite variety of noodles, macaroni, spaghetti and dumplings. There are twenty-nine varieties of green vegetables and fifteen varieties of beans. The detailed report shows that there are a few Irish potatoes eaten, weighing about half as much as the fresh fruit consumed, and one sixth as much as the weight of shrimps. The Irish potato was brought from Virginia by Sir Walter Raleigh and planted on his Irish estate, hence its name. From there the potato spread to all parts of Europe and was brought to China by the Dutch. In Thibet it is known as 'Dutch Wheat.' Unimportant potato patches are to be found in many parts of China, but I have never heard pi any place where the potato is an important article of diet or is given any consideration as a food supply. Another food of American origin, Indian corn, is much more popular. The residents of Shantung consume more Indian corn than rice.

A second analysis of the food consumption prepared by Shantung Christian University is also of considerable interest, as it shows the comparative percentages of expenditure compared to the average American expenditure. I have no British figures suitable for comparison, but they would not differ materially from the American figures.

A study of these figures will convince almost anyone that a very strong case can be presented for the adoption by Britons and Americans of a modified form of the Chinese diet. It probably wouldn't be possible to.

	China Percentage	American Percentage
Meat and fish	6.	23.
Milk	0.	10.
Eggs	2.	5.
Bread, cereals and beans	72.	13.
Butter, fats, sugar	4.	15.
Fruit and vegetables	14.	16.
Other foods	2.	7.

reduce their food bills to approximately the amount of the Chinese budget, but the food bill could be cut in half without allowing anyone to go hungry. There wouldn't be so many fat women, but there would be more slim girlish figures and fewer doctor's bills. But, on the other hand, it would be difficult to find any argument about a change of diet convincing enough to make any impression on the Chinese.

Face is an important matter in China

15. Face Saved and Face Lost

Although the word is not a new one, the Chinese have added to the richness of the English language by giving an added meaning and a new use to the word face. In its new, Sinological, meaning, it was for a century or more purely a China Coast word, unknown except on the Western shores of the Pacific, but in 1934 it was formally adopted and legalized by the editors of the Oxford Dictionary, who define:

lose face, of Chinaman, be humiliated.

save person's face, spare him from open shame.

These brief definitions give but little hint of the very important part that face plays in all affairs of life in China. It embodies a code of human relationships which enjoins on everyone the obligation, in all circumstance, to help his fellow-man to maintain his self-respect and to hold up his head in pride. In a way, it is a code of toleration and forbearance which enables Chinese to live together under crowded and highly competitive conditions with a minimum of friction. A man's misfortunes, or the results of his foolish acts, are not held up to derision, because that would make him lose face. In this way enmities are avoided and peace and harmony prevail. If one comes out the loser in a business deal, the victor does not push his advantage to the ultimate, but grants the unfortunate one some little concession so as to remove the sting of humiliation from his

199

defeat. It is at the same time a mental stimulus and a moral bulwark for the individual, as everyone more or less instinctively tries to avoid any act, or any course of conduct which might cause him to lose face, that is, be openly shamed or humiliated. On ethical grounds it is, of course, open to the charge of insincerity for, in great measure, the loss of face lies, not in the shamefulness of one's conduct, but in the misfortune of exposure.

No one in China is too lowly to treasure and guard his face, that is, his dignity and self-respect. And no foreign resident has ever accomplished anything in dealing with Chinese if he failed to take this factor into account. Those who know how to utilize it have found life pleasant and sometimes prosperous. Those who do not, find life unpleasant and full of hidden difficulties. Everyone's face must be respected. One may frequently and sharply reprimand a Chinese servant, make him do over and over again the tasks he has bungled, and still the household remains unruffled. But if the reprimand is delivered in front of others, especially in front of other servants, that is a quite a different matter. The unfortunate servant has 'lost face' and suffers an anguish difficult for the foreigner to understand. If the master or mistress continues to make him lose face by advertising his shortcomings to all within hearing, there will soon be a vacancy in the establishment. The boy or cook or coolie will sadly report that it is necessary for him to be absent for a few days to attend the funeral of his brother, and that is the last that is seen of him. A friend will arrive later to collect the wages due and to explain that the servant is suffering from a very severe illness and that the chances of his resuming his duties in the near future are so remote that a substitute had better be employed. There were many houseboys, cooks and coolies working in foreign homes in Shanghai at ridiculously low wages, who never thought of asking for an increase, but worked along contentedly year after year. On the other hand, there were many foreigners living perforce in hotels or boarding houses who could not keep house because no servants would work for them, no matter what wages were offered. Employment in their household would, in itself, have implied a loss of face, for their treatment of servants was well known, and any who accepted employment there would be subject to the ridicule of his fellows. Although such occurrences were very rare, there were instances of murderous attacks on foreigners by Chinese servants, and police officials who investigated such matters were of the opinion that most of these attacks were directly attributable to a loss of face. The foreigner had caused the boy or the cook such humiliation as to drive him to a murderous frenzy. Long hours, hard work, poor pay, an exacting or even an unreasonable mistress—all these things they will endure cheerfully and philosophically so long as they are not humiliated.

Sometimes the servant's face depends not only op the treatment his employer accords him, but also on what he thinks of the social status of his master. I once helped a boy to get a place as personal servant to a Shanghai bachelor. The wages were satisfactory, and I was very much surprised when he turned up a fortnight later with the announcement that he had quit and was looking for another job. It transpired that the bachelor had but two passions in life, horses and Scotch whisky, so he kept the boy up late at night serving whiskies and made him get up early to brew a pot of tea in preparation for the early morning ride. But it was not these long hours that distressed the boy. The bachelor spent so much time and money on whisky and horses that his wardrobe was a very sketchy affair. I have forgotten all the shameful details divulged to me by the horrified boy, but it appears that the bachelor had only three pairs of socks, and one of these was full of holes. The bachelor's indifference to an adequate supply of haberdashery was well known to all the other boys in the neighborhood and was the subject of frequent comment and servants' quarter jokes, and as a result no one could work for him without a serious loss of face. If he had been too poor to afford anything more, the boy said, it would have been a different matter, but he was shabby from sloth and indifference, thereby proving that he was not a proper gentleman.

Different occupations are graded according to the face they bestow on an employee. Banks probably rate the highest, and every bank has a long waiting list of sons of prominent families whose one ambition in life is to be employed by a bank. With them salary is no object. Indeed, many a wealthy Chinese father would bribe his son's way into a bank payroll and pay out more than the son could possibly earn in several years. Such employment not only gives face to the employee but reflects face on all members of the family. This desire for face-saving jobs has led to the development of a system of fraudulent promotion schemes which are peculiar to China. The promoter, usually of a bank or a shipping-company, goes through a fraudulent stock selling scheme —ornate offices, impressive office stationery, etc. He may sell some stock, but that is not his main objective, for it is easier and equally profitable to sell jobs. The staff of the prospective bank is filled over and over again, everyone from the cashier to the most junior office boy paying for his employment and putting up a cash deposit as security or, as it is known in Chinese phrase, 'honesty money.' By and by, when the opportunities have been exhausted, the promoter departs for some distant province, and that is the last his deluded employees ever see of him.

This sale of jobs in a fictitious concern is an old swindle in China, but the cinema vogue introduced a new version of it, which a gang of my fellow-Americans have worked with a fair degree of success. I had an opportunity to play a very useful part in this swindle myself. A man asked me to call on him at his hotel to discuss a big advertising campaign, and when I saw him he told me he was planning to open a beauty parlor in Shanghai and cater especially to Chinese girls of the wealthy classes. I didn't like the man's looks, and knew we would never get along very well together. Also, I couldn't see any possibility of beauty shop advertising amounting to very much, though he had thrown out hints that this was a different kind of a beauty shop in which large profits were to be made. So I told him beauty shop advertising was a little out of our line, and that he would probably get better service from one of the small Chinese agencies.

I didn't know at the time what a clever swindle he was preparing to operate. The beauty shop was only the blind or trap into which he lured his victims, and this was his method of operation. A pretty Chinese girl, a member of a wealthy family, became a patron of his shop and, after the first few visits, the manager of the shop, who pretended to have come from Hollywood, asked the girl if she had ever thought of going into the movies. Of course every girl, no matter what her nationality, has thought of becoming a movie star and every girl is interested and flattered by a question of that sort.

The next step was to have some test photographs made and, by a singular coincidence, a Hollywood casting director happened to be going through Shanghai just about the time and one inspection of the test pictures proved to him that this girl was just the type the movie studios were looking for—here was a girl who was the superior of Anna May Wong in every way. This was not difficult for the Chinese girl to believe, for Anna May Wong had visited China for the first time a few months previously and the Chinese girls made careful comparisons and were unimpressed by her.

The bogus Hollywood director offered the girl a contract at once on very flattering terms. However, there were a few little preliminaries to be attended, to before the contract was actually operative and the embryo star began to draw the enormous salary which had been promised her. She had to undergo some training which, though very simple, was also very expensive. After that, the swindle proceeded along its allotted course and the family of the girl continued to put up money until they discovered that the whole thing was a fake. This swindle was worked for a number of years in Shanghai, and neither of the swindlers was ever prosecuted, as the family which had been duped would lose too much face if the scheme was exposed.

When I started to organize my advertising agency, I at once encountered difficulties in the matter of face. There was no such thing as a properly organized agency, and the best known and most active representatives of the advertising profession consisted of gangs of coolies who pasted venereal disease circulars on blank walls.

Bandit or advertising man?

The advertising business not only had no face, but was not even respectable. I wanted to employ a young graduate of an American university who had taken a course in advertising at home and had worked for a year in an advertising agency in New York. His family had not learned until his return home that he had chosen advertising as his life work, and when they heard the sad news they were horrified. If he had announced that he intended to turn into a bandit or take up piracy, it would not have created much more consternation. He was very anxious to join my staff, but had to submit my offer of employment to a family conference. The decision was finally against me and he went to work tor an importing firm at half the salary I had offered him. His work was to handle advertising for this company but, as advertising was only a side line, one of its many activities, he could pretend to be in the mercantile business and thereby save the face of the family.

One of my earliest efforts was to give face to the advertising agency business, and I was entirely too successful for I soon had dozens of Chinese competitors. The business was much more exclusive when less reputable. When one of these competitors took a client away from us, my Chinese staff thought a great deal more about the face we had lost than of the profits. I would not be happy about it, but I bore up more philosophically than they.

When anyone, either foreigner or Chinese, was caught in some questionable dealing and haled into court, the popular discussion did not center around his guilt or innocence, but around the amount of face he had lost. If a printer delivered a poorly executed job to us, we did not appeal to his sense of fairness, honesty and justice to make the matter right, but pointed out to him the amount of face we would lose if we should send this job to our client, who would undoubtedly refuse to accept it. In order to save our face, he would do the job over again. The only time our cook stirred himself out of his usual lazy routine was when we had guests coming to dinner, for if there should be anything wrong with the meal the amount of face lost by the entire household would be incalculable. Our servants always enjoyed dinner parties, especially if they were elaborate with many guests. This would involve much extra work, but that was more than compensated for by the face gained to every one connected with a successful party. In my bachelor days, a dinner party I gave appeared simply miraculous to me, for the table was a thing of luxurious beauty with silver, china and linen, which I not only did not possess but had never seen before. The cook and the boy, realizing, as I did not, the humbleness and inadequacy of my equipment, had, on their own initiative, borrowed linen, silverware and glass from a neighbor who happened to be out of town. Thus my face was saved. On a business trip to England I bought several suits of clothing from a London tailor and, ten years later, I happened to notice that a suit my Chinese tailor had made for me was distinguished by a slightly frayed Regent Street label. When I asked him to explain this anachronism he said that as I discarded my old clothing he had removed the London labels and put them in the new clothing, as a London label gave me more face. As no one except the house servants was ever likely to see the labels, I don't know just how this possession of face on my part would manifest itself, but, at any rate, his intentions were of che best. All my suits were distinguished by London labels until the labels finally wore out.

Face makes promotions and salary adjustments very difficult problems in any office. Promotion of any employee out of the regular order of progression causes a loss of face to all those who have been passed over and they feel not only great humiliation but a keen sense of injustice. A single promotion of this sort can turn an efficient and harmonious office organization into an unruly conglomeration with enough animosities to supply a Noah's Ark. It is not at all unusual for a deserving employee who has proved his superior abilities to refuse a promotion, because he knows the feuds which would arise and be centered around him. Problems connected with adjustment of pay fall within the same category. Any pay increase which does not embrace the whole staff is bound to cause loss of face, heart-burnings and secret hostilities. The problem of giving one employee an increase and ignoring the others is a very difficult one to solve.

For a long time this fetish of face provided what appeared to be an insuperable obstacle to the development of athletics in China, for the loser in a contest, whether a team or an individual, felt such a humiliating loss of face that it was impossible to maintain regular sports schedules. Teams would even walk off the field during the progress of a game if they saw that defeat was inevitable. Since the physical development of the people formed an important part of the program for the building of a new China, this caused serious concern to the Chinese leaders but, after a decade of work, they managed to modify that idea. By means of provincial and national Olympic contests in which all the participants were honored and cheered and royally entertained, they accomplished what appeared to be the impossible, and built up a spirit of sportsmanship in which the vanquished accepted defeat without shame —that is, without as much shame as formerly.

In past generations, face was entirely a personal matter and its various conceptions were of very ancient origin, which did not take into account modern conditions of life. Later, under the guidance of Chinese leaders it came to assume entirely new aspects and was being widely used to accomplish the regeneration of China. The change in the attitude towards athletics was only one of many similar changes. Chinese have been notorious for their lack of public spirit. Filthy streets which would enrage the foreign visitor, who had no personal interest in the matter, were apparently unnoticed by the Chinese resident, who would spend a lifetime jumping over mud puddles and never take the trouble to fill one up. Thanks to the insistent teaching of Chinese leaders they finally came to understand that if the streets of a city are dirty the city has lost face and all the residents share in this municipal humiliation. In the days of the Manchus a quarter of a century earlier I would not have thought it possible, but I lived to see the residents of many Chinese cities take pride in the fact that their city was cleaner than a neighboring one. There was more street cleaning in the ten years beginning about 1925 than in any preceding ten centuries.

But the old traditions persisted in official life. Many an ambitious war lord started an unsuccessful revolt against the authority of the Central Government. In any other country the rebellious general would have been stripped of his honors, thrown into prison, perhaps executed for high treason. Not so in China. Such stern measures would cause such a loss of face to the war lord that even his bitterest enemy would not approve them. Instead he was frequently given a high rank and appointed on a commission to some distant and harmless duty, such as to investigate the use of submarines in Switzerland or the growing of potatoes in the Sahara Desert. This serves a very useful political purpose, for no animosities have been created among the adherents of the defeated general, and it is much easier to secure their loyalty. Some big foreign firms adopt a similar policy when, for any reason, they find it necessary to discharge an important member of the Chinese staff.

He is promoted by transfer to some branch office and, being able to read the handwriting on the wall, soon sends in his resignation, which is accepted with extravagant show of regret.

The great importance attached to face leads to many absurdities as any pretence invariably does. Motor-car numbers were never changed in Shanghai, the owner retaining the same number year after year. As the first license issued was No. 1 and new numbers followed in numerical order as new motor-cars were bought, a small number indicates that the owner of the car was one of the earliest motorists in Shanghai, thereby implying early and continued prosperity. All the early cars were bought by foreigners, for Chinese were very slow in accepting what they considered to be an expensive and dangerous toy. Soon after the Chinese began buying cars all the low numbers were in their possession. As opportunity offered they bought up the old cars for the sake of the license number, and in that way many a foreigner got a fancy price for a broken down old crock which would otherwise have been quite unsaleable.

Wealthy Chinese businessmen think that it gives them great face to come to the office late, thereby proving that they are not mere wage slaves and clock punchers. This led to the convention that all business calls should be paid in the afternoon. To call on a Chinese before noon would imply that he was of rather low standing and therefore had to get to work early, just like the coolies who swept the office. This custom is so well established, and a morning call is such an unusual occurrence that, when a Chinese of any importance called on me before noon, I couldn't help wondering what desperate need had caused this violation of the conventions. There was not a really big and successful afternoon paper in China, and the only reason I have been able to find for this was that morning papers were more popular because the Chinese businessman had so much time to read them before going to the office.

The rickshaw pullers paid an outrageously high rental

16. The Sacred Rice Bowl

In addition to consideration for the face of your fellow-man, there is another human obligation which is of possibly equal importance in China. You must not shame a man by making him lose face and also you must not destroy his livelihood or, as the expressive Chinese phrase goes, 'break his rice bowl.' It is quite in order to get the best of him in a business deal, to beat him down to the lowest possible price and then make another attack by demanding discounts, rebates and allowances. But to bring him to destitution, to cause him unnecessary loss, to take advantage of technicalities, to insist on him fullfilling a contract when he can only do so by impoverishing himself—all these things are looked on as being abhorrently inhuman. The right to live is inherent and he who deprives his fellow-man of that right is no better than a cannibal. There are, everything considered, surprisingly few lawsuits in China. One reason is that most business deals are between friends or relatives, and another that the powerful and well-organized trade guilds usually settle disputes in a friendly and common-sense manner without reference to courts of law. A third reason is that no matter how favorable a contract one party to a controversy may have, or how much another is indebted to him, he will seldom resort to a lawsuit to enforce a claim or collect an account which might throw the other party into bankruptcy. Those suits which are brought into the courts are usually fought with great bitterness because the two parties, before resorting to the employment of lawyers, have reduced themselves to such insane anger that they have forgotten all about friendship, face and broken rice bowls.

It must not be assumed that greedy avarice does not play its part in the life of China, for it does, and Shy-locks exist, though they are not common, and are held in universal detestation. Popular Chinese folk tales are full of stories of covetous old men who come to no good end and of the miser's store of wealth which always mysteriously disappears. Confucius divided the age of man into three parts instead of seven and warned old men against the sin of covetousness.[2] It is partly, because the character of Shylock produces such a thrill of horror that, of all the Shakespearian plays, The Merchant of Venice is the most popular for amateur production in China, and partly to the fact that Chinese girls like to play the part of Portia. Here is one foreign female character they can thoroughly understand, for Portia might have been a Chinese girl. I think they take the character of Shylock rather too literally, for a Chinese friend told me he couldn't understand why Shylock should insist on a pound of human flesh which was of no commercial value. He would have more readily understood the scene if the villain of the play had demanded a pound of pork.

To an Occidental, Chinese consideration for the other fellow's rice bowl is carried to a point where it becomes

---

[2] Confucian Analects, Book XVI, Chapter VII: 'Confucius said, "There are three things which the superior man guards against. In youth, when the physical powers are not yet settled, he guards against lust. When he is strong and the physical powers are full of vigor, he guards against quarrelsomeness. When he is old, and the animal powers are decayed, he guards against covetousness."'.

illogical and absurd. An employee of a foreign firm who is so obscure that he escapes the attention of the foreign manager may be hopelessly stupid and inefficient. Everyone around the place, including his Chinese superiors, who are presumed to discipline him, knows his inefficiency, covers up his mistakes and does his work for him. Of course, if he has been on the staff for a long time, and has friends or relatives in the office, there is more solicitude for him than would be the case if he were a comparative newcomer. But the sentiment is the same and the difference is only one of degree. In this connection a client of ours had an illuminating experience when the business depression made it necessary to reduce his payroll. He consulted the senior members of his staff about who should be discharged and, much to his surprise, found that they all agreed to the discharge of one of the best clerks in the place, but stubbornly resisted the suggestion that a stupid one be let out. When he finally got to the bottom of things he found that they had no qualms about discharging the clever employee, because he would have no difficulty in getting another position, but they knew that the stupid one would probably remain unemployed for a long time.

As practically all the Chinese living in the Philippines come from the Southern China port of Amoy, there was a lot of travel between the two places, and the American government formerly maintained a health officer in Amoy to examine immigrants and guard against the introduction of infectious diseases into the Philippines. Health statistics are bread and meat to a member of the public health service, and this doctor was very much perturbed over the fact that there were none in Amoy. In fact, there were no health statistics in Chinese cities at that time. Statistics were demanded by Washington and he set out to collect them himself by a method of his own devising. He detailed one of his assistants to make a weekly canvass of all the coffin shops in the city and find out how many coffins had been sold. He was correct in his assumption that the number of coffins sold would coincide rather accurately with the number of deaths, and in this way he could trace and measure the progress of epidemics. This rough and easy method of gathering vital statistics was inaugurated before, the annual visitations of cholera and plague, so as to establish the normal Amoy death rate, and when these two deadly diseases appeared the coffin sales went up as the doctor had anticipated they would, and he was able to plot the sinister curves on his charts.

Finally cooler weather came with autumn and the cholera and plague seasons ended. The doctor expected that his statistics would reflect this return to healthier conditions by a decrease in coffin sales, but, according to the weekly reports, the coffin business was just as thriving now as it had been during the worst of the epidemic. The thing was illogical and uncanny, for he knew the epidemics were over and that the city was suffering from no more than the usual and normal amount of sickness. With the aid of a sympathetic Chinese doctor, he made a thorough investigation and finally got to the bottom of the matter. One of the coffin makers explained the figures by saying that they knew the Chinese who was checking up on coffin sales for the American doctor was doing it on account of the deaths from plague and cholera, and they were afraid he would lose his employment if their report showed that there was no more of these diseases in the city, so they had continued to report the sales of approximately the same number of coffins as before. When assured that the employment of the doctor's clerk would not be affected by the number of coffins he reported sold, they agreed to send in reports of scrupulous correctness.

Troubles over the ricksha situation in Shanghai serve to provide a very striking illustration of the Chinese point of view on the subject of the rice bowl. For many years the Shanghai ricksha puller had been an oppressed and downtrodden laborer, who barely managed to make enough to keep body and soul together, while the owners of rickshas, by charging the pullers an outrageously high rental for the use of the vehicles, made tremendous profits and accumulated fortunes. Except for a few foreigners who took part in this exploitation of the pullers, every foreigner in Shanghai who gave any thought to the question set the ricksha owners down in his own mind as a rapacious bunch of wolves, and sympathized with the hard-working and poorly-paid puller. From time to time, over a period of years, various foreign organizations stirred up agitations for the relief of the puller, but the Chinese philanthropists never joined in these movements, though many attempts were made to get their support. In fact, the whole question appeared to be one in which the Chinese residents were not in the least interested, and they couldn't understand why the foreigners bothered so much about it. Finally conditions got so bad that the Shanghai Municipal Council, which controlled the affairs of the International Settlement, inaugurated a program which was designed to better the living conditions of the ricksha puller and, by reducing the rental charged by the owners, make it possible for him to earn a living wage. Almost without exception the foreigners living in Shanghai gave the movement their heartiest support, but also almost without exception, the Chinese were either antagonistic or indifferent during the period that the plan was under discussion. When the decision of the Council was finally annouced, the ricksha owners refused to agreed to any reduction in rental and declared a lockout, refusing to rent any rickshas, and thereby throwing some 35,000 pullers out of employment.

From the Chinese point of view, this put an entirely different complexion on the matter. For generations they had been content to see contemporary generations of poor coolies suffering all the hardships which accompany the most distressing poverty. But the moment the owners broke the coolies' rice bowls, poor and inadequate as the bowls were, by refusing to rent the rickshas, Chinese sentiment changed almost overnight and the owners found themselves entirely friendless. Chinese individual and public bodies denounced them in open letters to the newspapers. 'Cannibals' was the favorite taunt thrown at them. The ricksha tycoons weakened the second day and surrendered on the third, and the rental reductions went into effect.

There is never any question in the minds of the Chinese as to the responsibility of the individual who, for any reason whatever, deprives a man of his livelihood. The introduction of the automobile has led to the inevitable accidents and fatalities. These were, in fact, more numerous in China than elsewhere. Chinese had never been accustomed to any vehicle moving more rapidly than a wheelbarrow, and the motor-car was on them before they realized the necessity of getting out of the way. The universal rule was that the motorist must pay. It did not matter that he might be entirely blameless, that the injured man might have been guilty of the most criminal carelessness. So thoroughly was this understood that when there was a motor-car fatality or accident, the insurance companies always made a prompt settlement without ever allowing the matter to go to the courts. No doubt, in many cases, a legal decision would have been in favor of the insurance company, but no company dared to face the storm of indignation which would follow.

At one time I thought I owned a daily newspaper in Shanghai, and continued to think so until the friend who was backing me in the enterprise decided differently. During the period I was under this delusion I had to struggle with a printers' strike which developed a lot of ramifications. One of the strikers, in excess of zeal, waylaid a newsboy and destroyed all the papers he was delivering, so I had the striker arrested and charged. Very much to my surprise the Chinese judge took a very serious view of the matter and gave him a sentence of nine months. The next day his entire family moved in on me, demanding to know how they were going to live now that their rice-winner was imprisoned. It was useless for me to say that problem was no concern of mine. Their contention was that since I had sent him to prison and therefore made it impossible for him to keep the rice bowl filled, that responsibility devolved on me. I seemed to be the only person who did not look at it that way, so eventually I weakened and the family became pensioners. This kept up for several months. In the meantime the strike was settled, so I employed a lawyer to represent the striker and get him out of prison so that he could go to work again.

On a good many occasions we found it necessary and profitable in our business to appeal to the sanctity of the rice bowl. In almost all cities in the lower Yangtsze Valley there were taxes on all forms of outdoor advertising, which varied from city to city, with the result that a poster display cost twice as much in Ningpo as in Soochow. That was not the worst of it for, with a nice calculation of charging all that the traffic would bear, the local tax authorities sometimes raised the rates without notice, and we were at times confronted with the fact that we had a contract to paint advertisements in a certain town but that we could not carry out the contract without a very substantial loss, because the taxes were much more than we had calculated. However, that situation was not at all disconcerting and we wasted no time worrying about it. The head of the outdoor crew argued against the new rates and, if he could make no progress in any other way, showed our contracts and estimates of costs and the loss we would suffer, and cried:

'You cannot break, my master's rice bowl!' I was, of course, the rice consuming master referred to.

The appeal never failed, though sometimes we did not get as big a reduction as we hoped for. It would probably have been idle to make the appeal unless we were prepared to prove the actual danger the rice bowl was in, but once the official was convinced that the figures were correct and that we had made our contracts in good faith, he was on our side. Of course we could, with perfect logic, have reverted to foreign ideas and talked about preserving the life of the goose that lays the golden eggs, for the advertising geese of China did lay a lot of small but profitable eggs for the tax collectors. But I am sure we would have accomplished nothing with that entirely utilitarian appeal.

Now, in most countries it would not be of any particular advantage to gain the sympathies of a tax collector, for they do not assess the taxes and have no authority to change them. Fortunately, tax collecting was conducted on a more sensible basis in China, where reasonableness and the spirit of compromise always prevails over any legal formalities. The tax collector could not change the tax rate set by his superiors, but there was no reason why he should weary himself by going out to count all the signs we put up. So, by arrangement, we paid taxes on fifteen signs, but put up twenty. That is the way the amenities were observed, the tax rate was adjusted and brought down to a reasonable basis. No one's rice bowl was broken and everyone's face was saved.

Deceitful sings which deceive no one

The mutual respect for rice bowls led quite naturally to the formation of associations and guilds which were found in almost, every line of business except the newer ones such as advertising and publishing. The guilds of bankers, silk and rice dealers, were the richest and the oldest and their guild houses so ornate that tourists often mistook them for temples. In a restricted way, each one was a religious establishment, for it contained a shrine dedicated to the god who affords special protection to that particular guild. Some of the guilds had huge cash reserves and made generous contributions to funds for famine relief or other charitable purposes.

The guild organizations are so all-embracing that they included guilds of thieves and beggars. I have never, to my knowledge, ever met a member of the thieves' guild, for they had no representation in the International Settlement of

218

Shanghai. But a great many old residents who have spent years in the smaller up-country places have told me of their system of procedure. The head of the guild worked as the executive head of a theft prevention bureau and, by paying through him a small annual fee to the guild he guaranteed against any molestation by thieves. It was looked on by many as an ideal arrangement. For one thing, it relieved the local police force of a heavy load of responsibility for they seldom had to bother about thefts. As everyone who had any tempting valuables paid this small tribute to the guild, the thieves were able to lead honest lives in comfort and security without being compelled to practice their profession. I don't suppose any Chinese ever thought very seriously over the question of whether or not a thief deserved to have his rice bowl filled. The system made it possible for thieves and the honest citizenry to live together on cordial terms, a cordiality which was only disturbed when some amateur, who did not belong to the guild, purloined something from one of the guild's patrons. Then the members of the guild became thief catchers, and if they could not find and return the stolen article they compensated the owner for its loss. While there is no exaggeration about this brief note on the operations of the thieves' guild, it should be explained that it represents a picture of the past rather than the present, for with the organization of police and gendarmeries in many parts of the country, the thieves' guilds began to pass out of existence. It is said that many of them joined the police force.

I did get very well acquainted with the chief of a beggars' guild, who was one of the first acquaintances I made in China. It was in the summer of 1911 and the Yangtsze was suffering from a very severe flood. There has been a much more serious flood since then, but the 1911 flood was the most disastrous in the memory of any living man. I was sent to Hankow to write a series of news articles about the flood for the Shanghai newspaper on which I was working and also for a syndicate of American papers. Here I encountered my first difficulty in securing concrete facts and had my first experience with Chinese indifference to matters in which they have no direct personal concern. The flood was all about us at Hankow, the river was lull of wreckage, and the low-lying portions of the city itself were under water. Corpses which floated by with horrifying frequency testified to the fact that there was great loss of life, but no one seemed to have any idea of what the fatalities were or to care very much about the matter. One old French padre was doing a great deal of relief work, but when I asked him about the fatalities he said:

'We will mourn and bury our Christian dead but God must count the heathen.'

The editor of the one Chinese newspaper could give me no help. He was conducting his paper for the sole purpose of stirring up a revolution against the Manchus and was not interested in anything else. He was the editor I have already mentioned whose life was saved a few months later because his life was insured in a British company. I had employed an interpreter in Hankow and, after a day of fruitless work, I hinted to him that he would be discharged unless we could find some information that was worth interpreting. Then, for the first time, he did a sensible thing and. took me to see the head beggar.

He was a very intelligent and capable old man, with a venerable grey queue, and while answering my questions about the flood told me a great deal about the profession of begging as it was conducted in China. His father had been the head beggar before him, but his assumption of the office had been confirmed by all the beggars of the city and he became their autocratic head, acting as their business manager and official representative in all dealings with the police and tradespeople. Here, as in most other Chinese cities, begging had been thoroughly systematized. The beggars were apportioned between the streets under separate chiefs and all were under the control of the head beggar. No beggar was allowed off his own street in his professional capacity, nor could he beg there except on the first and the fifteenth day of each month. This arrangement had been made by the head beggar after many conferences with the merchant guilds and was an improvement over the administrative machinery he had inherited from his father. He was very proud of his achievement, as it enabled his people to loaf on all except two days of the month, and gave the least amount of annoyance to the shopkeepers. On the appointed days, the beggars, in company, would canvass their street, and the proprietor of each shop gave their chief the money to be divided between them. The amount given depended on the size of the shop, according to a well-regulated scale.

It was because of this admirable arrangement that the head beggar was so keenly interested in the flood and so well able to give me the details for which I had been searching. The flood had submerged a number of neighboring villages and many farms, sending the refugees scurrying towards the larger cities for shelter and food. They were encamped in large numbers just outside the Hankow city gates, while many of them had entered and were in the city itself, detailing to every passer-by the story of their misfortunes and threatening to die on the spot unless aid were forthcoming. This the head beggar naturally resented, and he grew very indignant as he told of the way in which these unorganized, non-union beggars were playing havoc with his own organization.

'The shopkeepers are all complaining to me,' he said, 'but what can I do? These refugees are competing with my own people and I can't get any protection from the officials, who throw open the city gates to any vagabond who wants to come in and beg. They do not belong to our guild, have no business here, and ought not to be allowed in the city.' He made his grievances so convincing that I agreed with him.

It is through their guilds that the Chinese have al-was enjoyed a rather democratic administration under a very autocratic government. Under the Manchu rule, the local magistrates, taotais, or prefects, possessed, in theory, almost unlimited powers. In practice they had at all times to be very careful not to run foul of the guild regulations, or to arouse public opinion to the point that all the guilds would combine against them. In the latter case, the guilds inaugurated a 'cessation of trade,' which was a combined strike, lockout and boycott. Workmen quit work and employees closed their doors. No one bought anything and the shopkeepers put up their shutters. The whole city took a holiday, or several of them, if the official was unusually stubborn.

The self-governing guilds naturally bred a democratic spirit and during the Republican revolution many of them gave valuable aid to the Republican cause. The first contribution to the funds of the revolutionists was made by a merchant guild at Hankow, and similar contributions from many other guilds enabled the republicans to keep on fighting and finally win against the monarchy. The guilds were well able to do this, for some of them are fabulously rich, owning carved and lacquered guild houses and boasting of millions of ounces of silver in their treasuries. In many cases their funds have been accumulating for centuries, for most of them have on their membership rolls the names of men whose fathers and grandfathers were members before them in an unbroken line for a dozen generations, and a few audaciously date their records from about 2,000 B.C. In a country as yet untroubled by statistics, it would be impossible to do more than guess at the aggregate wealth of the guilds, but all guesses would be expressed in hundreds of millions. However, this is a false measure of the guilds, whose importance lies, not in their wealth, but in their power to regulate all the commerce and industries of one-fourth of the world's population.

Business failures are rare, in China, for the guilds usually assume the obligations of the bankrupt, thereby preventing a disturbance of credits. It is seldom that a civil suit comes up for a trial in a Chinese court, for business disputes are almost invariably settled by the guilds. A Chinese silk dealer would laugh at the suggestion that anyone but a guild of silk merchants could decide a dispute in the silk trade, and when one sees the celerity with which such cases are settled in the unofficial guild courts, and the cheerfulness with which the verdicts are accepted, he is inclined to agree with the Chinese point of view.

"We cheat neither old nor young"

17. Several Ways That Are Dark

A good many competent observers, including some who have lived in China and have done business with the Chinese over the greater part of a lifetime, have testified in most enthusiastic terms to the honesty and fair dealing of the Sons of Han. The earliest foreign traders said that 'a Chinaman's word is as good as his bond,' and some contend that the saying still holds good. A great many others who are, presumably, equally competent observers, and have enjoyed similar opportunities to gain a practical working knowledge of Chinese business customs, can tell you long and distressing stories of devious turnings down the by-paths of ways that are dark and deceitful. They counter the saying about a Chinaman's word being as good as his bond by declaring that it may well be, because in most instances his bond isn't worth anything anyway; they can bring forth innumerable examples in proof, evidence which is direct, circumstantial and convincing. These two directly opposing statements of fact and expressions of opinion are very disconcerting to the outsider who has had no opportunity to acquire any first-hand knowledge and come to his own conclusions, and he naturally wonders which is right. The divergent views, of course, are very easily explained and, in a general way, each is right. The two parties who hold such

224

contradictory opinions have been in contact with different Chinese. One was fortunate in his associates and the other was not, and each has made the same mistake of assuming that his experiences were typical, and that the conduct of the Chinese he knew set the pattern for them all. Everyone, no matter what his country, knows that among his own fellow-countrymen there are honest and dishonest men, with a great number somewhere in between and, if he ever stopped to think about it, he should realize that the same condition very probably exists in other parts of the world, including China.

It is very easy to come to certain general conclusions about other people and nationalities, and with the imperfect mental and emotional equipment which we possess, very difficult to avoid doing so. When I was living in Tokyo, a Belgian, by means of some very clever misrepresentations defrauded me of a typewriter. So far as I can remember he was the first Belgian I had ever met. He was certainly the first one I had ever done any business with, and I made up my mind that he would be the last one. Some years later, when in business in Shanghai, I deliberately let a competitor take a Belgian advertising account that I could have had for the asking, because I had put representatives of that nationality on a mental blacklist and didn't want to have any dealings with them.

For fifteen years I disliked and distrusted the Belgians, and then I had a big shovel-full of very unsavory Belgian business dumped on me without my knowledge or consent and very much against my wishes. An Esthonian employee of mine had been taking a correspondence-school course in crime by reading American detective magazines and going to see the crook shows, and had got along very successfully until he committed the stupid error of forging my name to a check on a bank where I had no account. Before this mistake brought his homework activities to my attention, he had committed me to all kinds of obligations to a Belgian firm, had collected money in my name, and involved me in a tangle which would obviously be every expensive to me if the Belgians insisted on their rights, which is what I expected them to do. That was a very small part of what the Belgian had done when he got my typewriter by felonious means. But when I told them the story, they tore up their contract and left me with my own pound of flesh. In fact, if I had not insisted on compensating them, they would have shared a good part of the loss which legally and ethically fell on me. No one could have been more fair or generous.

The fact is very disconcerting to moralists, especially to those who are unable to disassociate morality and religion, but it is true that honesty, in its practical application to everyday affairs, is a very uncertain factor until translated into terms of business ethics and formulated into codes and standards of practice. The Yankee peddler who sold wooden nutmegs was not the scoundrel he is usually made out to be, because there was not, at that time, any definite standard of quality established for nutmegs, nor any code of ethics regarding nutmeg transaction. If the same man were alive to-day you could probably be perfectly safe in buying his nutmegs, because the world has become nutmeg conscious and the standard of quality a nutmeg must possess has become well established and is well known. Since practical honesty involves the application of codes of commercial ethics, rather than abstract theories of moral conduct, it stands to reason that the Chinese, with their centuries of trading experience, should have built up elaborate and complete codes covering all possible business relationships. That is what they have done and, as might be expected, the degrees of honesty as shown by differing codes of ethics follow occupational as well as individual lines of demarcation.

The silk merchants of China, who are also weavers, probably represent the oldest business in the country, if not in the world, for they were weaving and selling silk a thousand years or more before the birth of Christ and there has been no break in their activity. Their standards of manufacture have always been high. The Japanese had not been making silk for export a decade before they learned from foreigners how to give an artificial weight to their product, with the result that for many years there has been no such thing as pure Japanese silk. The Chinese had an equal opportunity to learn these sly tricks and practice them, but never availed themselves of the opportunity. Any Chinese silk dealer is glad to demonstrate the purity of his product by snipping off a piece and burning it in a saucer. Pure silk is the only substance that a flame will entirely consume without leaving a trace of ash. If there is the slightest adulteration, the tell-tale ash will appear. Because Chinese silk is pure and Chinese have confidence in its purity, it has always been sold by weight instead of by length. In all good shops there is no haggling over price; usually the policy of the shop is proclaimed by a sign reading:

'Prices are fixed. We cheat neither old nor young.'

The silversmiths also represent a very ancient craft with a strong guild and very rigid rules of conduct. Every piece of silverware bears the 'chop' or trademark of the shop which produced it, and in China this is treated with as much respect as the legend on a minted coin. It is a guarantee of the purity of the metal and also constitutes the most liberal and unconditional money-back guarantee any manufacturer in any country ever put on his product. No matter how old or battered the piece may be, the silversmith will always buy it back at a slight reduction from the original price. The homes of wealthy Chinese are crowded with silver vases and boxes which they buy, not only because they think they are highly ornamental, but also because they can, at any time, turn these ornaments into cash.

But in other lines of business the standards are not so high. For some reason which I have not heard satisfactorily explained, Chinese never built for permanence as the term is understood in other countries. Though many of their temples and palaces made a very impressive appearance they were never as substantial as they appeared to be and rarely outlasted the lifetime of the grandson of the builder. This was true even where plenty of good building stone was available. The 'hollow brick' method of construction, which is generally thought to be a modern architectural invention, was in use in China centuries ago. But it was not used to improve methods of construction. Its sole purpose was to make two thin bricks do the work of one big thick brick, thereby producing a flimsy building of deceitfully massive appearance and adding to the profits of the building contractor. One exception must be made to the statement that all construction was shoddy. Modern engineers would find it difficult to improve on either the design or the methods of construction of the Great Wall, which is still sound after more than 2,000 years of sun, frost and earthquakes. But this great defensive work was built by a military genius to keep out barbarian invaders and with no thought of the cost either in silver or human lives. The danger was a real one and flimsy walls would afford no protection. A hundred generations of Chinese builders have observed the Great Wall and admired it, but no one has sought to emulate it. Unless they are constantly and expertly watched, Chinese building contractors will use the cheapest material possible and even cheat on the quantity if they find an opportunity to do so. They excel in plaster work, because with it they can conceal their shoddy workmanship. The fact that they cannot conceal all the inferior material does not deter them from using it. Except in a few modern buildings erected under strict, foreign supervision, it is impossible to find, in the whole of China, a window with no imperfect panes. Foreign window-glass factories find in China a sale for the defective glass they could not sell in any other country,, and, in fact, this glass is known to the glass trade as 'China grade.'

An architect in Shanghai showed a Chinese contractor a picture of the Empire State Building and jokingly asked him how he would like to have a contract to put up a building like that.

'What a chance!' said the contractor, who also had a sense of humor. 'What a chance! I could leave out a whole floor and no one would know the difference!'

No doubt if there had ever been a demand for well-constructed houses, and for public buildings which would last through the centuries, a high standard of ethics would have been built up in the building trades, but this demand never existed and was in fact discouraged by the Manchu rulers, who restricted the size and style of houses that could be built by commoners, no matter how wealthy they might be.

The newer occupations, such as manufacturing and publishing, and the export trade, have not built up as yet any code of ethics worthy of the name. Chinese manufacturing almost invariably follows one disastrous cycle. The manufacturer starts with new equipment, turns out a good product and builds up a fair sale for his goods. When he has accomplished this much it seems to be impossible for him to resist the temptation to work off poor materials, the quality of his product deteriorates, his sales fall off, his business fails. Then someone buys him out, starts over again and runs through the same cycle. I have seen dozens of examples of it in the cigarette business. Most of the cigarettes in China were made by a British company so large that it was almost a monopoly. This made it a rather easy matter for a Chinese to start a factory, work up a little furore about smoking Chinese cigarettes instead of British, and so build up a profitable business in a new brand. As soon as he accomplished this the manufacturer reflected that he could add a great deal to his profits by using tobacco of a little cheaper price and poorer grade. It took some time for smokers to become conscious of a change in the quality of the cigarettes and, encouraged by the fact that use of the cheaper grades of tobacco had not affected sales, the manufacturer put in a few more economies. Then one day he found that his brand of cigarettes was expiring and that it was too late for him to do anything about it. It came to be taken for granted in the tobacco trade that no brand of cigarettes turned out by a Chinese factory would retain its popularity for more than a few years.

The Chinese manufacturer is also a graceless and shameless, but rather unsuccessful, imitator of trademarks. As soon as some foreign product which is easily manufactured builds up a good business in China, one or more Chinese manufacturers produce a product with packages and brand name which are similar. At one time we were advertising a sticky pomade which would keep the hair slicked down and gave heads the appearance of having been covered with lacquer. It enjoyed a good sale, because that was before it became fashionable for Chinese men to clip their hair short in the military or monkish fashion, and the hair on the Chinese male head is usually coarse and unruly. In a few weeks there was an imitation brand on the market, and an average of one or more new imitations appeared every month. We finally began collecting them, like new issues of postage stamps. At one time we had twenty-one varieties, but there we're a few rare issues that escaped us.

These imitations were very irritating, but I was never able to feel the amount of moral indignation they aroused in the breasts of my clients, because they never deceived anyone. In fact, I was always in some doubt as to how far they were intended to deceive. I think many of them were put out by the Chinese manufacturers because they didn't have the ability to get up something that was entirely original. In any town in the Yangtsze Valley one could find a number of shops which sold small batteries for use in flashlights. If you asked the shopkeeper for a well-known American brand he would oiler you the genuine article, but if you found the price too high, he would promptly offer you another battery with the same name and often an identical trade-mark and explain that he could sell this at a cheaper price because it was an imitation. It is not an easy matter to invent an entirely new design for a package or for anything else. That is what the fathers of America found out when they attempted to design a flag which could replace the separate standards of the thirteen colonies. The flag, when finally produced, turned out to be an exact copy of the flag of the Hon. East India Company except that our ancestors added two more stripes. With that exception, the only difference between the American flag and that of the 'John' company consists of later changes and additions. If any manufacturer to-day copied his competitor's trade-mark as unscrupulously as our forefathers copied the Hag of the East India Company, he would indubitably lose in a suit for trademark infringement. The fact that the Yankee traders of those days were offering strong competition to the British trading monopoly prompts the thought, possibly unpatriotic, that the similarity in flags was more than a coincidence.[3]

---

[3] In 1775, a committee was appointed by the Continental Congress to design a new flag which would provide a symbol of unity and which could be used by all of the thirteen colonies. The Committee performed their labors with a minimum of effort by copying the flag of the Hon. East India Company, but adding two additional stripes so as to bring the number up to thirteen, to correspond with the number of the colonies. In this flag the field was formed by the crosses of St. Andrew and St. George, just as in the Union Jack of to-day. Two years later, with open warfare between England and the American colonies, the inappropriateness of this Sag became apparent and on June 14, 1777, a new flag was adopted and the Union was replaced by a field of blue. The earlier flag officially disowned a few years ago by the adoption of June 14 as Flag Day. The story that Betsy Ross made the first flag from a sketch of Washington's is, unhappily, nothing more than a pleasing legend. See Encyclopaedia Britannica, 13th edition, Vol 9 pg 458.

The boy was suspected of being a Japanese spy

Any observant visitor to Shanghai when Shanghai was a tourist center must inevitably have come to the conclusion that the barbering business here was very prosperous and very highly organized for nine out of ten of the hundreds of shops bore the name 'Excelsior,' all apparently being units of one giant chain. But the connection between the individual shops existed solely in the similarity of names, for each shop was under individual ownership and management. One of the first of the American style barber shops that was established in 1912 was started by a Chinese barber from San Francisco who had worked in a shop called the Excelsior. So that was the name he gave his shop, and as other shops were started his competitors copied his sign. This went on year alter year until practically all of them had the same name.

While the Chinese manufacturer makes clumsy imitations of foreign labels and packages he seldom counterfeits them, an art at which the Japanese' are masters. The Japanese counterfeiting of well-known brands was an evil-smelling scandal before the turn of the century and conditions never improved. The center of operations was moved from Yokohama and Kobe to Dairen. There anyone could buy imitations of any well-known brand of Scotch whisky or English gin in bottles with labels which counterfeited the originals so cleverly that no one could tell the difference between the genuine and the imitation.

Probably half a century from now the Chinese publishers and advertising men will have built up a code of business conduct equal to that of their silk-weaving and silver-crafting fellow-countrymen, but there has not been any very substantial evidence that this will happen. Figures regarding newspaper circulations are as grossly exaggerated as they were in America before the Audit Bureau of Circulation compelled publishers, much against their will, to be honest. As we spent most of our client's money on advertising in Chinese newspapers the circulation figure was a matter of great importance to us. In the absence of any more accurate method we worked out several devious ways of arriving at our own conclusions regarding circulations. One method we used we called 'the acid test,' because it burned the chaff out of their circulation figures. We did not advertise free samples, but did give readers of the Chinese newspapers frequent opportunities to send us five to ten cents in stamps for which we would send them samples of vanishing cream, cold cream, pen nibs, toilet soap or a cure for infantile colic, which should have been better known than it was. Each remittance of postage stamps had to be accompanied by a coupon clipped from the advertisement, and by compiling and tabulating the coupon returns we arrived at a fair idea of the number of people who read a publication.

This acid test enabled us, on one occasion, to discover a publication which undoubtedly held the world's all-time record when it came to circulation figures, because the net paid circulation was absolute zero. The publication was a very well printed monthly magazine which, according to the publisher had 30,000 women readers. Its bulky pages were prosperously full of advertising. Our accountants liked it very much because the July issue came out in July instead of late in the autumn, which is the custom with many Chinese monthlies. It was very troublesome to explain to fussy New York and London auditors that the reason we had not included in our September invoice the charge for advertising in a July magazine was because that issue has not yet been published. One of our clients insisted on the use of this journal, and we ran a full page advertisement offering each one of 30,000 ladies a generous sample of vanishing cream for five cents in stamps. When the advertisement had appeared for three months without a single one of the 30,000 ladies evincing any curiosity about our generous offer, we began to think that there was something wrong and made an investigation, which disclosed the fact that the only copies of the magazine printed each month were those which were required to support invoices sent to the advertisers. And that was not all. The reading matter in the magazine was never changed, but was the same from month to month and had been so as far back as we could trace the record. The only change to be found from one month's issue to the next was in the advertising copy and in the date of issue m the cover page. And even that was not all. The text of the reading matter which appeared month after month and year after year did not have the slightest interest to women, or to men either, for it consisted of reprints from the columns of an old Shanghai newspaper. The publishers solicited advertising only from foreigners and assumed quite correctly that as they couldn't read Chinese anyway it didn't matter what was published. They did change the color of the cover each month, that being their only extravagance.

Over a period of more than ten years we received frequent letters from clients in New York, London and

Berlin demanding to know why we were not placing their advertising in this publication.

It is in the export business that the ways of the Chinese business man became the darkest. Chinese are not the only ones who have found it profitable and comparatively easy to sell to the export market goods which are not up to standard and feel secure in the knowledge that the deception will not be discovered until the cargo is unpacked in some distant port under circumstances which make it difficult to place the guilt on any one particular person. The aggressive selling methods adopted by Sir Thomas Lipton changed the big English demand from Chinese tea to Indian, but that would not have-been possible, or at any rate his success would not have been so easy, if the Chinese had maintained the quality of their product. Instead, they succumbed to the temptation of easy profits. There was a big demand for Chinese tea, and the suppliers found it -was a difficult matter to sell tea which had been adulterated or insufficiently cured. They were not alone in their attempt to make easy profits in this way. At the same time that the Chinese tea merchants were lowering the quality and the prestige of Chinese tea, British cotton goods dealers were doing the same thing with the products of the Manchester mills. British cotton cloth had always been sold in China with a labeled 'chop' or trade-mark and some of those chops became famous and popular. Then mills in China and Japan began operating in a big way, cutting prices and underselling Manchester. The British manufacturer met this competition by weaving a cheaper cloth which they sold under the old chop. This went on for a generation or more with the result that, with a few exceptions, a British treade-mark on cotton goods became of very doubtful value, and the British cotton goods business in China declined in the same way as and for the same reason, the Chinese tea business declined in Great Britain.

The large Chinese bean, which is known to commerce as the 'horse bean,' is the most humble of the bean family. It thrives on land which its more aristocratic relatives would be ashamed to thrust their roots into, and produces in abundance a crop which is so coarse that, while edible and nutritious, no human beings ever consume unless driven to do so by the direct necessity of famine. As an item of export trade this 'horse bean' has a very singular destination. It is shipped only to coal-mining countries and is consumed only by those unfortunate animals, the pit mules, who, by reason of their occupations, spend their lives in the darkness of the colliery tunnels. For some reason the Chinese horse bean is the favorite food of pit mules in collieries all over the world, keeps these poor animals in a fair state of health and prolongs their lives. The bean exporter who told me about it said there is vitamin D in the bean, which, in a way, makes up for the lack of sunlight.

Since this bean grows and produces like a hardy weed, it is unbelievably cheap. Hankow was the principal center of production and the beans never sold there at more than a few coppers a pound. In fact the beans constitute probably the cheapest food product known to commerce and it would not appear possible that there could be any profit in adulteration and that imitations should be impossible, but my exporter friend found out differently. After he had been exporting beans for several years he began receiving complaints that the beans comprising recent shipments had been found to be coated with clay, that in all the bags were found small lumps of mud. This was a mystery to my friend, for before shipment the bags had undergone the usual inspection and apparently contained nothing but sound dried beans with only the ordinary amount of dust and trash one might expect to find in a cheap cargo of this kind.

However, his suspicions were aroused and he made a personal and very careful inspection of a few bags of beans which were awaiting shipment. At first everything appeared to be in order. When a bag was opened up and the contents poured on the warehouse floor, it appeared to consist of nothing but dry beans. But a more careful examination showed that a few of the beans were broken squarely in two and these aroused his suspicions, for a sound bean does not break. He then made a minute examination of all the beans on the floor. He was an old hand at the Chinese export business, but he now encountered a new and almost unbelievably strange experience. About one out of every twenty of the apparently sound beans in the bag was nothing more than a bit of sun-baked clay moulded into the form of a bean. It was the same shape, color and weight, a commercially perfect replica. The fraud had apparently been detected only because someone had been careless enough to allow a few bags of beans to become so thoroughly watersoaked that the sundried pellets made in the shape of beans had resolved themselves back into the original Yangtsze mud from which they had been created.

He reflected that he had been exporting these beans for years, that his customers, who trusted him to ship good sound cargo, had paid him bean prices for a good many tons of Yangtsze River mud, and that thousands of poor pit mules had eaten clay beans. Thoroughly angry, he started to do a little amateur detective work. Partly by persistent effort and partly by a stroke of luck, he soon discovered, in the neighborhood of Hankow a clay bean factory. Equipped with a lot of wooden molds the factory workmen scooped clay from the banks of the Yangtsze, forced it into the molds to form pellets in the s shape of beans. These were set out in the sun to dry and if the sun was hot enough, as it usually is around Hankow during the bean harvest, it was a simple matter and a comparatively inexpensive process to make all the clay beans that the trade could absorb. The middlemen, who had contracted to supply the exporter with beans, bought these cheaper clay replicas at a low price and mixed them with the real beans in as generous a proportion as his conscience would allow and his caution would justify. It was a profitable enterprise for him and no one had really suffered except the pit mules.

Having discovered the deception and laid the whole plot bare, the exporter could do a little satisfactory chortling over his success as a sleuth. But his business was exporting beans, not doing detective work, and he was just as helpless and defenseless as he had been before. The clay beans were practically identical with the genuine bean in size, shape, weight and color. The only way one could be sure of telling the two apart would be by the individual examination into the life history of each bean, which obviously involved too much labor to be practical. Then he hit on an idea which was disastrous so far as the clay bean industry was concerned but gave the pit mules all the vitamins their owners were paying for. He built a small platform or mezzanine floor near the top of his warehouse, some fifteen to twenty feet above the ground floor. When he received the next consignment of beans the coolies were instructed to make delivery on the platform, open the bags and dump the beans on the concrete floor below. As the exporter had anticipated, the genuine beans could stand any kind of punishment of this sort, but the clay beans broke into bits. With great loss of face on the part of the middleman the broken beans were swept up, an adjustment, made on the contract, and the clay factory went out of business. So far as he knew that was the end of the great clay bean industry but my friend kept his testing platform intact and every now and then he had a few bags of beans dumped on the floor just for his own personal satisfaction and for the moral influence it might have.

In the sixth century B.C., when the great Chinese reformer, Confucius, was appointed governor of a small township in what is now the province of Shantung, he introduced several regulations which were designed to promote honest business methods. For example, farmers who were driving their livestock to market were not allowed to water the beasts while en route and so give them an artificial market weight. Merchants were also required to discard the false weights they were using and to weigh all goods on honest standardized scales. History records these innovations without making any comment as to how long these honest practices prevailed, but, as in the succeeding 25 centuries weights and measures were reformed many times we can assume that each reform was short-lived and had to be frequently revived.

Certainly when China was opened to foreign trade, about a century ago, a pint was not necessarily a pint, nor was a pound always a pound. Each was what the owner of the measure or the scale thought it should be, to be most profitable to him. British merchants, who were pioneers in China trade, insisted on knowing exactly what they were buying when they bought, and what they were selling when they sold, and the result was a series of trade treaties which, set down in terms of English ounces, pints and inches, was just what constituted legal weights and measures in China.

This restricted the Chinese trader in his dealings and eliminated one source of sure and easy profits to which he had been accustomed, but it wasn't very long before he found that the same results might be accomplished in another way by the use of, not exactly false, but slightly exaggerated invoices. For example, all paper is bought from the manufacturer by the pound but is sold by the ream, and if an invoice set forth that a certain poster paper was 43 lb. to the ream, very few would take the trouble to weigh the ream and find that it tips the scales at 39 lbs. If the posters had been printed it was then impossible to calculate the original weight of the paper stock.

False weights in all paper transactions became so common that no one but the amateur was deceived, Those of us who dealt in paper products soon learned from experience that 16 lb. bond paper was actually 14 lbs., that 43 lb. poster paper meant 39 lbs., that 130 lb. art paper would not under any circumstances weigh an ounce more than 110 lbs. We knew that this was true in spite of the fact that the printer was always able to produce an invoice from some highly reputable foreign firm which appeared to prove that the paper was of the weight he represented it to be. This supplying of false invoices to Chinese dealers by foreign firms was a rather general practice in all nationalities and was applied to many line of goods in addition to paper. In most cases the personal guilt of the foreign importer was rather difficult to appraise and would be impossible to prove. He usually knew that it was being done in his office, but was innocent of any knowledge of the details, because these were attended to by his Chinese associates and he could more or less truthfully say that he doesn't know anything about them.

I was discussing this matter of false invoices with a foreign importer and he told me that he had not only never made out a false invoice himself but had given all his Chinese employees strict instructions that they were not to do so.

'You must have lost a lot of business that way' I said sympathetically.

'Never lost a cent's worth,' he assured me. 'Whenever we sell goods to a Chinese dealer we give him a few blank forms and he can fill them out to suit himself'

Wooed by both, won by neither

18. Uncle Sam and John Bull As Exporters

When an export manager came to China to bestow the representation of his products on some deserving agent or distributor, he was usually rather shocked at the lack of enthusiasm with which his advances were met. Of course, if his product had been on the market for a long time and had a well-established sale, he would have plenty of agents to choose from, but if his company was unknown it was usually quite disillusioning to him to learn how completely and thoroughly it was unknown and what an entire lack of curiosity there was about it. Shanghai, where most of the foreign trade of China was centered, and most of the agents were located, is a big and busy city and singularly blase, with the combined sophistication of each of the seven seas. Douglas Fairbanks, Charlie Chaplin and Col. Lindbergh, to say nothing of innumerable British lords, American senators and continental princes have all been visitors and have all wandered through the shopping districts with no congestion of traffic. When American government officials of high degree visited us, the local American Chamber of Commerce had to fan local patriotism to a white heat in order to get any noticeable attention paid to them. If this had not been done, and the visitors had been left to bask in the unaided reflection of their own glory, I am afraid that most of the dignitaries would have left Shanghai feeling that the American colony had a singular lack of appreciation for the presence of greatness. Our British neighbors had to do the same thing, but the British notables seemed satisfied to get along with less limelight. This was just as well, for their countrymen are not so skillful as we are when it comes to working up impressive mass effects in artificial enthusiasm and f highly organized and noisy hospitality.

It was probably because representatives of all the nations of the world passed through our gates daily that we did not get excited over any of them but applauded instead our own small local heroes, and for a very similar reason the Shanghai importer appeared to be more interested in the old agencies he had than in the new one that were offered him. It seemed that every manufacturer in the world at some time or another tried to get an agent in Shanghai, and there were not enough agents to meet all the demands. As a result, no manufacturer of a product which was new to China had a very easy time establishing a satisfactory agency connection and he had to do so much looking around that § it usually took him weeks to accomplish what he thought could be done in a few days. While on his way out to China, he formed pretty definite ideas as to the kind of an agent he was going to appoint, but he usually ended up by appointing the first one he could talk into undertaking the work, who was in any way acceptable. This was true of all manufacturers, but, if he happened to be an American, he would find the agents a little more coy than if he was British or German, for American manufacturers had a reputation of fickleness which left much to be desired.

One of the local salesmen of a large firm of Shanghai importers went to his chief with a scheme which he felt would greatly increase the sales of the brand of American automobile tires for which they held the agency. The chief listened to him attentively and encouragingly until he became convinced that the sales program had a fair chance of being a success. Then he sent for the sales reports on this item, considered them carefully and made his decision.

'No,' he said, 'we are doing just as much business with this line as we want to do. If we carry out your suggestions and the sales increase, as I think they will, we will very probably lose the agency. The manufacturers will see the amount of business we are sending them, and will come to the conclusion that they can make more money by taking the agency away from us and establishing their own branch. Let this line rock along and work on something else, and don't write these tire people any enthusiastic letters about prospective sales and the big opportunities there are in the Chinese market.'

The manager was right. A few years later, as the sales continued to increase, a smart young man from Akron arrived one day, terminated the agency and established a branch of the home office. Since almost all agency agreements give the manufacturer the option of terminating them without compensation for the business and good will which have been built up, all the agent gets out of a change of this sort is the satisfaction of knowing that he has worked up a good business for the manufacturer and has lost the agency through his own efficiency. I have seen at least a dozen important American agencies taken away from firms in Shanghai in this manner, for no apparent reason other than the manufacturer's belief that he could enlarge his profits. In most cases, the profitable Chinese business which he took over had been built up entirely by the efforts of the old agents, and the bitter feelings with which they accepted the termination of their agency contracts can easily be imagined.

However, it does not appear, in all cases, to have been a cold-blooded analysis of sales returns and costs of operation and theoretical profits which prompted the opening of some of the branch offices in Shanghai. It is really remarkable how much vanity there is in supposedly astute business men, or how much romance, it is either vanity or the romantic idea that business is like an adventure story that, in many cases, provides the urge to make them open expensive branch offices all over the world. These branches broke out in Shanghai like measles during the boom years following the end of the First World War, and it is to be hoped that the manufacturers had a lot of fun out of their ventures, because they didn't make much money and most of them would have made a better showing on the balance sheet if they had not disturbed their old sales arrangements. When the depression made it necessary to cut out luxuries and useless window dressing in many lines of business, a great many of these branch offices were closed and the young men who opened them, slightly aged now, turned the business back to some local firm.

Apart from this passion for decorating their letterheads with the names of cities where their branch offices are located, the American manufacturers seem to enjoy changing their agencies in the hope, usually futile, that the new will be better than the old. This happened so frequently that when we got the renewal of an advertising appropriation from New York we always checked up before releasing the advertising to make sure that the same local agent was still functioning. We handled the advertising of quite a number of American manufacturers and, I cannot recall but two which did not change their Shanghai agency or establish a branch office in a period of ten years; some made three or four changes during that period. On the other hand, among an equally large number of British and continental clients

I ran recall only two which made any changes in their sales arrangements during the same period of time. My business brought me in daily contact with distributors and

244

sales agents of several nationalities and I know that they all felt that if they had a profitable British agency they had an asset of some permanent value to which they could afford to put their best efforts, but if it was an American agency, they had the uneasy feeling that it might be taken away from them any time on the whim of an export manager, and the American export managers, rightly or wrongly, had the reputation of being-very whimsical people. British manufacturers, on the other hand, might have found it advantageous and profitable to do a little more shifting of agencies than they did. Too many agencies of British companies felt such a sense of security that they made no .effort to increase sales but contented themselves with the unearned commissions which came to them without any effort. There were a number of Shanghai men with British agencies who had suspiciously low golf handicaps.

The system of hiring and firing, which is much more common in America than in any other country, may be a wholesome one so far as domestic business is concerned, but it was very disturbing in the export business, and American export managers appeared to hold rather insecure positions. In fact, it was the firing of old and the hiring of new managers that frequently provided the cause of the change in agencies, for the new man usually set in to improve on the organization of his predecessor by securing- a lot of new representatives. Every time I saw the name of a new export manager on a letter I knew that we were in for a lot of tedious correspondence in which we would travel through many new doors but finally get back to the place we started from. All knowledge was not confined to the 'old China hands,' who had usually, if truth must be told, acquired more disillusionments than knowledge, but the new export manager had acquired neither.

This hiring and firing-by American firms cost me quite a little time and money on one of my visits to America. We were handling the advertising of a large motor-car company and, when he heard of my impending trip to America, the Far Eastern Manager of the company insisted that I should visit their Detroit head office for a conference on advertising in China, and gave me letters of introduction to five different executives. There were several differences of opinion and misunderstandings which he thought I could straighten out on this visit, and he believed it would give me some mental stimulus if I would spend a few days at the fountainhead of the world's automotive knowledge. As soon as I could arrange to do so, I left New York for Detroit, taxied many miles through the uninteresting streets of that mass production city and finally reached the imposing head office of the company. I hadn't taken the trouble to wire for an appointment, because my friend had assured me that, barring a golf game, any one of the five executives would drop anything he was doing and go into conference with me as soon as I sent in my card. I gave the most important letter of introduction to the young lady at one of the many reception desks, but she soon returned with the information that the man to whom the letter was addressed was no longer with the company. She didn't know where he was but thought he was in. New York. The second letter brought the same information, so in order to save time, I gave her the three remaining letters and asked her to deliver one to the first man she could locate. She came back with the sad news that not one of them was now connected with the company and that not one of them was in Detroit. I didn't like the idea of having made this long trip with no accomplishments, so I gave her a few of my business cards and said:

'I have been handling the advertising of this company in China for several years. At the request of your Far Eastern Manager, I made a special trip from New York to Detroit to talk to the men in your export department. I wish you would go out there and tell them this and see if any of them has ever heard of me or if anyone wants to see me.'

She must have done a thorough job of it, for she "was gone a long time, but when she returned it was only to report that no one had heard of me and no one wanted to see me. So I took a drive around Belle Isle and caught the next train to New York. I reflected that the only satisfaction I could get out of the incident would be the story I would have to tell my friend in Osaka, but even that was denied me, for when I got back to the Far East a few months later I found that he also had been removed from the payroll.

American stenographers are too efficient

A manufacturer's agent living in Shanghai confided to me some years ago:

'I have found out how to handle New York export managers. Write them plenty of letters. They have a lot of fun answering them, and send the carbon copies to the general manager to show how busy they are. About all an export manager can do is to write letters anyway, and it is only fair to give them plenty of opportunities. Of course, they must have a reasonable number of orders, but if you write them enough letters they won't grouse so much about the size or infrequency of the orders.'

This man remained in business for many years and so his system must have had some merits. The export managers, by reason of their isolation, must carry on a voluminous correspondence, but theirs is not the only department in American business concerns which produces ready letter writers. The number of letters, and the length of tire letters, which American businessmen seem to find it necessary to write amaze the businessmen of other nationalities—all except the Spaniard. He is even more long winded, and can, without rhetorical difficulty, quote Aleman or Cervantes and give you an idea of the weather he is enjoying and the state of his health at the time of writing. The responsibility for American verbosity, I feel sure, lies with the very efficient American stenographer, and the temptation to garrulousness provided by the skill of her fingers. In some offices it seems that letter writing has finally become a major undertaking, like writing for publication, and not a means to an end. There is no one who appears to be quite so well satisfied with the result of a day's work as the American businessman who has dictated so many letters that his secretary has to work overtime transcribing them. The first practical evidence I had of the existence of the depression in America came when I noticed that the letters I received were fewer and shorter. Obviously, it had been necessary to reduce the staff of stenographers.

It is my candid opinion, after reading these letters for about twenty years, that half the typewriters in America could be scrapped and half the stenographers married off, and the wheels of business would run just as fast and with a good deal less noise and waste effort. Businesses in other countries are conducted successfully with only a fraction of the amount of correspondence Americans appear to find necessary. Every man whose business is to dictate letters should be compelled to read over, at the beginning of every business day, the copies of letters he dictated, one year before and see for himself how many of them were twice as long as necessary, and how many were not necessary at all.

It may have been unjust, but I could not escape the feeling that a great many of the letters I received were not written to me, but for the benefit of the executive who looked over the carbon copies. If the letter was from one of the New York advertising agencies, it was always obvious that the carbon copies should create quite a good impression on the client, who could easily see that the agent was alert and was looking out for his best interests. The English typists are not so skillful and so the Englishman is not subject to the same temptation to verbosity. Once I received, by the same mail, letters from New York and London correspondents. The letters were especially welcome, for each was a renewal for the ensuing year of advertising which we had in each instance been carrying on for a decade or more.

The letter from New York covered several typewritten pages of instructions, supported by formal orders, schedule of insertion dates, etc. In the letter, we were admonished to be careful to get the best positions possible for the advertising, see that the publishers didn't place competing advertising on the same page, look out for poor printing, contact the distributors occasionally to keep them contented and see how sales were going, etc. In other words, we were exhorted to do just what any advertising agent would do as a matter of the usual routine and just what they had been telling us to do, annually, for more than ten years. In fact, in a properly organized office, it would disturb the routine and be a lot of trouble to avoid doing all these things. The final paragraph was almost lyrical in its appeal to me to do the right thing by this account.

It didn't take the Englishman long to dictate his letter. In fact it was so short that I suspect he wrote it, out by hand and then had it typed. The letter read:

'Dear Sir,

We beg to acknowledge receipt of your favour of the 17th ult. and to advise you of our approval of the revised advertising schedules contained therein. Trusting that this business, will receive your usual careful attention, we are, Dear Sirs,

Yours faithfully.'

I believe it was an English nobleman who, when away on a hunting trip, wrote to his wife:

'Madam, it is very cold and I have killed two sheep.'

While the Englishman's terse letters are more than satisfactory in ordinary business correspondence, the average English correspondent is hopeless when it comes to writing a selling letter. Give an American the least bit of encouragement and he will bombard you with sales letters designed to convince you of the superiority of the goods he is selling. The Englishman's idea of a good, snappy, sales letter is, 'In response to your inquiry we beg to quote—'

While the American writes many and lengthy letters he does not always compose them very carefully. When an important business letter is written to be dispatched several hundred miles across the sea, it should be checked and double checked to make sure that it is clear and complete. Most letters from English firms bear a number of initials, showing that the letter has been read by several people. It is a far cry from that practice to the rubber stamp on some American letters which informs you that a letter has been dictated but not read, or to the fact that in many American offices it appears that everyone except the office boy is allowed to write and sign letters. I recall one bit of carelessness on the part of a letter writer which caused us a lot of bother and some unnecessary expense. A letter which we received countermanded the instructions contained in an earlier letter which, it was said, was dated January 16. We looked through our files, could find no communication of that date and assumed that it had been delayed in the mails and would show up later. The letter did not arrive and then a Chinese office boy made the interesting discovery that January 16 was a Sunday, so obviously some other date, was meant. We finally had to send a cable asking the correct date, as it might have referred to any one of several January letters. Now, if your correspondent has a registered cable address, and any one of a dozen or more cable code books, you can send quite a long message at a cost which is not excessive, but this concern, although engaged in overseas; trade, had no registered cable address and apparently did not possess a code book. We had to pay cable tolls on the whole name and street and city address of the firm and send the message in plain language, and the costs were too large to be cheerful about. In the end, we learned that the letter referred to was dated January 6.

There are very few people who will dispute the statement that when it comes to the technique of advertising and merchandising Uncle Sam is far ahead of John Bull, though far behind him in other factors which influence the sales in export markets. The most striking example of Uncle Sam's superior merchandising methods is found in the packaging by which the manufacturers of the two countries present their goods to their customers. A great many of the English packages of brands which have a world-wide sale were designed several generations ago, before typography had reached its present high stage of development or the modern art of package design had ever been heard of. They were, however, the best that could be produced at the time, which is more than can be said of the modern British package, for the manufacturer makes little or no use of the expert modern talent which could be supplied by any commercial art studio in England. He turns out the best product it is possible for him to make, and, having done that, he appears to consider that he has done all that a manufacturer could be expected to do. There are probably a good many honest differences of expert opinion as to which of the two nations is the most artistic, but there can be no doubt about the fact that the American manufacturer was the first to discover that art is a valuable aid in the selling of goods. When, in 1882, Oscar Wilde toured the country from New York to San Francisco, he scolded Americans for their lack of appreciation of art, for the ugly surroundings which they endured so complacently. He found nothing to admire, but if he were alive today, he would undoubtedly give American manufacturers a word of praise for their packages.

And he would probably exhort his fellow Britons to follow the American example. The safety razor I formerly used was of British manufacture and design. It was a very fine piece of workmanship and, as safety razors go, was a rather expensive article. But there was no hint of the existence of a superior article in the case enclosing the razor. Anyone who saw it for the first time might easily imagine that it was a tin of sardines of rather novel proportions. Any American manufacturer would, with little or no additional cost, produce a package of dignified beauty, in keeping with the high quality of the razor itself, and, by this method, make the article more saleable. In fact, any Chinese in my art department could- have designed a more attractive package than this one.

There is the same indifference to style and beauty in British advertising, and lack of care or indifference in the typography and lay-out. But in one way, in the export field, the Briton is a better advertiser and merchandiser than the American. I have never known the latter to make or even discuss any plans beyond those which are to be put into execution at once. All appear to make their plans on the assumption that the world will come to an end at the close of their next financial year. And with the first approach of a slump in sales he visualizes early dissolution. The Englishman has seen sales slump before and knows that somehow or other their business has continued for a good many years and is not going to come to a sudden end. This difference may partly be psychological, but it is partly due to the difference in company organization. Too many American manufacturers have found that they could make more money by floating stock companies and speculating in their own stock than by earning legitimate dividends. The result has been over-capitalization and hungry stockholders whose only interest in the business is in the figure showing quarterly earnings. Most of the big British companies were privately owned. They had, as a rule, much larger reserves than American companies and were not so easily thrown into a panic by a temporary drop in sales. One of these British clients, by the way, used his cash reserves to cut quite a generous slice out of his advertising costs, for he paid for a year's advertising in advance, and we were able to get such liberal cash discounts for him that he actually earned 18% on his money. We often got our American appropriations and detailed instructions quarter by quarter. The Englishman took a more long-range view of things. „His firm has been doing business for a long time and he assumed that it was going to be in business next year and the year after. He made plans not only for the current year, but for the years which he knew would follow.

The British manufacturer, once he has produced an article which is saleable, seldom changes it, and stubbornly resists any suggestion that it might be improved. In fact, it is not much of an exaggeration to say that he seldom makes any change or improvement until circumstances compel him to do so. So far as the Chinese market is concerned, this conservatism is a help rather than a hindrance to sales, for the Chinese customer is equally conservative. So long as an article is satisfactory he sees no reason for altering it and is likely to look with some suspicion on any change. His experience has made him skeptical and he finds it much easier to believe that a product has been changed so as to reduce the cost of manufacture at the expense of the quality than to believe that the manufacturer has voluntarily started in to produce a better piece of goods with no increase in price.

This conservative attitude on the part of the British manufacturers provided a striking contrast to the constant search for change on the part of the American. Sometimes this did not bring the reward that should follow honest and earnest effort.

The electric flashlight found a wide market as soon as it was introduced into China and there" was a very large sale for the small electric batteries which went with the flashlight. A friend of ours secured the agency for a well-known American battery and in a short time built up a surprisingly big sale for which we took some credit, as we were handling the advertising. Then someone in the factory came to the conclusion that the package could be improved and expert package designers were put to work. Without any warning that a change was even contemplated, a big shipment of batteries arrived in the new package, characterized by a few broad .stripes instead of many thin stripes. There was no doubt that the psychology of the new package was correct, for it gave an impression of sturdiness which was entirely lacking in the old package. But the Chinese consumer didn't know that. All that he knew was that this was a new package, which he at once concluded must be a Japanese imitation and therefore inferior. We had to scrap all the advertising picturing the old battery and then spend most of the advertising appropriation explaining that the new battery was really just the same as the old.

All this naturally slowed up sales and they were just returning to normal when we suffered a body blow even more serious by another manifestation of efficiency. It was an engineer this time. He had gone through the records of domestic sales and found that all batteries were not only sold but consumed within six weeks from the time of production. Without thinking about the nice little business that was being built up in China, he came to the conclusion that it was a waste of money to make a battery which would outlast its allotted period of usefulness. The experts set to work to produce a battery which would last just as long as it was necessary for it to last, and no longer, thereby providing a saleable and satisfactory article at a substantial reduction in factory costs. We didn't know anything about this change until angry dealers along the Yangtsze refused to pay their bills on the justifiable grounds, that the batteries would not work. Their span of life which had been so expertly allotted by the efficiency experts had expired while the batteries were on the way to China. The batteries should then have been wrapped in an old sail and dropped over the side, after the manner of burials at sea. That was the end of our promising battery business, for less efficient manufacturers took all our business away from us.

British and Americans were more active in the export trade than any other nationalities. So far as China was concerned, there were but two other nationalities who offered any serious competition, Japanese and German. With the Japanese out of the field, each of the two great English-speaking nations would do a great deal more business, not only in China, but in other parts of the world. But Japan contributed nothing new to the world's variety of merchandise, nor has Japan ever gained a foothold in world trade because of any superiority in methods of manufacture or merchandising. Japanese competition has been successful solely on the basis of price—low costs of production made possible by the most shameless exploitation of cheap labor. In the markets of the world Japan conducted a perpetual bargain sale of sweat shop goods.

German competition fell within a different category. The German enjoyed no essential advantage over either John Bull or Uncle Sam when it came to costs of production. In his merchandising methods, he displayed all the faults and all the virtues of both, but there was one essential difference, he worked very much harder and took fewer holidays. He was more energetic than the American, much more energetic than the Englishman, who, all in all, is probably the world's most leisurely business man.

The French manufacturer has never had to work for his export business and as a result he hasn't very much. He did not employ any export managers, because he depended on French soldiers to hold colonies which soldiers of past generations had conquered, and on French legislators who would build up a tariff wall high enough to keep all competition out. His conception of an ideal market was one in which no one else had any chance to compete and he had only to make the goods with no brain fag or expense over selling or advertising. The French statesmen of last century, anxious to be given full credit for their achievements, coddled him into the belief that they could take care of all the sales exploitation he needed. When France began lagging behind in exports the statesmen tried to waken the manufacturer and get him to go to work. They appointed commercial attaches and in a mild way copied the work of the United States Department of Commerce. But they did not succeed in awakening him, and a friend of mine in the French consular service told me in 1936 that the only response they got were a few-lazy grunts.

Sales of French goods to China amounted to less than 1 ½ % of China's total importations. Australia, Belgium, British India, Canada, Germany, Japan, Siam, United States, all exceeded her. Germany's trade, with China was almost ten times that of France.

Chinese eat a lot of apples

19. An Apple a Day

Let's take apples as a good, practical example of the opportunities afforded by the Chinese market with which I, as an advertising agent, had to familiarize myself. Apples are grown in all temperate zones, there are few crop failures, they are comparatively cheap, easier than most fruit to pack and ship, and undoubtedly provide a very popular and healthy food. They can be eaten as they fall from the tree or can be cooked in a number of appetizing ways. They can be stewed, fried, roasted, baked or made into cider or salads. An individual apple can be conveniently and cleanly divided into segments of the most meager or most generous proportions, thus lending itself to small retail sale or to consumption on the communistic or family plan. Because of these and other reasons, an apple is, among all the fruits, the easiest to market. Suppose we could convince the 400 million potential Chinese customers that an apple a-day would keep the doctor away.

Apart from the matter of dependable supply, cheap price and satisfactory shipping qualities, an apple has, as a problem of selling to the Chinese, a good many factors which are encouraging. The Chinese believe that everything they eat has some medicinal value, so they would be less skeptical about the health-giving properties of apples than most other people. A great many Americans, in spite of

257

several decades of advertising, are still doubtful about there being iron in raisins, but the Chinese are not, though it is a comparatively new story to them. It didn't take very much advertising to convince them that the eating of raisins would make them healthily ferriferous, because they were curing their ills with fruits, herbs and other vegetable products more than ten centuries before the birth of Christ, and the idea was not a novel one to them. Although very few apples are grown in the country, Chinese eat a lot of them which are imported from Korea, and some which come from America and New Zealand. So there is no question of overcoming any food prejudices or breaking down any strong sales resistance. It is only a question of making the present scattered demand for apples universal.

When working out figures of prospective sales it is best to be conservative, even when all" the factors are so favorable that failure seems impossible, so we will assume that the advertising and sales campaign will not be an entire success, and that only half the people will become apple consumers. This will leave out the old who have lost their teeth, and the young whose dentition is incomplete and for whom orange juice would be more appropriate. Then, since one cannot expect rigid consistency in any human undertaking, let us assume that one half of the charter members of Apple-a-Day Club will not stick to the diet but get tired and discontinue it after the first month or so. Finally, in order to be thoroughly cautious, and arouse no false hopes, let us cut this conservative estimate of Chinese apple consumption from the orthodox regularity one might wish for, and assume that the remaining consumers will eat an average of an apple every other day. This would give us a daily consumption of fifty million apples, not an unreasonable amount for such a tremendous population once our advertising campaign has convinced them of the benefits to be derived. Medium-sized apples will pack 200 to the box (an approximate bushel) and there are

258

twenty-five boxes in a ship-ton, so this would mean 10,000 ship-tons of apples daily. Figured in terms of tonnage that is a lot of apples —more than the average single ship could carry, even if it had no other cargo. Gosh, when you get down to details, the scheme is not practical. If all the ships which formerly called at Shanghai did nothing but carry apples they could take care of only a fraction of the business. Besides, if there were enough ships to bring them here, the Chinese railways and river boats couldn't haul them away. And also, if we sold all these apples to the Chinese, there wouldn't be any apples left for the rest of the world.

Any time an export manager wants to enjoy a pleasant day-dream of the future, in which fame and prosperity will unite to banish daily cares, all he has to do is to take a pencil and a pad of paper and start figuring out what sales he could make if he could only find an advertising agent clever enough to induce a reasonable proportion of China's 400 million customers to buy his goods. Merchants wore out quill-pens on the same pleasant speculations long before graphite pencils, calculating machines and advertising agents began to play an important part in the affairs of the business world. So long as people of one country make goods to sell to others, so long as ships cross the ocean and international trade exists, the golden illusion of the sales which may be made to China's industrious millions will always be an intriguing one. No matter what you may be selling, your business in China should be enormous, if the Chinese who should buy your goods would only do so.

China's trade with foreign countries embraces, with a few regional interruptions, a period of almost 2,000 years, but it has only been during the comparatively recent period covered by the past century that foreign traders began coming to China to sell rather than to buy. Before that period China was the greatest manufacturing nation on earth, produced the finest goods and in the greatest quantities. Chinese silks were sold in Rome in the first century A.D., and were probably sold to Arabian traders before that time. Silks in ancient China were provided for the comfort of the aged, were woven for warmth as well as beauty, and were much heavier than the silk produced today. This did not suit the Roman ladies, who separated the threads from the Chinese cloth, spun them finer, and then wove garments of a cobweb transparency which shocked the respectable. Reformers of the day made as much fuss about it as reformers of the present generation made about the one-piece bathing suit, and with as little effect. Silk, in which they had a monopoly, was not the only article the Chinese exported to Rome. In spite of the-difficulties and expense of transportation, Chinese tools of iron and steel were sold in Rome during this period, and, because of their superior quality, brought such high prices that the trade was a profitable one, and Chinese tools became famous throughout the civilized world.

About a thousand years later (during the Sung dynasty), Chinese porcelain, which was then in the childhood of its development, reached a stage of perfection so far ahead of that represented by the rude earthenware of other countries that the wealthy in Europe and the Near East bought the jars and vases as fast as they could be imported, often paying weight for weight in silver. The European scientists had puzzled unsuccessfully over how silk was made, and now porcelain gave them a new mystery which they were also unable to solve. The Dutch traders, who had imported huge quantities of silk, introduced Chinese tea to Europe in the sixteenth century, and for more than 200 years it provided a big and profitable export business. It was, in a way, a third mystery, for it was strange to the herbalists of Europe. It was not until a few centuries before the discovery of America that the Chinese learned of the existence of cotton, brought seed from Persia and began to grow 'the cloth plant.' They were novices at growing cotton, but they introduced into the spinning and weaving of the new textile the advanced technique of silk manufacture, which they had known for at least 4,000 years, and so became both as to quantity and quality the world's premier manufacturers of cotton cloth. During the sixteenth, seventeenth and eighteenth centuries and for some time after that, the best cotton cloth available anywhere in the world came from the hand-looms of China. No gentleman in America during Colonial days thought he was fashionably dressed unless he had on a pair of knee breeches made of Chinese hand-woven cotton, and no lady thought her wardrobe complete without at least one dress of Canton silk.

During all of this period, the West had very little to sell that the Chinese wanted. From the earliest times they bought sandalwood, peacock feathers, spices, elephant tusks and precious stones, and these continued to be in demand, but articles like these do not fill the hold with cargo, and generations of traders saw ships come to China half empty or in ballast and return to home ports fully laden with the rich produce of China. The discovery that ginseng, a root to which the Chinese attribute great medicinal value, grew wild in the hills of New England, enabled some early American traders to make some easy fortunes, for it could be had for the expense of digging it, and it sold in China for very high prices. The cargo of the first American ship to call at Canton, 1784, consisted principally of ginseng, and that continued for some years to be a very important American export. But, valuable as it was, the cargoes of ginseng would not meet the costs of the produce America bought, nor could any other country sell to the Chinese enough goods to pay for what was bought. An essential part of the cargo of every ship coming to China to trade at this time consisted of kegs of Spanish or Mexican silver dollars, for the balance of trade was all in China's favor and, in the absence of banking facilities, trade was on a cash basis paid for in silver.

Without wishing to revive a controversy which was long ago interred without benefit of clergy, I may say that the persistence of the hated opium traffic in China was due to the fact that opium was, at that time, the only commodity the British and American traders could sell to the Chinese in sufficient quantity to meet a substantial part of their payment for cargoes of silk and tea: In spite of the tons of opium shipped to China and sold at high prices, the money the Chinese paid for opium was never enough to meet the costs of purchases made from China. Silver dollars continued to pour into China for several generations, to be spent, hoarded or melted and converted into tea pots, vases and ornaments. Many were kept in circulation for a, century or more before they were bought up by China's modern mint and recoined as Chinese dollars. Some of them were worn smooth in domestic trade, but never left China's shores, because the Chinese found nothing in the West worth exchanging them for. From the dawn of history everything produced by China had been superior to anything produced by the barbarians.

The Chinese assumed that this was a condition of affairs which would last forever and paid but scant attention to the goods the foreign trader had to sell. The first serious blow their inordinate pride suffered came when they discovered that the barbarians could really produce good merchandise. This indifference to the products of Europe continued until some time during the middle part of last century, when the tide turned and the sale of foreign goods to Chinese became more important and more profitable to foreign traders than the sale of Chinese goods to the West. It started with the invention of the cotton gin and the application, in Manchester, of power machinery to the manufacture of cotton cloth. This English machine-made cloth was not as strong or of such good quality as the product of the Chinese hand-loom, but it was very much cheaper and every shipload sent to China found a ready sale at prices which represented a satisfactory profit to the manufacturers and the middlemen. For a few decades preceding the turn of the century more than fifty cents out of every dollar the Chinese spent for foreign goods went for the purchase of cotton goods. Manchester got the bulk of this trade, but the New England business in Manchuria was important enough for the United States to negotiate the opening of Manchurian ports to foreign trade.

The China trade has not only been a fascinating one in theory, but has also been, in the main, a profitable one, and there are many 'made in China' fortunes in various parts of the world. As each generation of manufacturers has brought new products to the world's markets, consumers have been found in China and new fortunes have been made. From sandalwood, peacock feathers, ginseng and opium, China's trade turned to cotton goods, candles, and kerosene. These more recent articles replaced older products as producers of fortunes and now newer products are replacing them. Kerosene oil came in to cut down the sale of candles. Later batteries for flashlights provided strong competition to kerosene and created such a vogue in peripatetic illumination that the formerly huge business in storm lanterns died, one might say, overnight.[4] But while the kerosene business slowed up, the oil companies began dotting the countryside with filling stations to supply gasoline to those who travel China's thousands of miles of new motor roads. The sons of men who bought carriage whips began buying spark plugs. With changing demand and changing supply, China's millions have bought many different things, and they have always been steady

---

4 The great popularity of the flashlight in China is due to a rather curious reason. Chinese country people have an inveterate fear of burglars and bandits and know that when they walk through the fields with a lighted lantern bandits can easily follow their movements. The flashlight is flashed on as needed and is more difficult to follow.

customers, they could always be depended on to absorb a good proportion of the world's surplus products. Of recent years they bought such a wide variety of things that a list of them would look like the text of a Chicago mail order catalogue. But, while a few are wealthy, the average purchasing power has been low, and a very small proportion has ever become more than theoretical customers who are interesting for statistical purposes, but valueless from the standpoint of actual sales. It is doubtful if more than ten million Chinese could afford to buy an apple a day without diminishing their bowls of rice or noodles.

During the first thirty-five years of the present century, China's purchases of foreign goods showed a constantly changing picture of the wants of the Chinese people. In 1900 the total sale of cigarettes in China was 300 million, or less than one per person per annum. Ten years later it had jumped to 7,500 million or, say, about 19 per annum. In another ten years it was 22,000 million or 60 per annum. In 1936 it amounted to 80,000 million or, practically a daily cigarette for every male resident of the country. In the meantime, the sale of imported cotton goods dropped from more than 50% of the total to less than 3%. Importations of 'candles, soaps, oils, fats, waxes, gums and resins' later amounted to more than importations of cotton cloth. This did not mean a decrease in the demand for cotton goods, but the development of a new source of supply. Most of the cotton goods bought by the Chinese in recent years were produced in local mills owned by Japanese, Chinese and British.

The old British merchant told me many stories

The Chinese were a long time making up their minds that they wanted any of the modern articles manufactured by the West, but once they started buying they found that they wanted everything they could afford to buy and a good deal more. The catalogue of China's wants is no longer restricted by ignorance and prejudice, but solely by ability to purchase. In fact, China's 400 million customers face the same, problem as that which confronts the lady who has a shopping list which calls for an expenditure of $10 and has only $4.95 in her purse. Before anything is purchased, it is necessary to give careful consideration to the value and desirability of that article in comparison with similar articles, and also in comparison with a number of other articles of an entirely different nature. This was true of small as well as large purchases and was strikingly illustrated by the annual summer slump in the cigarette business. The many varieties of melons which come on the

265

market in June provide about the only uncooked food the Chinese eat and there is a universal demand for them, but many cannot afford the twin luxuries of melons and cigarettes. As a result, some gave up cigarettes for melons, and cigarette consumption did not resume normal proportions until the melon season was over, in the early autumn.

Thus, every sale that is made in China is the result of successful competition not only with similar articles made by a competitor, but with a wide variety of other things with which it would not appear to have any particular connection. The apple eater, for example, would, like the melon eater, have to choose between fruit and cigarettes and then, if the choice fell on fruit, apples would have to run the gamut of all other fruits before a sale was made. This introduces into the selling of goods to China complications which are measured by the geometric rather than the arithmetical progression, and adds grey hairs to the heads of sales managers and advertising agents.

Compared with the complexities of selling in China in modern times, marketing during the boom days of the clipper ships and the early days of the Manchester mills was a very simple matter. When I first came to China, twenty-five years ago, I had a great many talks with an old British merchant whose experience went back more than fifty years, and so embraced a part of that halcyon period. He never got tired of telling me about how simple it was to do business then, what a leisurely life one could lead and how certain the profits were. He was very bitter about the modern commercial methods, the petty trading and bargaining one had to do to make any profits or even to make ends meet. In his boyhood days, business was conducted along quite different lines. The firm with which he had served his apprenticeship as a clerk maintained two main offices, one in London and one in Shanghai, with partners in charge of each office. The London partner bought cotton cloth which was shipped to the Shanghai office and sold at auction. The proceeds of this sale were invested in tea, which was shipped to London and sold at auction to buy more cotton, which was sold to buy more tea which was sold—and so on ad infinitum. It was a continuous process, and was looked on at that time as a rather hustling business, as each ship arriving in Shanghai carried a cargo of cotton cloth, and each departing ship carried a cargo of tea. There was little to do between the arrival of ships. Sometimes as many as two ships arrived and departed in the same month and then there were busy days to be talked about for months.

The old merchant maintained that this was the only genuinely honest and above-board system of selling. What he had heard of modern advertising and high pressure selling methods which were practiced elsewhere, and were beginning to be introduced in Shanghai, filled him with profound disgust. They savored to him of trickiness, if not of downright dishonesty. His contention was that, when a Chinese bought a bale of cotton cloth at auction sale, he was paying exactly what it was worth on the Shanghai market, no more and no less. The goods offered for sale were always on display in the auction room, to be freely examined by all, and there could never be any question of a claim because of damaged cargo or misrepresentation of quality. In these later unregenerate days he had to quote prices subject to confirmation by cable from London, shade his prices and cut his profits in order to meet rascally competition, knuckle under to what he knew to be unjust claims. He had to worry now about whether or not his customers would pay their bills. In the old days, everything had been cash on the nail. The fact that the business was always profitable to his firm did not diminish his enthusiasm for the system.

It was an economical and in many ways an ideal method of selling. The book-keeping in London and Shanghai was so simple that the partners themselves could take care of it.

There were usually steady profits and, occasionally, a delightful windfall, as when a cargo of choice tea was the first of the season to reach London, or when a cargo of cotton cloth arrived in Shanghai at a period when other ships had been delayed, and found a market depleted of stocks.[5] The modern curse of over-production had not only never been heard of but had never been dreamed of. The English markets could always consume all the tea shipped to London and the Chinese market could always consume all the cotton goods shipped to Shanghai. Prices might fluctuate, but never below a point where sales would be unprofitable. In fact, the only really important problem the partners in this pleasant business had to decide was whether they should continue to invest their surplus in increasingly larger cargoes of tea and cotton or divide some of the profits.

Those good old days are gone and are remembered by but few. The sale of cotton cloth by auction, running to millions of dollars annually, continued into the present century and then lingered on to become finally one of the casualties of the First World War. After that there were a few cotton goods auctions in Shanghai, but they were of no importance. The Shanghai auctioneers confined their activities to disposing of unclaimed cargo and bankrupt stock and the household goods of residents going home. Sir Thomas Lipton's advertising and aggressive selling methods,

---

5 The completion of the Suez Canal enabled a Shanghai tea dealer to set all London talking by his enterprising selling methods, lie loaded an entire sailing ship with tea and accompanied the cargo as far as Marseilles. From that port, he went by the fastest possible route to London with samples of his tea and had the entire cargo sold by the time his ship arrived. A competitor, whose ship actually was first to anchor in the Thames, found the market already well supplied. No super-cargo had ever before arrived on the London tea market in advance of his ship, and there was some difference of opinion both in London and in Shanghai as to the ethics of this procedure. The unfortunate competitors were outspoken in their denunciation of this sly trick.

coincident with Chinese chicanery in the production and curing of their own tea, turned British taste from the delicately-flavored Chinese to the heavy Indian teas, and it has been many years since there was an auction of Chinese tea in London.

The easy old days were replaced by regular schedules of steamer sailings, merchandising managers, sales conferences and advertising agents. A very large proportion of the foreigners living in China were, like myself, primarily interested in selling goods to as many as possible of China's 400 million customers. We made market surveys, speculated on what articles they would buy, how the article should be packaged, how advertised, and what merchandising methods should be followed. The problems were the same as those we might attempt to solve at home, with added complications and difficulties, and competition from every country that boasts a factory. None of us ever prospered to the extent we thought our work justified, but we had compensations. The work was always interesting and, in spite of our years of disillusionment, all of us secretly cherished the thought that a reasonable number of the 400 million might buy our goods next year.

CPSIA information can be obtained at www.ICGtesting.com
Printed in the USA
BVOW06s1922110116

432524BV00028B/285/P

9 780968 045909